LIFE AND WORK OF

PESTALOZZI

PESTALOZZI.

*(From an engraved portrait in the 1827 London edition
of " Hints to Parents.")*

LIFE AND WORK

OF

PESTALOZZI

BY

J. A. GREEN, M.A.

PROFESSOR OF EDUCATION IN THE UNIVERSITY OF SHEFFIELD

LONDON: W. B. CLIVE

University Tutorial Press Ld

HIGH ST., NEW OXFORD ST., W.C.

1913

PREFACE.

Although this book incorporates the whole of my *Pestalozzi's Educational Ideas* first published in 1905, it has been so much altered and enlarged as to be in effect a new presentation of Pestalozzi's Educational Doctrines.

In addition to more or less incidental changes and expansion in the original text, I have added a special chapter on Pestalozzi's Fundamental Principles, and given new translations of the *Diary*, the *Pamphlet of 1800*, the *Prospectus* of the short-lived school at Münchenbuchsee, the *Report to Parents*, and the first of the *Letters on the Education of the Children of the Poor*. The *Prospectus* and the *Report* have not, so far as I know, appeared before in English. Yet it is hardly possible to understand Pestalozzi without them.

My indebtedness to Wiget's articles in Vols. XXIII. and XXIV. of the *Jahrbücher des Vereins für Wissenschaftliche Pädagogik* will be obvious to all who know that admirable exposition of Pestalozzi. Wiget has been my mainstay, though I have used Natorp very freely in Chapter VII. and elsewhere. In addition, I have made use of Schmid's *Geschichte der Erziehung*, Vol. IV., Part 2; Schmidt's *Geschichte der Pädagogik*, Vol. IV.; Hunziker's *Geschichte der Schweizerischen Volkschule*, and Scherer's *Die Pestalozzische Pädagogik*.

The biographical chapters are based chiefly upon Morf, *Zur Biographie Pestalozzi,* the biography prefixed to Mann's edition of Pestalozzi's *Ausgewählte Werke,* and upon that of Seyffarth (Pestalozzi's *Sämtliche Werke,* Vol. I.).

Thanks to the opportunity afforded by the inclusion of a new selection of Pestalozzi's writings in Arnold's *Educational Classics,* I am enabled to make most of my references to what is, I hope, an accurate English rendering of the original text. Along with the translations in this volume, that book makes it possible for English students to obtain an adequate idea of Pestalozzi at first hand.

The Bibliography in Chapter XXII. is based upon that of Israel in Vol. XXV. of the *Monumenta Germaniæ Pedagogica,* which, extensive as it is, makes no reference to the *Letters on Early Education* written by Pestalozzi to J. P. Greaves and published in English in 1827.

My debt to those who helped me in the earlier work remains. In addition I have to thank my wife for the preparation of the indexes.

J. A. GREEN.

THE UNIVERSITY, SHEFFIELD.
    August 1912.

REFERENCES IN THE TEXT.

G = *Educational Writings of Pestalozzi.* Edited by
     J. A. GREEN and F. COLLIE. (E. Arnold.)

M = MANN'S *Pestalozzi's Ausgewählte Werke.*

S = SEYFFARTH'S *Pestalozzi's Sämtliche Werke.*

TABLE OF CONTENTS.

PART I.—BIOGRAPHICAL.

PART II.—EXPOSITORY.

vii

PART III.—DOCUMENTARY.

PART I.

LIFE AND WORK OF PESTALOZZI.

CHAPTER I.

GENERAL HISTORICAL INTRODUCTION.

THE History of Education in Western Europe, as a branch of the History of Culture in general, *Renaissance and Reformation.—Verbalism of the Schools.* takes a new point of departure in the Renaissance of the fourteenth and fifteenth centuries. Great intellectual movements necessarily bring in their train changes in the theory and practice of education, and, reversing the point of view, one may regard the practice of contemporary schools as an index to the penetrative effect of new ideas and new modes of thought which from time to time stir the current of intellectual life.

"During the Middle Ages man had lived enveloped in a cowl." [1] His intellectual outlook was dominated by an ascetic Church which emphasised the fleeting character of life in this world and taught that abstinence and self-mortification were the chief ends of man.

There were many signs, however, that the human spirit was becoming impatient of the intellectual strait-jacket

---

[1] *A Short History of the Renaissance in Italy*, Symonds, p. 5.

which Church tradition and practice imposed upon it; and the downfall of Constantinople in 1453, which led to the migration of the scholars of that city to Italy, gave a new impetus to the revival of classical studies which had already begun there. Quite suddenly, as it were, the Italians, with the Florentines in the forefront, discovered a native literature and a native civilisation older than the Church, which itself was alien in origin. In it they found a new rule of life which made the most of this world. Personal distinction became a cult. Curiosity was stimulated. Humane as opposed to ecclesiastical learning became the object of ambition among students.

The spirit of the Italian Renaissance spread over the whole of Western Europe, and after a long and bitter struggle the traditional teaching of the higher schools and Universities had to adapt itself to more modern needs. The invention of printing told in favour of the new learning. The limitations which ecclesiastical tradition and the relative scarcity of books had put upon the schools were removed; Greek studies were revived, and the prose of Cicero, as a basis for the study of Latin, replaced the rhymed grammars which had for centuries held sway.

But whilst the Renaissance did much to stimulate the intellectual life of the higher schools, its effect upon education as a whole was not immediately and entirely good. The events of this period, for example, caused the severance of what, for convenience, we call primary and secondary education. A gulf was fixed between them which few countries have even yet been able to bridge satisfactorily. With all its faults, the Church of the Middle Ages was distinctly a democratic institution; it always kept open the way for the clever boy from the parish song school, which provided the priest with his choir boys, to the school of the monastery or cathedral, which introduced its pupils more or less adequately to the whole range of Mediaeval studies embraced in the seven Liberal Arts. From such a school the boy might beg his way to one or other of the great teaching corporations—universities, as they came to be called—which developed in the thirteenth and fourteenth centuries, and there pursue more specialised studies at the feet of the greatest masters.

Universities and grammar schools were so altered in character by the Renaissance that the direct line of continuity from the primary school upwards was broken. The boy who knew his psalter by heart and could intone the responses accurately was not in a position to take up the new studies of the grammar schools, which were becoming less and less subordinate to mere ecclesiastical needs. Educational changes, in fact, threatened to carry higher education right away from the control of the Church, and thus to break up what had been a fairly effective educational ladder.

Then came the Reformation. For Luther the elementary school was the centre of interest. It followed from his doctrine of direct individual responsibility in the matter of salvation that every person should be put in a position to find out for himself his duty to God. Everyone must be able to read the Bible, and, since the language of the people was not the language of the accepted version, he himself translated the Bible into the vulgar tongue. But his view of the function of the school was just as narrow as that of the Mediaeval Churchman. It was to be as much the handmaid of the Church as ever. Indeed, the school was a necessary adjunct to the latter's work, for it followed from Luther's doctrine that education should be compulsory and universal. All children, boys and girls, must learn to read the Bible and must know the

catechism which Luther himself had written for them—
"the spelling-book of their religion," as he called it—
and the State should use its powers to compel neglectful
parents to send their children to school.

Learning for its own sake did not appeal to Luther.
The violence of his methods of controversy and his anti-
humanistic attitude threatened to detach the new learning
entirely from the Reformation as they had estranged
Erasmus. In this respect the situation was saved by
Luther's friend Melancthon, who was a scholar first and
then a reformer. Through him schools which were at once
Protestant and Classical were founded in many German
States—schools which were the prototype of the modern
gymnasium. By publishing Greek and Latin grammars
and other school books, as well as by advising upon the
appointment of teachers, Melancthon contributed enormously to their success.

As a counter-stroke on the Roman Catholic side, a magnificent system of classical schools was organised by the
Jesuits in the interests of the Church. In France, at
least, these schools were unrivalled, and for two centuries
they held the field of secondary education almost unchal-
lenged.

But what the Reformation had done, directly and
indirectly, for education in Central Europe was
The New largely undone by the devastating effects of
Scientific the Thirty Years' War. At the same time,
Spirit. the ancient classical culture which now completely captured the higher schools was being threatened
in its turn by a new point of view, which refused to look
upon the writings of the ancient Greeks as the ultimate
source of wisdom. It was pointedly urged that the New
Learning had only substituted one authority for another,
the philosophy of the Greeks and the literary form of

Cicero for the dogma of the Church and the rhymed grammar of Alexander de Villa Dei. In 1620 Bacon published the *Novum Organum*, in which he gave expression to a growing revolt against the attitude of mind involved in the practice of the schools and universities. It was not in books but in experience that truth was to be found. All ideas which do not come from experience are "idols" which darken men's minds and conceal the true nature of things. Words themselves often blind us to the truth. Men must cease to quote Aristotle as the final authority. They must learn to read in Nature's book, in which many secrets lie hid.

Bold investigators had already challenged the truth of many traditional conceptions. The Ptolemaic theory of the universe was giving way before the calculations of the mathematicians and the observations of the astronomers. Bacon himself did not realise the force of his own words; he rejected the theory of Copernicus and doubted the use of the telescope while Galileo was making his startling discoveries. Yet he gave literary form to a widespread feeling that it was a vicious point of view which regarded everything knowable as having been discovered by the ancient Greeks and as being expounded in their books, and that, therefore, the best education a youth could have was a literary one such as Erasmus would have approved, or rather such as the Jesuits were giving in their schools.

Literary and grammatical studies were attacked from another quarter. What Rabelais had said of the verbal sophistries of the scholastics, Montaigne repeated in politer language in reference to the already degenerate word-teaching of the Humanists. In their zeal to acquire a polished Latin style, the later Humanists thought more of form than of substance in their compositions. Ability to say nothing at all with fluency and elegance is after all not a satisfactory result of an elaborate course of education, and though the Humanists never meant anything of the sort, it was to something like it that education was leading. Hence arose the cry for things as well as words. Language training was admittedly necessary, for Latin was still the language of the learned world, and instruction in Latin must still continue to be the central feature of the school curriculum. But need it be taught as if it had no connection with the real world? Could it not be used to impart knowledge?

This sort of problem was much discussed in the seventeenth century. Even in the interest of the language itself it was maintained that Latin should, from the outset, be associated with the world as children know it. When the words have a genuine content they will be learned all the more rapidly.

To make the doctrine applicable to early lessons in Latin, Comenius published an illustrated Latin primer (*Orbis Pictus*) in 1658, the forerunner of all our modern instructive picture-books for children. "There is nothing in the intellect which has not found its way there through the senses," was the guiding principle of the new school. Comenius did much more to bring the new spirit and the new regard for Nature into relation with the whole problem of education than to write a first Latin book, but his *Great Didactic* (1628), which is by far the most exhaustive educational work of the seventeenth century, had little influence upon the practice of the schools. The darkness of the period of the Thirty Years' War (1618-1648) was too dense to be pierced by the light of a treatise upon education, however brilliant it might have been. Amongst his contemporaries and for some generations later the book was practically unknown.

The wonderful achievements which followed upon the birth of the scientific spirit had another **The Enlight-** effect, which in its turn affected the pro- **enment.** blem of education. The human intellect had achieved such triumph that men began to look upon reason itself as the final test of truth. The taint of intellectual arrogance which characterises eighteenth-century thought is in part perhaps justified by the proud record of the seventeenth—the century of Galileo, Kepler, Harvey, Descartes, Pascal, Boyle, Newton, and Leibniz. Nature and Reason were the watchwords which now guided men in every sphere of thought. What mankind as a whole believed was natural, what was natural was reasonable. The two terms are scarcely to be distinguished.

Thus, almost side by side with the great strife of sects which followed the Thirty Years' War, there grew up a school which looked upon the externals of religion and the varying dogmas of churches as unreasonable in their very particularism, and which advocated a "natural" religion. Its creed was exhausted by belief in the existence of God, in the immortality of the soul, and in compensation for the ills of this world by the rewards of the next. These were doctrines universally held, and were therefore natural.

The application of the idea, Nature or Reason, to every sphere of human activity is the characteristic feature of eighteenth-century German thought, of the German Enlightenment (*Aufklärung*) as it is usually called. The stimulus came from England (through France), and especially from the writings of Hobbes and Locke. We have seen the direction it took in religion : its ethics were founded upon the natural self-love of man, modified by his equally natural, though duly subordinate, interest in the welfare of others. It was "natural" to wish to make the best of this life, and both religion and ethics had a utilitarian *raison d'être*. Its treatment of political theory is especially characteristic of its arrogance and of its method.

Since what appealed to reason was true for these thinkers, they had no temptation to go outside their immediate environment in order to find out how things came to be what they were. The aim was to arrive at a reasonable theory which would connect the facts as they saw them, the civilisation of European States on the one hand and the ill-understood barbarism of Africa on the other. The ideas of the state of nature and of the social contract, which were the bases of the political philosophy of Hobbes, Locke, and Rousseau, were invented and ingeniously adapted to explain the particular form of Government which the writer was concerned to condemn or to defend.[1] The failure to realise the fact that historic development is in itself a natural phenomenon was one of the most conspicuous defects of the "enlightened" thought of the eighteenth century.

The particular point of view which we have described had considerable influence upon both the theory and the practice of education.

In the first place, its rational outlook influenced the educational work that arose out of a religious
Pietism. revival which stirred Germany in the first half of the eighteenth century. This religious movement was a natural reaction from the rigid insistence upon dogmatic differences which were rife even amongst the Protestants themselves. More importance was attached to forms of

[1] The student will find a simple exposition of the political theories here referred to in Sir Frederick Pollock's *History of the Science of Politics*, Chap. III.

words than to inner convictions which find expression in
conduct, and as a protest, first Spener in Frankfort-on-
Maine, and then Francke (1663-1727) in Halle, preached
that religion was primarily a matter for the heart.

Thus the "Pietist" movement—a sort of continental
Wesleyanism within the Lutheran Church—began, and
under Francke's leadership it took up the cause of education. Religion was to be its central theme, but it was to
be a religion of the heart. Catechisms mattered little.
The school was to be, as it were, a continuous children's
mission. More than half of the whole day in the primary
school was given to religious instruction and religious
exercises.

Francke's own foundation at Halle embraced a free
school for the poor, an orphan school, a school for the
children of townspeople, a middle school, a higher school,
a girls' high school, and a training college. The institution
still exists, and is a conspicuous monument both to the
man and the movement he initiated. Owing to the influence of the "Enlightenment," what was at first a purely
religious movement in education took a utilitarian turn, to
which fact the German *Realschule* [1] owes its origin. The
idea was first expressed in a project of Francke's to add to
his many-sided work in Halle another school in which the
sons of country gentlemen and merchants who did not
intend to proceed to the university might learn subjects
specially suited to their future careers. *Non scholae sed
vitae discendum* was the principle underlying Semler's

[1] The *Realschule* is in Germany a secondary school of the second
grade. The curriculum is modern. Latin is usually excluded.
Modern languages and science are the chief subjects of study.
The leaving age is 16. It corresponds most nearly to our municipal
secondary schools, which have developed out of the old higher
grade schools.

plan for carrying out Francke's suggestion, in the sketch of which, published in 1708, the term *Realschule* was first used. "In this school the pupil shall be trained in those sciences which are indispensable to his daily life." It is the utilitarian idea of the "Enlightenment" grafted upon a movement at first strictly religious in character.

But the typical German schoolmasters of the "Enlighten-

Rousseau and the Philanthropinists.

ment" were the Philanthropinists, who took their inspiration from Rousseau. In 1762 Rousseau published *Emile*,[1] a book which, with all its faults, created an educational atmosphere in Western Europe such as would have favoured the temporary success of the wildest attempt to carry out a "natural" education as Rousseau conceived it. In words of passionate eloquence he combined the ideas of Locke and Montaigne upon the education of a gentleman's son with his own views upon the rottenness of society and the banefulness of that culture in which his contemporaries took so much pride, and produced a scheme of "natural" education in which artifice itself becomes a cult.

Emile is an orphan to whose education a grown man of fine psychological insight is sacrificed for twenty-five years. The lad is removed from society altogether, and his tutor is his perpetual companion. He learns nothing until the psychological moment arrives; that is to say, until he feels an actual need. Books especially are "taboo." There is to be no hurry. If the boy is left alone all will go well. Emile is not to learn either to read or to write until he is twelve, and then only if he wishes. Things are his teachers, and he is to feel no other limitation and no other stimulus than that due to things. He does not learn science, he discovers it.

[1] A complete translation of the *Emile* is now published in "Everyman's Library."

What then is the tutor's business? His work is to create the environment, to see that the boy is placed in educative situations and to be ready to help his pupil out of difficulties when the moment is ripe. In this "natural" way the boy's physical, intellectual, and moral development are furthered until he is ready to play a man's part in a society of which he knows nothing. The general attitude of the book towards contemporary educational practices was that everything was wrong, and, in order to be right, it was only necessary to do the opposite of what the world generally was doing.

In spite of its follies and contradictions, *Emile* was an epoch-making book. It interested people in education as they had never been interested before, and it taught people to look at the problem from the child's point of view, to regard the perfection of the child *qua* child as the important thing at the moment, instead of trying to make of him an epitome of the adult. Singularly enough, Rousseau thought only of education as necessary to the upper classes. The children of the poor got their education in the struggle of life itself. In this respect he did not rise to the logical outcome of the "Enlightenment," which taught the dignity of man.

The very year after *Emile* appeared, De la Chalotais published an essay on national education which attracted wide attention. It was in the main a polemic against the Jesuits, who controlled higher education in France. Education was an affair of the State, he said, not of the Church. Thus he initiated the movement which has led to State intervention and control in most European countries, although Chalotais himself cared only for the education of the well-to-do.

Amongst the readers of Rousseau and Chalotais was Basedow, at that time a teacher of repute in Altona. He

had already written books (mainly theological) in which
novel views on education were advanced. He now conceived himself as destined to reform the educational institutions of his native country, and indeed of Europe
generally. He sketched his plans and appealed to
"Friends of Humanity" for money to publish them in
detail. Money poured in and what was intended to be an
elementary introduction to knowledge in general for use
in the house was issued. It was republished later as *The
Elementary Work* (*Das Elementarwerk*). Not unlike
Cassell's *Popular Educator* in idea, it was a collection
of all the knowledge necessary to the education of youth
from the beginning up to the fifteenth year for the use
of parents, teachers, and private tutors. Along with it, a
folio containing a hundred copper-plate illustrations was
issued.

In 1774, under the patronage of the Prince, he opened
at Dessau a school which he called the Philanthropinum,
because it was to educate "friends of humanity." This
educational venture attracted wide attention in Germany,
and although, after many vicissitudes, the school had to be
closed in 1793, it had really accomplished a great work :
numerous schools were founded on the Dessau model both
in Germany and Switzerland. In their educational theory
and practice, the followers of Basedow applied the principles
of the "Enlightenment" directly to the school. They
abolished the catechism ; and whilst they tolerated all forms
of religion, they taught in the school only the principles of
natural religion ; they appealed here, as in all subjects of
instruction, to reason.

Throughout, their aims were strictly utilitarian. Naturally they taught best those subjects which would be useful
to the children in later life. To enable the children to
learn quickly they adopted Rousseau's principle of teach-

ing through things.   Teaching from direct experience was
carried on almost to the point of absurdity.[1]   Discipline
was gentle.   In order to provide their boys with the
necessary motive power, they relied chiefly on an elaborate
system of numerical marks which brought valued privileges
to the successful.   They attached great importance to
soundness of body, and, to that end, they encouraged open-
air life, active out-door games, excursions into the woods,
bathing, fencing, etc.

But the Philanthropinists did not touch the problem of
popular education.   The spirit of the " En-
The Social Motive in Education. lightenment" made itself felt, however, upon
a number of ruling princes, and conspicuously
upon Frederic the Great and Maria Theresa.
The Prussian king gave up the barbarous idea that the
greater the ignorance of the people the easier they are to
govern, and at his instance the education laws of 1763 and
1765 were passed, in which it was laid down that elementary
education was a State concern, and attendance at school was
made compulsory for all children from 5 to 13 years of
age.   A great reorganisation of Prussian schools followed.
Amongst the most conspicuous workers in this field was
an Augustine monk, Felbiger, who did admirable service
in a Catholic province.   His success induced Queen Maria
Theresa to invite him to undertake a similar work for the
whole of Austria, where the suppression of the Jesuits in
1773 had produced considerable educational disturbance.

Not only Princes but noblemen also occasionally took
an enlightened view of their functions.   Chief amongst

[1] The student who has read *Swiss Family Robinson* will know
exactly what their ideals of education and instruction were.
Though the authorship of this book is disputed, there is little
doubt that it was the work of one of the Philanthropinists, probably either Campe or Salzmann.

these was Rochow in Prussia. He lived amongst his people and realised their ignorance. By founding and fostering schools, and by writing school books, he hoped to improve their intellectual and moral condition. As a whole, however, the nobility held aloof from such reforms as were attempted, and the people themselves were not really reached by what were purely external influences. The interest of the upper and educated classes in popular education was in the main academic. It required a shock like the battle of Jena (1806) to stir them to their depths and to open their ears to the philosopher Fichte, whose burning eloquence led Prussia to undertake seriously the organisation of a national system of schools.

Long before that, however, the study of social problems had become a fashion. There were numerous societies and many journals devoted to the discussion of social and moral problems. Every centre of intellectual activity amused itself in this way. The organisation of prize competitions for essays upon set subjects was a favourite method of provoking interest.[1] Here and there, of course, deeper convictions and abler men combined to produce serious contributions to the subject. Amongst the best of such societies was the Helvetic Society in Zürich, and the *Ephemerides*, published by Iselin in Basel, was conspicuous amongst the serious journals of the time.

Education was, therefore, in the air in the latter half of the eighteenth century, and behind it was a new motive—philanthropy, love of mankind. Western Europe, thanks to the Revolution and its literary antecedents, was talking and writing about social reforms based upon the rights of man. In Switzer-

Position in Switzerland.

---

[1] Rousseau's earliest literary work was a competitive essay in which he maintained that human culture in all its forms was pernicious in its effects.

land, which was of course closely connected with Rousseau, improvement in education was a leading feature of the programme for social betterment. The political position of the Swiss peasantry, which was little to be distinguished from serfdom, prevented anything being done on a large scale. But some members of the privileged classes attempted to follow in a smaller way Rochow's example and to improve the lot of their dependents—notably Tscharner and Daniel Fellenberg. The former wrote a " Guide for Country Schoolmasters " (1772) and important " Letters upon the Education of poor country children" in the *Ephemerides*. Lavater's "Christian Booklets for Children " (1769) and Iselin's " Essay on the improvement of public education in a republican business town " (1772) are alike interesting examples of the practical interest taken in education, and are typical of the widespread influence of the Philanthropinists, to whose work and methods both men had given their support.

In towns like Zürich practical school reforms were introduced, but the political position of Switzerland as a whole was exceedingly unfavourable. Small as the territory was, it was in no sense a unity. A loose confederation of eighteen tiny sovereign and twenty-seven semi-independent States, it was beset with all the vices of parochialism, and until the Revolution of 1798, carried through at the point of French bayonets, broke up the confederacy and established a central executive it was not possible to do anything for education as a whole. The new government— the Swiss Directory—only lasted from May 1799 to March 1803, but under the lead of Stapfer, its Minister of Arts and Science, who was unexpectedly called from the Professorship of Philosophy and Philology at Berne to this office, a brave attempt was made to put popular education on a sound footing. How badly action was needed may be judged from contemporary accounts. In Canton Zürich there were some 350 country schools of which less than a hundred had buildings of their own, and such buildings as there were could not have been more unfit for their purpose.

" As I opened the door, an oppressive feeling of dampness struck me. Packed in a dark corner our country's greatest treasure—its youth—were sitting, compelled to breathe the hot air reeking with thick foul mist. The windows are never cleaned, the room is never aired. The children are so closely heaped together that it is impossible to get out without climbing over the seats and tables." Most of the schools were in private houses : " I keep school in my own house, and have only one room for both my household and the school. I receive no rent and no allowance for school furniture," writes one of the masters. Occasionally the schoolmaster had to hold school in different houses in turn. Schoolmasters were usually badly paid, and necessarily had to combine schoolkeeping with some other business.[1]

An interesting story which is told by the biographer of Oberlin, a clergyman who did heroic work for his people in the Alsatian parish of which he had charge, shows that this description of Swiss schools applies with equal force to the schools of other lands. When his predecessor in the parish took up his charge he asked to be shown the principal schoolhouse. He was taken to a miserable cottage where a number of children were crowded together without any occupation, and in so wild and noisy a state that he could with difficulty get a reply to his inquiries for the master.

"There he is," said one of them, pointing to a withered old man, who lay on a bed in one corner of the room. " Are you the schoolmaster, my good friend ? " enquired Stouber.

What Schools were like elsewhere.

---

[1] *Vide Morf*, Vol. I., pp. 18 ff.

"Yes, sir." "And what do you teach the children?" "Nothing, sir." "Why, then, were you made school-master?" "Why, sir, I had been taking care of the pigs for the countryside for many years, and when I got too old and feeble for that, they sent me here to take care of the children." [1] This was not exceptional in Alsace in the eighteenth century.

But we may come nearer home and read the reports of the Committee of Council on Education for 1847—nearly a hundred years after Stouber's experience. "The school was held in a miserable room over the stable ; it was lighted by two small glazed windows and was very low; in one corner were a broken bench, some sacks, and a worn-out basket; another corner was boarded off for storing tiles and mortar belonging to the chapel. The furniture con-sisted of one small square table for the master, two larger ones for the children, and a few benches, all in a wretched state of repair. There were several panes of glass broken in the window ; in one place paper served the place of glass, and in another a slate to keep out the rain."

"The master was formerly a labourer—he has never been trained to teach." [2]

The art of keeping school was not, therefore, far advanced. The children's duty was to learn and the schoolmaster's duty was to hear their lessons. Twice each " school meeting " he made the round of his pupils, each one of whom was learning his particular piece of work in his own way. Class teaching as we know it was unheard of in the village school. The children learned to read, to say by heart the church catechism, selected portions of the Bible, and many prayers. Writing was usually only taught when parents particularly wished it, and even the elements of arithmetic were

---

[1] *Memoirs of Oberlin*, p. 9.
[2] Committee of Council on Education : Report on Wales, 1847.

regarded by many schoolmasters as a luxury with which they themselves could well-nigh dispense.

Of method in teaching, as we understand it, there was no thought. A child would come to school not knowing his alphabet. The teacher would show it to him in his book, say it to him once pointing to the letters and tell him to sit down and learn it. In an hour and a half he would come again to test him. This process would go on for many weeks, until finally the child could say it through and thus was ready to take the next step. Want of method and ignorance on the part of the teacher were made up for by an abundant use of the rod. The children hated the school, and learned nothing there that could possibly help them to lead self-respecting lives.

It was in times like these that Pestalozzi came upon the scene. How much there was to be done for education we can in part realise by comparing our present elementary schools with the accounts just given. From Pestalozzi more than from any other man came the spirit which has enabled the great educational reforms of the nineteenth century to be carried through, but Pestalozzi was a child of his own age in so far at least as he gave expression to some of its leading motives ; he did not in any sense create an enthusiasm for education. It was there waiting for some definite guidance, and this at least Pestalozzi helped to give. Above all, what was wanted at that time was a man who knew the people and their needs intimately, not from without, as a nobleman like Rochow or a king like Frederic the Great might know them, but from within ; a man who had lived in their midst, who had suffered with them, and fathomed the depths of their moral and intellectual distress.

CHAPTER II.

(1746-1773)

Heinrich Pestalozzi was born January 12th, 1746, in Zürich, where his family, together with other Italian Protestant refugees, had settled in the middle of the sixteenth century. His father was a surgeon and oculist of some repute when he died in his thirty-third year, Pestalozzi, the second of three children, being only five years old. The family means were so straightened, that it was only through the services of a devoted but quite uneducated woman, Babeli, that his mother was able to make both ends meet. His early life was spent in an atmosphere of loving self-sacrifice.

Early Environment and Education.

Naturally sensitive in temperament, all the circumstances of that time were calculated to appeal to his feelings in the highest degree, and his father's early death deprived him of what might have been a strong correcting influence, and thus have spared him many of the troubles of his later life. Nevertheless his environment was the source of much that is most characteristic of his educational doctrine. As we shall see later, his " idea of elementary education," so far at least as it is concerned with moral and religious training, is an honourable monument to the home life

19

which gave it birth. "It is at once the product of, and an expression of gratitude for, all that his mother and Babeli had been to him."

Physically always a weakling, Pestalozzi, the "mother's boy," in spite of intellectual gifts of a high order, did not shine at school. He was always the butt for his schoolfellows' practical jokes, and he did not please his teachers, who saw no promise in a pupil who could neither spell correctly, nor write legibly, and who, besides, had no head for arithmetic.

Pestalozzi's school and college courses lasted from 1751-1765. The schools of the city were rather loosely organised, but above the elementary schools there were two Latin schools of equal rank, both of which Pestalozzi attended. They led up to the *Collegium Humanitatis*, which provided two year courses in Arts, and above this was the *Collegium Carolinum*, which catered especially for theological students, though others were admitted. Pestalozzi passed through the *Collegium Humanitatis* and was also for two years in the *Carolinum*. It was here especially that his education began to exercise a real influence upon him.

The teachers included men of European reputation. The period was one of critical importance in the History of German Literature. French thought and French literary standards had hitherto been dominant in Germany. Now it was the turn of England, and particularly of Shakespeare. Thanks to this new influence, a new spirit of freedom entered into literary effort. There followed the *Sturm und Drang* period in which the advocates of French classicism on the one hand and of English licence (as the opposing forces called it) on the other struggled for mastery. The Moderns were centred chiefly in Leipzic and Zürich. Two of the teachers at the Zürich Gymnasium, Bodmer and Breitinger, were in the van of the reform forces.

Bodmer had been one of the first to recognise the merit of Klopstock's *Messias*, the earliest literary product of the new spirit that was invading Germany. Celebrities of the time always found a warm welcome and a congenial atmosphere in the Swiss city. When Klopstock, then a literary veteran, visited Zürich, he found there, especially in the younger men, keen literary interest and susceptibility, to which his presence gave a powerful impulse.

He was followed there by Wieland and other writers, one of whom wrote: "Zürich is really an incomparable place, not only on account of its magnificent situation, which is quite unique, but also on account of the number of intellectually eminent men you meet there. Whilst in great Berlin I do not think you would find more than three or four men of genius and taste, in tiny Zürich I have come across at least twenty." Although Pestalozzi was only six years old at the time of these historic visits to Zürich, their influence had not died away when he was old enough to be affected by it.

Breitinger was Professor of Greek and Hebrew when Pestalozzi entered the Gymnasium. He regarded those languages as the chief source of wisdom for all times and all peoples, and he knew how to make his pupils look upon them from the same point of view. "He was the type of a good teacher," says Morf, and he was loved and honoured as a father by his pupils.

Bodmer taught history and politics. He conversed with his pupils rather than lectured to them. In the classroom, and on the walks he frequently took with his pupils, his intercourse inspired them with intense love of freedom and justice, and many famous citizens of Zürich owed both guidance and inspiration to him.

Pestalozzi's sensitive nature was particularly susceptible to the influence of such teachers. He carried their ideals frequently into extremes of practice. They enjoined simplicity of life and the practice of bodily endurance and hardening. Pestalozzi became a vegetarian, and slept on the hard floor of his room without clothes and without covering, until outraged nature brought him back again into more reasonable ways. Ideals of freedom, moral, intellectual, and political, were advanced as things worth living and fighting for. Pestalozzi, in the midst of a political struggle which at times threatened to bring him into serious trouble, whipped himself till he bled that he might be able to bear the pain of any punishment his ardour should bring upon him.

Writing in his old age of his schooldays, whilst recognising the value of the intellectual stimulus he received, he tells us that there was a conspicuous want of practical reference in the lessons they had, and that this tended to produce a dreamy idealism in the boys which made them unfit to deal with the concrete facts of life.[1] Nevertheless, great achievement has usually come from men who have devoted themselves to what others have called the wild dreams of unpractical idealists, and perhaps we owe more to the training Pestalozzi received at the hands of his Zürich teachers than he himself could have realised.

Pestalozzi's interest in social and political questions was further fostered by his holiday visits to his grandfather, a devoted clergyman in Höngg, a village in the near neighbourhood of Zürich. He accompanied his grandfather in his visits to the school and the houses of his people. There he learnt to know the country peasantry at first hand.

If we may trust his memory in later life, he found something of the old Swiss spirit lingering on amongst

[1] Cp. *Swansong*, § 163 (G.).

them, and his picture of the school in Höngg, which in spite of the technical weakness of the work done, stood in intimate relation with the home life of the children and exercised a powerful influence upon its pupils in training them to be attentive, obedient, diligent, and persevering, is a pleasing one. In fact he found village life and village institutions in much healthier condition than life and institutions in Zürich. The towns were first to suffer from the industrialism that was just beginning.

He saw how little the "A B C and Catechism schools" did for the people, and he realised the disastrous consequences for both mind and body, that came from the general practice of sending little children as early as possible to the factories which were then springing up in and around Zürich. The ignorance of the people, their suffering, and their inability to help themselves made a deep impression upon him. Already the resolution to devote his life to helping them had taken shape in his mind. "Ever since my boyhood my heart has yearned to stop at its source, the wretchedness into which I saw the people had sunk."

His education was intended as a preparation for the ministry. As a clergyman, he expected to have abundant opportunity for carrying out his plans, but the circumstances of the time, coupled with his failure in his first sermon, led him to regard the law as offering perhaps the most direct means of achieving his purpose. But his youthful ardour for political justice, for truth and right, brought him into such acute conflict with the authorities, that he had to give up all hope of a public career.

Political interest in Switzerland at the time centred in the struggle between the citizens of Geneva and its ruling families. Although nominally a republic the government of the city was practically a

Politics.

hereditary oligarchy.[1] During the greater part of the
sixteenth century, the citizens had been chiefly engaged in
the defence of the town from external attack, and powers
of government had been provisionally vested in leading
families, which they continued to exercise after all danger
from without had disappeared. So long as they remembered to what circumstances they owed their position, their
administration was conciliatory and passed without chal-
lenge, but they gradually assumed further powers and began
to look upon their privileged position as a sacred right.

Towards the end of the seventeenth century, the citizens
ventured to question these privileges and to demand a
share in the government of the city. In 1738 they secured
the unconditional right to make representations to the
Magistracy, but the events of 1762 showed how illusory
this right was. In that year the Genevan oligarchs, in
imitation of the Parliament of Paris, condemned Rousseau's
Emile and *Social Contract* as dangerous to the State and
the Christian religion, and sentence of imprisonment was
passed upon the author. The citizens appealed against
this judgment, and asked that it should be withdrawn, but
the petition was refused, and the Magistracy claimed that
any petition which they thought proper to refuse, *ipso facto*
fell to the ground.

Naturally the people of Zürich watched this struggle
very closely. The leading men of the town and the
majority of the people looked with suspicion upon all

---

[1] Geneva owed its form of government to Calvin. "Those who
only think of Calvin as a theologian know little of the extent of his
genius," writes Rousseau in a footnote to the *Social Contract*, II. 7.
It was a republic in many ways analogous to one of the ancient city
states of Greece, and it owed its political independence and its
special character in a great degree to its Lycurgus, Calvin (cp.
Ritchie, *Natural Rights*, p. 50).

attempts to alter the character of existing institutions by popularising them. But Bodmer and those whom he influenced felt differently. They took up the cause of the citizens of Geneva with the utmost warmth, and Bodmer founded the Helvetic Society (1765) in the hope of advancing the cause of popular freedom. The young Pestalozzi was a particularly active member. Rousseau's teachings were a gospel to these patriots.

" My own visionary tendencies were stimulated to a pitch of extraordinary enthusiasm when I read that dream book (*Emile*) of his. I compared the education which I had received at home and at school with that which Rousseau demanded for Emile, and felt how wretchedly inadequate it all was." [1] His political ideals were equally disturbing. Many of his friends were so affected by the " return to nature " idea that they looked to agriculture as the ideal career. " It is wonderful how some of our best students have taken up the idea of becoming farmers. They have already gone to help with the harvest as a sort of apprenticeship, to see if they can endure the heat, the sweat, and the rain," wrote Bodmer in 1765. In the same year, the patriots founded a weekly newspaper, the *Erin-nerer*, to which Pestalozzi was a frequent contributor.

As politics were forbidden to the journal, it was devoted to the discussion of social, educational, and moral questions. Pestalozzi's own contributions are modestly expressed in the form of wishes. " A young man," he wrote, " who cuts so small a figure in his native land as I do, has no right to pass adverse judgments or to demand reform; that is not his business. So, at least, men tell me every day. But surely I may give expression to my wishes ! Who would forbid me that or even take it ill of me ? I will therefore just wish and give my wishes to the

[1] *Swansong*, § 16 (G.).

world in print. May the man who laughs me and my wishes out of court enjoy the blessings of reform! "

Then follows the Litany of this youth of nineteen who sees in comic stories, indecent pictures, bad companions, slanderous gossip, unhygienic living, and lazy dollish womenfolk—all so characteristic of the time—the chief sources of social evil.

"Would that some citizen would print a book containing sound principles of education in language simple enough for the humblest to understand, and that some wealthy philanthropist would make it possible to distribute it freely and gratis amongst the people and that they would read it! But what a lot that is to wish all at once!!" Pestalozzi's interest in education as an instrument of social betterment shown thus early, remained with him until his death.

The political situation did not grow easier, and the Zürich councillors were getting impatient with the active young members of the Helvetic Society who had brought to light several cases of official corruption, thereby making enemies on every hand. The decision to send troops to coerce the recalcitrant citizens of Geneva added greatly to the excitement, and Pestalozzi, as one of the most zealous of the patriots, was suspected of being an accessory to the escape of the author of a lampoon directed against the authorities. Although he was shown to be innocent, he was under arrest for three days, and the offended magistrates never forgave him for his part in these matters. As long as he lived he was a dangerous demagogue in their eyes.

Thus was destroyed any lingering hope that Pestalozzi may have had of following a legal career. His **The Farm at Neuhof.** most intimate friend advised him to give up all thoughts of public life and to seek the quiet pleasures of a country calling. The example of his fellow students occurred to Pestalozzi. He decided to burn his manuscripts, and to become a farmer, helped in his decision, no doubt, by his desire soon to be in a position to marry a lady who shared his interests and hopes, for he saw himself contributing to the elevation of the country people as his agricultural schemes took shape in his mind.

At that time Tschisseli's agricultural success at Kirchberg, a village in the Bernese Emmenthal, had attracted widespread attention. He had converted a large tract of apparently worthless land into a number of valuable farms, thereby establishing the welfare of five villages. Many people went to learn his methods, Pestalozzi among them (1767). After a year with Tschisseli, Pestalozzi spent his small patrimony in purchasing some fifteen acres of land not unsuited to his purpose in the neighbourhood of Zürich. He obtained the financial support of a Zürich banker, burdened himself with more land than he could manage, and in 1769, after many misgivings on the side of her parents, he married Anna Schulthess, the daughter of a well-to-do merchant in the city.

He had already begun to build a house on his newly acquired but heavily mortgaged property. He called it "Neuhof," and when they made it their home the "ideal life" seemed at last to have begun for Pestalozzi. But he was unbusinesslike to the last degree, and misfortune soon overtook him. From the beginning his enterprise was doomed to failure. He was cheated on every hand, and his strenuous but ill-directed efforts could not prevent the ruin which unfriendly comment was quick to foretell.

Unfavourable but authoritative reports led the banker to withdraw his support, and Pestalozzi, although he was always unequal to business detail, endeavoured to retrieve his position by adding a wool-spinning business to that of the farm. Naturally his difficulties increased, debts accumulated, and ruin was imminent. Family friends had exhausted their patience and their means in their endeavours to help him. Some drastic change must be made or he and his wife would have to leave their home, endeared as it had been to them by the birth of their son, whose education was Pestalozzi's only joy during this anxious period.

This was in fact his first concrete study of the educational problem, and his diary has preserved for us the observations and experiments he made upon the four-year-old boy :—

The Diary. [1] *Jan. 27th*, 1774.—I showed him water, and pointed out how swiftly it ran down the mountain side ; he was delighted. I went a stone-throw or two further down, he followed me, and said to the water : " Wait for me, water. I shall be back directly." I presently led him to the same little stream, but lower down the hill. " Oh look, the water is coming too, it comes from up there, and goes away further down ! " We followed the water, and I said to him several times : " The water runs downhill." I went through the names of several animals with him, saying : " Dogs and cats are animals, but Uncle Tati and Klaus are men."

Thereupon I asked him, " Now what is an ox, what is a cow, a calf, a mouse, our Klaus, Igf Roth, an elephant, the pastor, a lamb, a baby goat ? " He nearly always told me right, and when he answered wrong his answer

[1] The German text from which this is translated is given in Vol. III. of the collected edition (Seyffarth) of his works. The original documents, which are only fragments, were left by Niederer to the City Library of Zürich.

was always accompanied by one of those peculiar smiles of his which show that he is in a teasing mood. This " not wishing to say it right " seems to me a humorous attempt on his part to get his own way, and to pretend, in some sort, that things can be made what he wishes them to be; it requires to be closely watched.

Afterwards I asked him : " What is ' dead ' ? " " Dead," was his reply. " And that (little goat), is it an animal ? " " It is dead too." " And is the bed an animal ? " " No." " Why ? " " Don't know." I saw that ideas of life and death, of free movement and the impossibility of such movement are necessary to him to distinguish animals and men from inanimate things, and made a note of this as an idea for future development.

Jan. 29th.—I thought if I let Babeli remain in the room, and if I ran and played with him in the open air first of all, I might hope to keep him a long time at his lessons. His activity out of doors showed me that the teacher must be strong himself if he proposes to capture the good-will of his boys by playing with them out of doors. I saw the strength of the baby body in quite a beautiful light.

Jan. 30th.—He found his reading lesson rather a bore, but as I had made up my mind that he should work a little every day whether he wished or no, it is better that he should realise this at once. I left him no choice between his task and my displeasure with the consequent punishment of being confined in a room by himself. After this he gave way, and learned his lessons merrily.

I showed him that wood floats in water, but that a stone sinks to the bottom. In the afternoon he went to Brunegg with the maid. (31st) Away at Königsfelden.

Feb. 1*st.*—The seriousness of lessons was interfered with through fear of the cough which had troubled him in the night. I taught him the names of most of the external parts of the body as an exercise in Latin, and also the meaning of such words as "outside" and "inside," "below" and "above," "middle" and "sides" by means of figures and objects. I showed him how snow turns to water when brought indoors. I found it an advantage in these lessons to make use of capricious changes of tone—now loud, now soft—or changing from a sort of chanting tone to one mixed with sharpness. But whither does all this eccentricity lead?

A few days ago he saw some pigs being killed, and to-day he wanted to imitate the process and begged for the knife. They put a belt round him; he took a piece of wood and placed everything in order. During this game, mamma called out "Jacqueli" to him. "No, mamma," he answered, "you must call me Mr. Butcher."

Feb. 2*nd.*—He knows the names of the first few numbers; I have been trying to teach him their meaning. My experience would have made it clear to the dullest intellect, how the command of words which are not associated with correct ideas of things blocks the way to truth. The habit of not distinguishing intrinsic differences between the various words which denote numbers was now fixed. It proved a great obstacle to attention. 7, 8, 9 were to him like 3, 5, 17, and all were of equal value; I could not get over the difficulty at all. Why have I been so foolishly anxious to teach him such important words without at the same time giving him the ideas connected with them? It would have been perfectly easy not to let him say "3" till he had learnt the value of "2" in all sorts of materials. How easily he would then have learnt to count, and how much I have deviated from the way of nature in this over-haste! May I never forget these truths, so important for wisdom and virtue!

To-day, finding himself alone, he went to the wine cask and filled his little glass. The maid came up, whereupon he at once said, "Mamma gave me permission." He did not want to learn his A B C. The roundabout ways which he takes to avoid it, the conditions which he lays down, his quickness in catching at something else, his habit of demanding everything which he wants and cannot easily get, on condition of giving in return a promise to try and read and do his lessons well—all this has attracted my attention for some time, and I feel that I must watch these tricks carefully. The purchase of a violin gave him intense pleasure, but circumstances prevented my deriving as much advantage from it as I hoped to do.

Feb. 3rd.—Again I felt the consequences of my mistake in letting him learn to count. If all words learnt without any idea of their meaning throw our minds into such hope-less confusion, how shall we ever be able to arrive at real truth? I pray that God may teach me the sacred laws by which He leads us slowly and in a thousand different ways to the attainment of clear and complete ideas for which all words are signs. What infinite confusion it must cause in the child's mind when symbols are acquired with-out his knowing what they stand for; and when the words we use in our intercourse with him represent partial and even incorrect ideas, the daily accumulation of error goes on apace without our knowing anything of it. Working backwards against error is so difficult, but going forward in simple truth is so natural and easy.

To-day he had an indigestion pain, he wriggled about and said, "It is hurting me." Mamma said, "I will look (and see what is the matter), Jacqueli." "You can't see anything" was the answer. On this extremely cold day I could not endure being in the hall, although *he* had endured it. I was very sorry.

Feb. 4th.—I was in Königsfelden, and the day was lost to me, as far as Jacques was concerned. An attack of rheumatic fever frightened us; Herr Koller (the doctor) came in the evening. We had a great deal of trouble to get him to take the slightest thing. Herr Koller advised us that, when he was quite well, we should now and then give him harmless but unpleasant drinks and powders, so that, in case of need, he would not mind so much. I saw the soundness of the idea at once, and I should like to put it as an educational precept in the following general terms—Every accomplishment, act of self-control, etc., which is only rarely called for, shóuld be practised before the emergency arises, for at the crisis circumstances will make what is unusual exceedingly difficult to accomplish, in spite of its importance.

Feb. 5th.—The persistence of a little fever and further absence from home prevented me from making full use of this day either.

They practised him in counting, and cut out paper figures, with scissors, in his presence. He imitated, apparently quite innocently, the gestures and tones of other people. Ought I to do anything to check this instinctive method of increasing his general knowledge? In trying to widen his knowledge and to make him more alert by allowing him to practise his powers of imitation on every-day occurrences am I encouraging impertinence, which is probably seeking the occasion (whatever means one may take against it) to take root? How am I to distinguish it from quite innocent imitation, and how can these little vices be checked? Perhaps in this way: "My child, you may imitate everything that is beautiful, both in speech and attitude, but you must not copy anything that is ugly, for you surely do not wish to become ugly yourself."

Feb. 6th to 12th.—The presence of Jacques Schulthess, my own absence from home, and continued consideration for the little one's health account for these empty days— not neglect for which an apology is due.

Feb. 13th.—The consideration we have shown to him on account of illness has had unlooked-for consequences; his self-will is visibly stronger. I took up one of his nuts to crack it; he thought I wanted to eat it, and began to shriek and cry and screw up his face in all sorts of ways. I looked at him coldly, and, without saying anything, I took another, and calmly ate both of them in front of him. He went on crying; I held the mirror before his face; he fled, as usual, to hide himself.

I admired the simple wisdom of our servant Klaus, in a conversation we had to-day. I am always interested in the unsophisticated opinions of informally educated men. "Klaus," said I, "Jacques has a good memory, hasn't he?" "Yes," he said, "but you are overworking him." "I am often afraid of that myself," I answered, "but don't you think that I should notice it in the child if it were so; his spirits would flag and he would become timid and uneasy. If I saw anything of the sort, I should at once take the greatest possible care." "Ah, you are not then forgetting these things; I feared you were." "O Klaus, all the wisdom in the world is not worth the loss of health and happiness in its acquisition. As long as the boy's face beams with mirth and high spirits, I have no fears. Short moments of dejection which are followed immediately by new joys and pleasures are not depressing in their effects."

So much for Klaus. To see peace and happiness springing from obedience and order is a real training for social life. It is the character of our experiences as a whole which determines the cast of our mind. But we should avoid disorder and excitement and see that the prevailing atmosphere is orderly and peaceful. Much pleasure can be got from quiet patient search for butterflies, for example. Do not cram knowledge into your boy. Bring varied objects to his notice and show them in many different lights. See that the boy's eyes and ears are always open, but do not often ask for his opinion. When you do, let it be about things which he is putting to use.

Ask his opinion as Nature does yours; she does not ask you to judge of the breadth of the ditch alongside which you are walking; she only shows it to you and you may possibly consider the question; but the ditch which goes right across your path and which you must pass over— *that* you must think about. So in every case when you can lead the child to put into practice what he has learnt, then it is natural and necessary to call for his views. I say, when he is face to face with a genuine problem, then is the time for judgment, but as a rule the child should simply observe and pass on.

Feb. 14*th*.—To-day things went off well; he learnt willingly. I played with him, was a horseman—butcher—what he wished. I gave him cooked apples now and then. He wanted to eat them all, and looked for his spoon; I said he must not take his spoon, that if he took it I would put

the dish aside; but if he learnt well I would give him some
more.   He left the spoon alone.

I made him draw straight lines and an upright perpendicular line.   Herr Füssli said to me: "Everything that
they do should be quite complete.   Let there be no going
on from *a* to *b* till *a* is perfectly known—and so in everything.   Never be in a hurry to proceed to the next point,
but remain at the first one till it has been thoroughly
mastered, in this way you will avoid confusion in the
future."   Order, accuracy, completeness, perfection—how
strongly I feel that my character was not properly developed in these points in my earliest years.   These same
failings are now a source of danger to my child—the
temptation to yield to the exuberance of his feelings, to be
satisfied with quick showy success, and, blinded by his
brilliance in many things, to forget or ignore particular
faults.   Lack of development is concealed by a semblance
of development.   Do not let me forget: Everything complete and nothing in a hurry—order, accuracy, completeness,
and perfection.

I will form his ideals quite early by the definite accomplishments of each day.   I will press forward, always doing
something, always developing, but always looking backwards, taking no forward step till every gap is filled up.
Everything complete, everything in order, no confusion.
Satisfied that everything possible has been done, without
inflicting any injury whatever, having made no concessions
to vanity, and given up everything for the sake of truth.
Great projects !

The way in which I appeal to the boy's memory has caused
me some difficulty to-day.   Is it possible that his feeble
young body will be injured by attention and by effort of
memory, or that his weak brain will be so burdened by the
many hundreds of words that his mental powers will suffer ?

I do not think so. Just consider the number of words in a single language, and what powers of memory it requires, and yet no one has ever imagined that the learning of the mother tongue is too great a burden for the youthful brain.

The organs of sight are capable of seeing after very slight practice, and this power is a lasting one; the organs of hearing are in the same way capable of hearing. It is only sharp contrasts which are harmful. Much seeing and hearing only strengthen these organs and make them more accurate, but thunder and bright sunshine weaken them.

If ten other languages were taught in the same way in which Nature teaches the first, they would only strengthen the powers of the mind, but unnaturally hard and violent exertion is not good for the mind, though its consequences cannot be attributed to lack of memory power. I notice that I do not follow Nature sufficiently in the way in which I teach Latin. I ought to accustom myself more to talking always in Latin. Nevertheless I am satisfied with Jacques' progress.

Feb. 15th.—One of my child's habits is worth noting. It indicates capacity very clearly, though it also shows the need for care on my part. Everything which he wants, he asks for only after having first of all met some particular objection which he thinks may stand in the way of his request, or after giving a reason which he thinks will induce us to grant it, such as :—" Mamma, I won't break it." "I won't ever tell lies." "I will learn my lessons if I may have it." "I won't ever want another."

He always says something of this sort before he asks a favour. We must not allow these roundabout ways to be of any profit to him; we must prize much more highly the

straightforward expression of his wishes; when he asks
for anything in this way we must make him ask again in
direct fashion, and then often refuse his request, pointing
out to him that we do so just because he did not, at first,
say straight out what he wanted. Also when he tries to
avoid something he does not usually say, for example, " I
don't want to have my hair combed," but " I will learn my
lessons," showing that he knows how much I excuse him
for the sake of his lessons. This is a new point for consideration. How far may this policy of excusing him be
carried, without serious harm ?

A few weeks ago a calf was fastened up in the entrance
to the stable. It was not the usual place, and he thought
it was loose. I showed him the rope by which it was tied,
but it was of no avail; he was frightened and would not
stay there on any account. After that I refused to allow
him to go into the stable again. Some weeks have passed
since then, and now he wants to go into the stable. " I
won't cry," he said, " the little calf is fastened up ; come
too, Papa, dear Papa, and I will say my poetry in the
stable."

You must lead your son by the hand into the great open
lecture hall of Nature, and teach him there, with mountains and valleys on every side. In Nature's great class-
room his ear will be open to your suggestive leading. He
will be compensated for the difficulty of his language
lessons by the freedom he enjoys. But at such times let
Nature be his teacher rather than you. Do not insist on
his following your words when natural objects distract his
attention. If he is sensitive to Nature's call, and you are
content to follow in her wake, then should a bird or a
caterpillar catch his eye, your language lesson must go.
Bird and caterpillar will teach him more and better than
you. Be quiet therefore.

This, of course, does not apply to the lesson hours given up to the acquisition of necessary technique. These must be few and absolutely undisturbed. The boy himself must not imagine it possible to escape from this duty. If he thought there were the smallest chance, a feeling of unrest would be set up which never comes otherwise. The natural longing for freedom must be absolutely checked, then no trouble will follow. A wise man once told me that the most beautiful nuns were to be seen in the strictest convents where all hope of freedom was gone, but that in other convents, where there was a certain measure of liberty, extreme misery prevailed. He said that this difference was most striking.

He who has learnt to restrain his desires may rise to complete self-conquest. But to be wavering between fear and hope, to hope, not frankly, but secretly with fear and trembling—that is as deadly as poison, and worse than any confinement.

So far as the freedom of your children must be restrained in order to prepare them for the duties of social life, let this restraint be absolute, and let there be no hope whatever of escape, then they will find self-conquest easy, and the enjoyment of the freedom which you can give them later will destroy the impression of the restraint you had to enforce at first, for it is the prevailing sensations which determine character. Much pleasure combined with some self-restraint give strength and vigour to the mind, but too much restraint weakens courage and induces general despondency.

Character is the result of the sum total of the strongest impressions, the fewer and weaker impressions are rendered ineffectual by the others. Herein lies the possible remedy for errors in education. Note too the falseness and uselessness of the dogma that a few chance impressions could ruin the whole structure of a good education.

Feb. 15*th.*—He is very obstinate and self-assertive. To-day I punished him twice to try and cure him. He went so far that he tried to take a piece of barley sugar, not indeed out of my mouth, but out of my hand, and broke into a passionate burst of anger when I held him back, put the piece of sugar near his mouth, and then quietly ate it myself.

Feb. 16*th and* 17*th.*—To avoid provoking opposition we must guard against the ordinary dogmatic tone of teachers —which often approaches that of the Almighty Himself —and we must take more care in alternating games and work; we must not restrict freedom unduly; we must arrange the regular hours for work more carefully in order that the rest of what he learns should bear no trace of labour—how important this is! I taught him how to hold his piece of chalk. Trifling as this is, I must never allow him to hold it in the wrong way again.

Feb. 18*th.*—I walked about a good deal with him to-day. How inexpert I am in making purposeful use of different situations and circumstances! M. (Merki) met the carpenter and asked him to pay the bill which he owed him. "M.," said Jacques, "do not worry the carpenter!"

Feb. 19*th.*—It gives me a great deal of trouble trying to avoid the conventional pedantry of the teacher. Where am I to draw the dividing line between freedom and obedience,—that obedience which must be practised so early as a preparation for social life?

ARGUMENTS IN FAVOUR OF FREEDOM.	ARGUMENTS IN FAVOUR OF OBEDIENCE.

Every restriction of freedom causes dislike for the restraining cause.

Experience shows that it is those children who have been most restricted who prove unfit for later freedom.

It is impossible to check children in their desires without exciting various passions. Freedom wisely directed opens eyes and ears.

It brings peace, equanimity, and pleasure to the hearts of the children.

Even complete freedom presupposes a guidance which makes the child dependent, but only on the nature of things and not on the arbitrary will of men.

No education is possible without it, for even in the most advantageous circumstances we could never leave the child to do just what he wanted.

There are a hundred circumstances when death would be the speedy result of unrestrained freedom.

In social life various habits and accomplishments are necessary which could not possibly be formed if the child were given unlimited freedom. The passions are not rooted out through freedom ; their development is only checked. Emile trembles with pride at having outdone the juggler. And even Rousseau speaks of the danger of fire and of difficult characteristics which must be kept in check, in a way which assumes the child's social dependency. There are individuals for whom a childhood passed in entire freedom would unfailingly mean an adolescence weighed down by bonds and fetters.

Which side is right ? We must not seek truth from one point of view only. Freedom is good, but so is obedience also. We must bring together what Rousseau has separated. Convinced that the wretchedness of man came from restrictions to his liberty, he assigned no limits to freedom. Let us make use of what is wise in his principles. Let the teacher recognise that freedom is good, let him not try to force on his young charges just to gratify his own vanity.

Let the child be as free as possible, treasure every moment which may be conducive to freedom, peace, and equanimity. Do not teach by words anything which you can teach by actual experience of things as they are. Let him see, and hear, and find out, and fall, and get up again, and make mistakes—never let words take the place of actions; what he can do by himself he must do. Let him always be busy and active and, most of the time, free. You will find that Nature is a better teacher than man.

But when it is necessary to teach him to obey, then let his freedom itself prove the need. Remember that all restraint is a sign of mistrust; and, if this feeling should germinate, all your labour has been in vain; make certain then of your child's affections, make yourself necessary to him, let him have no gayer and more obliging companion, none whom he would rather have by him to make him merry, than you. He should have confidence in you; if he often asks for something which you do not approve of, tell him the consequences and leave him free to do as he likes, but make the consequences quite plain to him, and always show him the right way.

If he goes aside into the mud and sticks there, lift him out of it ; warn him a hundred times, and then, if he neglects to make use of the warnings, let him get into unpleasant— even extremely unpleasant, predicaments.

If you can so direct things that their natural consequences, as far as they affect him, agree with the advice and warnings which he has received from you, then none of the restrictions you may find it necessary to inflict upon him will arouse antagonism enough to outweigh the many instances in which his confidence in you have been justified.

He will obey a wise teacher, a father who gives just warnings, but his guides must only command when necessary ; no caprice, no pride, no fancies for unnecessary knowledge should occasion commands. If some command is necessary, wait, if possible, for the occasion when the nature of things makes the fault obvious, and when its consequences will make the child see the reasonableness of the command.

If, for example, I wish to forbid his annoying practice of touching all sorts of things, I go about it in this way : I put two bowls on the table, one cold, one extremely hot, and wash my hands in the cold one and place the hot one in such a position that the little one is certain to touch it and so burn his hand. " People should not touch things which they know nothing about " is my only remark as I soothe the pain of the burn with some oil. A few days later I put some hot eggs in the same place ; he immediately takes hold of them and burns himself again. Then I say, " I don't like you to be always burning yourself ; leave things alone till you know something about them ; you should have asked me what it was that stood on the table and whether you might touch it." When he has been treated like this, you will not lose his confidence. Afterwards I insist that "Things on the table must not be touched."

I know, however, that good as this sort of thing may be, it is not always possible, though I think that if the teacher is careful to use this method whenever he can, he will find that it applies in most cases. His general treatment must never be arbitrary : he will certainly prevent the few direct commands that are necessary from affecting the child's trustfulness. The child has much necessary and seemingly meaningless labour in preparing for the duties, conventions, and accomplishments of social life. I cannot make a citizen of him without, for example, setting him early to work, and there is much that he cannot yet quite understand and which is contrary to his principle of doing nothing which he does not himself see to be necessary.

What is to be done in such cases? I take it for granted you have worked with all your might to win the child's trust; you are necessary to his happiness, and you are not disposed to be arbitrary in your requirements. Then exercise all possible care and thought in training the child to proper obedience; duty and obedience will become a pleasure to him. I do not say that you must not soon impart some general knowledge, but while he is still enjoying his freedom take up some study, which you must be careful to present to him in its pleasantest and (in the child's eyes) most attractive aspect. Watch him carefully; do not overburden him. Away with work and let's to pleasure! Do you take as much interest in his pleasures as he takes in your work? Let all things combine to render both obedience and work pleasurable.

From the mass of human knowledge, choose those studies which are easiest for children and which have the greatest charm for them, in order to accustom them to work which requires them to sit still for an hour. Let the natural instinct for imitation guide you here. You have a stove in your room. Make a drawing of it; if your child in the course of a whole year should not succeed in drawing a proper stove, he will at least have grown accustomed to sitting still and working. The comparison of mathematical figures and sizes is good material for games, and through these games shrewdness may be encouraged.

What an admirable preparation for social life it is to take care of a garden of one's own, to collect larvae and beetles, and to preserve them with industry, neatness, and order! What a check on wild and lazy ways, and yet how far removed from all knowledge which is unsuitable for children, who indeed should scarcely ever read in any other book than that of Nature !

The more you strive to reduce both work and discipline to a minimum, and to make your commands as pleasant as possible, the more imperative it is that your commands when given should be obeyed. Duty and obedience should be indissoluble bonds, and should lead to pleasure. But blind obedience is also necessary in some few cases. It may be remarked that one thing is important if obedience is to be easily won, namely, that there should be no ambiguity in the children's minds as to what is forbidden and what is not. Nothing leads to such bitter indignation as uncertainty about what will be punished as wrong-doing ; and to punish an innocent child means the loss of his affection. We must not imagine that the child ought to know instinctively what is likely to cause damage or what is of importance in our eyes.

So ends this brief fragment of a diary. It reveals clearly not only the influence of Rousseau upon Pestalozzi, but the independence of his young disciple. " Let us make use of what is wise in his principles," he writes. Notice too how many of the problems which agitate the modern schoolmaster are touched by Pestalozzi—sometimes, of course, " after Rousseau." Things before words, the discipline of consequences, meaningful occupation, the severity of the " drill " lesson in relation to the times in which the child is free (or feels free) to follow his own bent, the " psychological moment " for instruction. It is an admirable illustration of Dewey's words : " From the side of the child, the problem is to see how his experience already contains within itself elements—facts and truths— of just the same sort as those entering into formulated study ; and, what is of more importance, of how it contains within itself the attitudes, the motives, and the interests which have operated in developing and organising the subject-matter to the plane which it now occupies." [1]

We may note too that the charge of neglect in the matter of his son's early education which Pestalozzi brought against himself in his old age seems hardly justified. The whole document breathes a wholesome pedagogic spirit remarkable in one who had yet to realise his own particular genius.

[1] *Vide* Dewey, *The School and the Child*, p. 25.

CHAPTER III.

EDUCATIONAL AND LITERARY WORK AT NEUHOF.

(1774-1798)

It was the practice of the farmers of the neighbourhood
to take orphan apprentices from the parish
authorities. If sufficiently overworked and
underfed, these poor children proved profitable
to their masters, but the ultimate effect on the
children themselves was disastrous in the extreme. Ignorant and entirely dependent upon others, they developed
into hopelessly degraded men and women.

The Education of Neglected Children.

Although no state action had yet been taken in respect
of popular education the condition of the poor and of their
children was much discussed. Pestalozzi had recently
joined the Helvetic Society of Schinznach which for
more than a decade had played a prominent part in the
development of Swiss thought. Here he came into touch
with Iselin, Gessner, Tscharner, Füssli, Bonstetten and
others who were destined to be associated with him in
his later work. At their meetings educational problems
were discussed and the idea of industrial schools found
favour. In 1765 they discussed a proposal to purchase a
farm for the purpose. Tscharner, said to be the person on
whom Pestalozzi modelled the Squire Arner in his story of
Leonard and Gertrude, wrote a long series of letters to
the *Ephemerides*, an important periodical of the time
appearing under the editorship of Iselin in which he

developed the scheme, long a favourite dream of his. But nothing was done and Pestalozzi, who had already shown his interest in his village by introducing the wool-spinning industry, was feeling more and more convinced of the need of action.

It was not the poverty of the poor he pitied: he and his wife were poor, but they had intellectual interests which helped them to bear the burden of poverty without personal degradation.   He longed to be able to teach the people how to live self-respecting lives.   Finally, he decided to make an effort.   He would convert Neuhof into a school, in which the children of the very poor might be so trained, physically, morally, and intellectually, that they should look upon work as a means of self-help and as a source of personal freedom rather than as a sign of their dependence and degradation.

He straightway opened his doors to twenty such children, and in spite of opposition from his wife's family the scheme matured and Pestalozzi ventured to publish an appeal for help.   A number of people were interested.   Of these Iselin was the most important.   He published Pestalozzi's appeal, which followed shortly after the series which Tscharner had written, and which were mentioned above.

Pestalozzi outlined his scheme of making Neuhof a self-supporting industrial school.   His experience had already shown him that this was possible if the institution could once be set on its feet.   He had found that simple vege-tarian diet suited the children admirably and that it was not hard work that hindered the development of poor children but the irregular life they led.   He asked, there-fore, not for gifts but for a loan which he would begin to repay in ten years' time, and in return he promised to give his whole time and thought to the problem of educating poor neglected children.   In summer they would work in the fields, in winter they were to spin and weave. The girls were to be specially instructed in housecraft, sewing, and gardening. In the intervals and even whilst engaged in handwork they were to receive instruction in the elements of reading, writing, and arithmetic.*

Iselin commended this appeal to the notice of his readers and it was successful enough to allow Pestalozzi at once to increase his numbers (1775).

But the work was full of unexpected difficulties, some of which he described in the third of a series of letters to Tscharner who sent them to Iselin for publication.

These letters are important as showing how definite, **Letters on the Education of Poor Children.** even at this early period, were Pestalozzi's ideas upon the education of poor children. At the outset he lays it down that, inasmuch as it is generally true that each generation of mankind will exercise its powers chiefly in the same circumstances, and in the face of the same limitations and difficulties as its predecessors, it is most essential that what we do for children in their learning time should in no way incapacitate them for the kind of life they may be expected to lead later on. The most important application of this general truth he finds in the bringing up of the children of the poor for the most difficult of all life's callings—poverty.

" The poor must be trained to poverty." In such state institutions as exist this fundamental principle has been overlooked. They have left undeveloped in the children just the qualities which poverty itself would have brought out and in consequence they are really nothing less than " nurseries of men unaccustomed to industry " and there-

* *Vide* the text of the letter printed in Vol. 3 of Seyffarth's edition of Pestalozzi's Works, pp. 243-6,

fore quite unfit to endure the mischances and limitations of poverty. Any school for the training of the children of the poor must be primarily an industrial school, and one only needs to see the work done in their homes by children of six years of age, steadily increasing in efficiency year by year, to realise the possibility of combining industrial and mental training.

Yet Pestalozzi is not blind to the higher aims of education, for he thinks it quite as possible to train character in an industrial school as in any other. The essential thing is earnestness of purpose. "By the heart alone can the heart be guided."

As for the physical side of education he thinks an industrial school offers indisputable advantages. Three years' experience has convinced him that intelligently planned and lovingly directed industrial work has much less evil effect upon growth and stamina than is commonly thought; indeed, he has seen many cases of children who, when taken out of the idle wretchedness in which they were pining away, have been restored to ruddy health and strength by steady work at the spinning-wheel.

The practical difficulties and disappointments he had had to meet were in no way minimised. Experience had in part at least disillusioned him. Children hardened in bad habits are not readily amenable to kindly treatment. Their training is a long and painful process not seldom ending in failure. They are often ungrateful and parents frequently encourage their ingratitude, even inducing them to leave the school, perhaps just when they are decently clad, on the plea that their benefactor is waxing rich upon the fruits of the children's involuntary labours.

The greatest difficulty of all is to develop a religious feeling in children who always have lived, and always will live, in the midst of evil. There is only one way, that of awakening in them a lively belief in God as One who requites in their proper measure both good and evil, and in Jesus as their Saviour. One must pray with them morning and evening, asking God to preserve their hearts in innocence.

Pestalozzi's first pedagogic venture was thus an attempt to develop in grossly neglected children the elements of humanity, which his faith assured him existed even in the most degraded. To carry out his aim he thought it worth while " to live for years like a beggar among beggars, in order to teach them to live like men." His successes were numerous enough to convince him that human nature as a whole might be ennobled by the organisation of industry in the service of education. He believed that schools of this kind once started would become self-supporting and even provide a surplus which might be applied to the foundation of new schools. A steadily increasing number of children might thus be rescued from the miseries which generations of oppression, poverty, and neglect had entailed.

Unfortunately Pestalozzi was not the man to give practical effect to such an attractive scheme. Self-sacrificing devotion to lofty ideals, except in conjunction with business capacity, can not bring permanent success to pioneer effort. Subscriptions only postpone the day of reckoning. In 1779 the financial crisis came, the institution had to be closed, and had it not been for the help of friends Pestalozzi and his family would have been homeless.

Neuhof was, however, saved to them though they were reduced to the bitterest poverty. His family connections abandoned him altogether, and most of those who had shown interest in his philanthropic schemes forsook him. Keenly as he felt his position Pestalozzi grieved most for the cause which his failure had discredited,

It was at this time, or thereabouts, that an old servant of another branch of his family came to his assistance. She undertook the management of the house. Before she came they were often short of food, in spite of the fact that the garden was large enough to supply their needs and more. All this was put to rights. She won Pestalozzi's confidence so completely that he made her the heroine of his first story, and thirty years later he mentions her as an active member of his much enlarged household. Elizabeth Näf was her name, though the only authority for that is an entry in the diary of Pestalozzi's wife. He himself does not mention her by name, though in conversation with Ramsauer he once said, " I should turn in my grave and be unhappy in heaven itself, if I did not believe that she would be more honoured than me after my death."

His faith in his ideas was stronger than ever. " I had made a great effort, I had learned great truths, and gained invaluable experience. My conviction of the importance of what was fundamental to my views and my confidence in my work were never greater than at the moment in which it had to all appearances completely broken down."

"The Evening Hours of a Hermit."

" If I had to live on bread and water for years, and to work in the humblest cottage in order to attain my object, I would laugh at any danger, and would be certain of ultimate success, even in my greatest need. I will do a work such as no man has yet done, one which shall have the greatest possible results for the people."

Iselin and one or two others remained steadfast friends, and the former suggested that he should continue the pursuit of his object by writing. Ready to do anything which would keep his family from starving, Pestalozzi began what is generally called his period of literary activity by publishing anonymously in the *Ephemerides* a series of aphorisms entitled *The Evening Hours of a Hermit* (1780). They were addressed to "the shepherds of the people and the wise of the earth." Written in an hour of the deepest gloom, they bear the impress of the moment of their origin, yet in Raumer's words* they furnish "the programme and key of Pestalozzi's pedagogical system, the plan of a gifted architect who is convinced of the value of the work which destiny has prevented him from carrying out." Niederer† speaks of them as containing the earliest outline statement of the whole range of Pestalozzian principles.

The author of the aphorisms sees mankind vaguely yet profoundly dissatisfied with life, the meaning and purpose of which men do not understand. Those who might be expected to help in this emergency can do nothing—Pastors make no effort to understand the nature and the needs of their flock. In his blindness and ignorance man gropes for the truth which is only to be found in the innermost recesses of his own nature. The infant in arms, who is learning lessons of love and gratitude, is on the way to it. Faith and love are at its base, but the whole truth is un-attainable. Man, however, does not need it. His range of knowledge is limited. In the natural order it begins in his immediate neighbourhood and in his most intimate relations. Thence it extends its bounds, but at each expanse it directs itself again to the middle point, the fructifying centre of truth. True human wisdom rests firmly on the basis of an intimate knowledge of what lies nearest to it, and on the trained capacity for dealing wisely with its most immediate concerns.

All men need to be elevated to true wisdom, which is the universal aim of education. To this general aim all

* *Geschichte der Pädagogik*, Vol. II., p. 381.
† *Wochenschrift für Menschenbildung*, 1807, Nos. 13 and 14.

specialised education must be subordinate. The way of education is the way of nature, therefore the minds of children should not be forced into distant fields or be led into the confusion of word teaching before they have been inclined toward truth and wisdom by first-hand acquaintance with the realities of their surroundings. First the thing, then the word.

All man's native capacities and powers should have the opportunity to develop by use and exercise. First in importance is the moral culture of the individual, for all human wisdom rests on the power of a good heart, obedient to truth. This is the universal aim of all education. But man is fundamentally social and he must be educated for society as well as for himself. In this respect the family is pre-eminently the educative factor. In it all human relations are typified and all man's finest feelings are rooted. The child's love for his parents is the starting place of his love for God, which is the source of all restfulness in life ; and the rulers of men should see in the relations of fathers to their children the noblest pattern of their own obligations to their people.*

As we shall see in later chapters, some of the most characteristic of Pestalozzi's educational doctrines are here suggested. But the aphorisms, or, as they have been called, Pestalozzi's educational creed, attracted little notice at the time.

His next literary venture was a more practical and concrete contribution to the literature of social

"Leonard and Gertrude": Gertrude's Home School.

and educational reform. The holiday visits to his grandfather in his boyhood and the last eleven years at Neuhof had brought him into intimate contact with the poor. He had him-

---

* The full text of this document is given in G., pp. 15-32.

self suffered poverty, and, as Pestolozzi said, only those who have themselves been poor really know how the poor live. These experiences were the source of the story *Leonard and Gertrude*, which was published in 1781 and was afterwards extended to four volumes, the last three of which were published in 1783, 1785, and 1787 respectively.

Pestalozzi knew the village life of his native country as few of his contemporaries knew it, and in the first part of *Leonard and Gertrude* he is concerned especially with showing exactly the condition of affairs. In his simple story he makes clear the far-reaching effects of a corrupt officialdom. Every household in the small community of Bonnal suffers from the malicious influence of the man who combines the offices of village innkeeper and land agent. The whole atmosphere is contaminated and the people have for the most part sunk into poverty and degradation. There is, however, one exception, the household of his heroine, Gertrude, who is the model wife and mother. She saves her husband, Leonard, from the toils of the unscrupulous tavernkeeper, and through her action Arner, the new squire, who is anxious to do his duty to his people, initiates reforms which ultimately lead to the dismissal of the arch offender.

In simple convincing pictures the household of Gertrude is described. Her talks with her children, their eager response and ready helpfulness in the work of the household, their little acts of self-sacrifice in their mutual devotion extended under their mother's wise guidance to suffering neighbours, are all set forth so tenderly that one cannot help feeling that the pictures come from Pestalozzi's recollections of his own child life. Here we have in the concrete the doctrine which is characteristic of all Pestalozzi's teaching, that family life is the greatest of all educative factors, that the mother is God's appointed teacher, before whom all others sink into insignificance.

In the second book the problem of education comes rather more prominently forward, and in this respect Gertrude's household is again the centre of interest. The squire, his friend Glüphi, and the parish clergyman are coming to the conclusion that permanent reform is not to be expected unless they begin with the children. They cannot do much for the parents and they begin to realise that children entirely brought up in vicious home surroundings cannot be saved from moral ruin; on the other hand, if the home teaching is leavened with the Christian spirit, neither the incapacity of a schoolmaster nor the machinations of a wicked official could do serious harm.

In the third book a cotton-spinner, Meyer, who has seen the mischievous influence of improvidence on the efficiency of his workpeople, suggests that reforms should be instituted which would bring the schools into the most intimate contact with the actual lives of the children, and stimulate into activity the whole range of the children's powers applied to the circumstances in which God had placed them. The idea appeals to Arner and Glüphi, but how is such a school to be set up? Meyer suggests that Gertrude can tell them, for "she has worked wonders in the education of her own children, and converted her cotton-spinning room into a schoolroom which cannot be surpassed. Each of her children is just what it should be at its age."

They go to see her, and beg her to proceed as if no one were there. The family has just finished breakfast. The children help their mother to clear away, sit down to their work, and begin to sing their morning hymn. Gertrude reads a chapter from the Bible, the children repeat the most striking passages after her until they know them by heart. She explains nothing, as the lesson is meant for the heart, not for the head. The work is arranged according to its difficulty. The little ones who cannot spin, pick over the cotton and take out the dirty pieces. They are not hurried into reading and writing; the first thing is to teach them to speak. With an old A B C book they learn to pronounce the whole series of possible German syllables, but Gertrude attached greater importance to actual conversation.

It is what they *do* together that is really educative. "Except spinning, sewing, and the other household arts of which she is a master, Gertrude knows little beyond the beginnings of drawing and writing and nothing at all of what may be called technical education. Yet she contrives to lay the broad foundations for such an education. The children can measure exactly with their eyes; their hands are steady, their imagination is exercised upon their Bible stories, and their feeling for the beautiful, since it rests on their lively belief in God, is lofty and sound. The life of their wise and pious mother, in the fulness and loftiness of its truth, passes over wholly into theirs."

She counted with them how many steps it took to cross the room, how many panes there were in the window, how many fingers they had, the number of threads they were spinning; she taught them the bases of measurement by exercises in the sensory appreciation of long and short, narrow and wide, pointed and blunt, round and angular, and as they prepared their meals, or made the fire, or helped to carry the water and the wood, she made them realise the action of fire, of water, of air, of wind, of smoke, the difference between water standing in the tub and running in the brook, the various forms it took as ice, rain, hail, etc., its influence in dissolving the salt and in putting out fire.

She never took them one step further than they could advance from their own observation, and in whatever they did they were made to feel conscious of their own power and anxious to bring it into action.

The result of the visit was that Glüphi decided to become a schoolmaster in Bonnal, and to try to **The Village School in Bonnal.** introduce into the school the spirit and methods of Gertrude. He realised that whilst the child believed thoroughly in his parents, he did not at once put faith in his schoolmaster. The latter must, therefore, approach him in the parental method and manner, and make the child feel that the schoolmaster, like his parents, was most concerned to make him an independent personality, an end best reached by thinking more of what the child could do than of how much he knew. Current objections to popular education arose from wrong views as to what such an education should provide. Merely to remove ignorance was not to educate men. It was an incomplete view of the problem. Above all, it failed to appreciate the necessity of taking into account the actual situation of each individual child.

The fourth book continues the account of reforms in Bonnal. Gertrude gives Glüphi much good advice. "It is useful and right that the children should get knowledge and be taught to do things at school, but it is not in these points that home education is especially wanting; the most important thing is that they should become something that is good and right, and the many-sidedness of the school in respect of stimulus and guidance is its great advantage over the home—that view of its functions the schoolmaster should especially keep in mind. The children should acquire the habit of doing right, and an unshakeable determination to maintain it."

Of course there are times of difficulty, and the villagers

themselves often seem hopelessly inaccessible to higher
ideas. Gertrude, however, never loses faith. "A man
may live for a time without faith and love, without intelligence, and in absolute idleness ; but his capacity for love,
for intelligence, and for work never dies altogether. And
if that is true of a single man it is even truer of a whole
village." The schoolmaster in particular is discouraged,
but Gertrude urges him to think more of the children and
less of himself. He makes many mistakes in spite of his
high-minded efforts, and at one time seems to be losing
his influence with the children entirely.

A chance visit from the cotton-spinner teaches him
a fruitful lesson. The visitor tells the children a Bible
story in their own home language and at once finds access
to their hearts. Little incidents of this kind teach him to
study the children themselves, their peculiarities of speech,
their ways of thought, their individual dispositions, and
gradually his mistaken view that they were incorrigible
disappeared, and progress from that moment is rapid.
The school approximates more and more to the home ideal.
"When this does not happen," says the author, " the school
is rather a forcing-house in which the children are bent to
this or that form, than an institution which aims at the
free and harmonious unfolding of the whole range of
human powers and capacities." Hitherto, although the
squire has sent complete equipment for practical work, on
Gertrude's advice Glüphi has refrained from using it.
First, he must win the children's confidence and love.
Bible talks, Bible reading, and genuine interest in their
personal concerns finally bring success. Then a capable
woman is added to the staff, the spinning-wheels are
brought in, and actual hand work becomes the central
feature of the school machinery.

Important as practical training is, Glüphi always makes

it subordinate to character training. He had abandoned the empty verbalism of catechism teaching current in those days and substituted for it the simplest religious teaching, which centred in God's love for His children, combined with the habit of diligent work and kindly action. Work is a prime instrument in moral education in the Bonnal school. In the same way intellectual education is directed to the support of the moral ideal. "The head should be as bright and clear within as the silent moon in the heavens." Children are not born muddle-headed and Glüphi tries to preserve their native clearness by insisting on their seeing accurately and hearing properly; he educates them to willing effort by exercising their powers of calm attention and by refraining from burdening their memories with meaningless words.

In this respect Glüphi's teaching methods illustrate another characteristically Pestalozzian principle. As we shall see later Pestalozzi looked upon accurate observation as the fundamental requirement in the acquisition of knowledge. Glüphi teaches through the senses, he takes care that his children see and hear rightly, not merely in order that they may remember more easily, but because "the habit of accurate observation is the first step to practical wisdom."

Later in his life Pestalozzi planned a fifth and a sixth volume, but the MS. of the fifth was lost on its way to Paris, and the sixth was probably never written. The first volume he had called "a book for the people," the later volumes he regarded as written for the educated.

Morf sums up the contents of the four volumes in the words: "Glüphi takes Gertrude's household as a model for his school, and in the course of its history he approaches more and more closely to her proceedings. The parish clergyman brings his cure of souls into harmonious relation with Gertrude's home life and Glüphi's school efforts, and the work of these three persons in the house, the school, and the church is helped on by Arner, who brings to their aid the highest powers of the State, and these four primary institutions of mankind, working in harmony, give rise to a true education for and a nobler life amongst the people. The middle point is the home; its influence extends over into the school and finally brings about a new life in the whole village. State, Church and School work with the family towards a common end, but all learn from the mother, in whom centres the highest activity, because she follows simply nature's voice and the dictates of a heart educated only through Faith and Love."

The first volume proved a great success, but its author's object was not attained. People liked the story, but nothing further came of it. He wrote *Christopher and Elizabeth*, which was published in 1782. It consists of some thirty conversations in which Christopher, an intelligent farmer, discusses with his family, chapter by chapter, the history of Bonnal. Elizabeth his wife, Josiah his eldest servant, and Frederic his son are the chief personages. Its object was to point the moral of the successful story with greater clearness, but its didactic tone was not calculated to bring it into favour with the readers for whom it was intended. As a whole it is intolerably dull, but there are interesting pages in it.* The same year saw the beginning and end of a weekly newspaper, the *Schweizerblatt*, under Pestalozzi's editorship.

Exactly fifty-two numbers appeared. The contents were mainly from the editor's own pen, and con-
Schweizer-blatt.
sisted partly of critical comments upon the social and educational conditions of the time and partly of short stories, sketches and dramatised

* For example *vide* G., pp. 41 ff.

scenes representing current news of life. In many of them we have Pestalozzi at his best. How lovingly for example he describes the contented cobbler at work:—

"In one of the villages in my neighbourhood there stands, in the first little narrow lane near the church, a certain house. Fifteen years ago it was only a little old cottage, even its roof was scarcely whole, its window-frames were rotten, and in the upper storey there were no windows at all, while as for the others there were no panes in most of them and paper had been placed over the openings and attached by shoemaker's resin. The front door was going to pieces and the window shutters threatened to tear away from their fastenings and fall into the street.

"One summer day the window was open and I saw a man sitting at his work table. He sat there all alone and hard at work, his shirt sleeves pushed up beyond his elbows so as to display his strong sinewy arms, and stitching away at his shoes with such zeal and energy that I stood still for a time to gaze at him. He did not see me, for he was sitting with his back to the window. He sang a merry song as he pulled right sturdily at his thread, and when he used his shoemaker's hammer he whistled in time to his blows. About the tenth part of a skin of leather for soles and a small piece of calf's hide lay neatly piled together on the bench. A lot of old shoes stood in a row near the stove, one or two pairs of new ones stood beside a book of devotions and a Bible on a little shelf at the man's side, but otherwise there was nothing in the room—except a few more tools. There was also, however, no dust or dirt on the floor, it was almost as clean and tidy as the table: not the smallest fragment of leather lay scattered about, everything had its proper place on the table and in the room. The basin in which the leather was steeped was in the darkest corner of the room, and no water had been spilt round about it.

"After a time a woman came into the room. She was poorly clad but clean and healthy, and her expression was serious and thoughtful rather than merry. Nevertheless, she smiled at her husband as she handed him the platter of food which she had in her hand, and he answered her smile with such an energetic nod that his cap fell off. He then put his shoes on one side, stood up and finally sat down on the other side of the table so that I now came within his range of vision and was obliged to go on for fear he should ask me what I wanted. Those are poor people, but they are orderly and methodical and things are not so much amiss with them—these were my only reflections as I went away."

The later volumes of *Leonard and Gertrude* were less successful than the first. The circle of readers grew less with each new part. His style is not in itself attractive, and only those who were keenly alive to social needs and dangers, philanthropists and the more thoughtful members of the governing classes, took the trouble to wade through the prolixities of the later volumes. Readers of this class were too few to make the books a source of profit to Pestalozzi, but he was brought by their means into direct contact with many men of power and influence.

Distinguished visitors to Zürich made pilgrimages to Pestalozzi's cottage. Amongst them was Nicolovius, subsequently a Prussian Minister of State, who has left tender recollections of his relations with Pestalozzi in his hermit days. Nearly thirty years later (1809) in a letter to Yverdun he said, "The hours in Neuhof are as fresh in my mind as if they were of yesterday. How glad I am to think that you are at work and as inspiring as ever. May I be privileged to see you once again in full activity."

His correspondents were numerous ; amongst them were German, Italian, and Austrian ministers of the highest rank, who wrote to him for advice upon social questions which were forcing themselves upon the anxious attention of their governments.

Of the readers of *Leonard and Gertrude*, probably nobody owed more to it than Fellenberg, with whom Pestalozzi was later in his life to have many, not always pleasant, dealings. Fellenberg himself said, "The book made a deep impression upon me, and every time I read it I was more and more convinced of its truth, and it was in an access of deep feeling caused by reading it that I vowed to my mother that I would devote my life to the poor and forsaken children." *

This may well have happened shortly after a visit which Pestalozzi paid to the elder Fellenberg in 1783, of which visit his son has left an interesting account. " I was sitting with my aunt under a large lime tree in front of the castle of Wildenstein, attentively observing while talking to her what was going on in the yard. We suddenly saw a man, clothed in a singular manner, with a thick beard and long black hair, ascending with rapid steps the avenue to the castle. My aunt, alarmed at the man's appearance, sought in her pockets for something to give him, to induce him to withdraw. At the same time I saw my father, who in the meantime had left the castle, hastening eagerly to embrace him. . . . I learned afterwards he was highly distinguished for his benevolent temper and devotion to the best interests of humanity. It was on this occasion that I heard for the first time the name of Pestalozzi." †

* *Vide* Mod. Germ. Ped., xxv., p. 58.
† *Letters from Hofwyl*, by a Parent, p. 49,

A visit to his sister in Leipzic at this time was made memorable to Pestalozzi from the fact that he met Goethe, Wieland, and Herder there. He took the opportunity also of visiting many Training Colleges for Teachers, though he does not seem to have expressed any views concerning the impressions they made upon him.

"The Enquiries into the Course of Nature," etc.

On his return to Neuhof (1793) he met Fichte, whose *Addresses to the German Nation* (1807-8) were to kindle German enthusiasm for education as the one means of national salvation. Fichte saw in Pestalozzi's principles the key to the solution of the educational problem, and at his suggestion Pestalozzi set himself to write a philosophical account of his views upon human nature and the problem of its development. After three years' hard work he published (1797) *Enquiries into the Course of Nature in the Development of the Human Race.* Although to those who have Pestalozzi's whole career before them the book is distinctly interesting, one cannot be surprised that it found few readers at the time of its publication. As he himself sorrowfully admits in the edition of 1821, "scarcely anyone had noticed the book, although it had been before the public for more than twenty years."* Its interest for us lies in the fact that on the one hand we see in it how his fundamental principles are related to the philosophical thought of the time, and on the other hand we find in it a general account of the ethical basis of Pestalozzi's pedagogy.

These "Enquiries" were the last product of his eighteen years of literary work. During the greater part of this time Pestalozzi and his family suffered many privations. His wife was now a chronic invalid, and only the help of

* For text of this work *vide* G., pp. 53 f.

his faithful servant, who had established the most rigid economy in the household, enabled the family to hold together. To add to his troubles his only son returned home from his apprenticeship in Basel in a delicate state of health.

His literary work had not, however, been exclusively educational, though the social and political welfare of his countrymen was always its leading motive. He had written (1780) a competitive essay on the treatment at law of a crime[1] which was prevalent enough to stir Schiller to write indignant verses upon it—the murder of illegitimate children by their unhappy mothers. It is a remarkably outspoken plea for the rights of such children and for the considerate treatment of their erring parents. "An illegitimate child is no more a burden to the State than a child born in lawful wedlock, except in so far as it is badly brought up. An illegitimate child will, on the contrary, be a source of strength and blessing to mankind and to its own land, if it is rightly cared for. And so for the parents, such a child will be an instrument for their betterment if they may give it freely the love which is its due."

In 1792 he had received the entirely unsought honour of election to the citizenship of France. This did not prevent his writing, in 1793, a strong protest against the unrest the republic was deliberately inspiring in neighbouring states.[2]

There were other minor political writings which at least show the keenness with which their author followed public

---

[1] *Uber Gesetz-Gebung und Kindermord, Wahrheiten und Träume, Nachforschungen und Bilder.*

[2] *Ja oder Nein?* 1793. *Ausserungen uber die bürgerliche Stimmung der europäischen Menschheit in den obern und untern Ständen. Von einem freien Mann.*

events; and, lastly, he had published a book of fables
with the express hope of making men think intelligently
of public matters. Concrete teaching, he thought, would
be more effective than cold philosophising. He had in the
Preface to the third volume of *Leonard and Gertrude*
spoken of that as an A B C book, and it is as a sort of
commentary on *Leonard and Gertrude* that we must regard
these fables.[1] Two or three examples must suffice to show
the style and content of the book.

THE ORIGIN OF MOUNTAINS (19).

The earth fell once to wondering how the mountains had been
able to rise to such heights upon her surface. They answered her,
saying: "It all came about simply through the hardening of the
materials of which you yourself are made."

Comment.—"The hardening process may produce many great
mountains, but the higher these portions of the earth become, the
less fruitful are their summits; and where their tops stand covered
with everlasting snow, there neither trees nor grass will grow."

THE SONG OF THE BIRDS (21).

When Leander was passing through a wood in which the birds
were singing, he said "How gentle is the weather!" but when he
saw no birds in the trees, he said "A north wind must be blowing
here."

On this Pestalozzi comments: "That is all very true, but the
traveller who judged of the condition of the poor who have to work
in wind and in rain, in heat and in frost, from what he saw of the
protected life of the palace would make many mistakes."

THE OLD TOWER (34).

An old tower was crumbling away; tiles and bricks were constantly falling down.

The poor creature who lived in it was angry that he could not

---

[1] *Figuren zu meinem A B C Buch oder zu den Anfangs-Gründen
Meines Denkens*, 1797.

conceal its condition, and, in order to do so, had the stuff which fell each day collected and put under another wall.

His neighbour who saw this said, "But that will not keep your tower from falling!" "I know that well enough, but I must clear this rubbish away," said the man. On which his neighbour repeated, "That will do the tower no good."

"Yes, I know; but be quiet and do not worry me with your remarks about my misfortunes. I am satisfied if people do not see them."

His neighbour was silent, but watched him pityingly. The man understood the look and said, "I am now quite happy if I can only persuade myself that nobody thinks me miserable."

Comment.—"Do not ask me, reader, who it is that lives in that tower; if you are anxious to help him—I dare not name him." [1]

His cup of sorrow was full to overflowing. Only one of his many undertakings during the thirty years of his married life had prospered. Yet it is to this period of trial that the world owes the Pestalozzi to whom it finally gave ear. When he had taken his young wife to Neuhof his thoughts had been naturally turned to the provision of a comfortable home, in which he might enjoy with his family those rural pleasures which his friend had advised him to seek, the life which his youthful contemporaries at the high school had idealised as the happiest and most natural man could lead. As a greyhaired man of fifty, his bitter experiences had long ago convinced him of the vanity of pursuing purely external objects. His only wish now was for an opportunity of carrying through a plan which

[1] More of these fables are given in Biber's *Life of Pestalozzi* (1821); some of these are reprinted in Holman's *Pestalozzi*. There were 239 sections, the latter of which become longer and less allegorical in their style. They close, for example, with a conversation between two friends on the differences between a natural life in the woods and life as it is lived in society. It is, of course, reminiscent of the work to which he had been at this time especially devoting himself.

had little connection with his own worldly prosperity. The idea of reforming the education of the children of the poor had now become the dream of his life.

He had begun his active life full of enthusiasm for Rousseau's ideas. He had christened his only son *Jacques,* out of admiration for the author of *Emile,* in the literal inspiration of which he was almost a believer. But at Neuhof Pestalozzi learned to distinguish the letter from the spirit of Rousseau's teaching, "to reconcile the kernel of truth it contained with the facts of life, and to see in that kernel the secret of an education which should build up the strength of the people." At Neuhof, too, he learned to know the people as they knew one another. He had suffered with them. What this had taught him we may read in *Leonard and Gertrude.*

Intimate acquaintance with the most degraded of men had convinced him that the germ of good is not completely choked in any man, and that it only needs favourable environment to bring it to life. He had made a noble effort to bring the children of the lowest classes out of their surroundings and to solve the problem of their education. His failure only proved to him that the task was too great for private effort, that the resources of the State were required if reform on a large scale was to be attempted. Finally, the events of the time convinced him that the duty of the State was not ended when it had abolished serfdom, that, indeed, the step would be a dangerous one unless it were associated with schemes for educating the people.

CHAPTER IV.

PESTALOZZI AS SCHOOLMASTER—WORK AT STANZ.

Under circumstances of the kind detailed in the preceding chapter, Pestalozzi decided to change his calling once again. He would give up literature and become a schoolmaster.

Political Situation.

" The country was at this time under the government of an Assembly, constituted after the pattern of the *Directoire Exécutif* in France, and Pestalozzi, who was at an earlier period identified in feeling with the party now in power, though his sympathies had been alienated when the cause of liberty was contaminated by excess and violence, still counted the more wise and moderate of them among his friends. The most influential of these was Legrand, one of the " directors," who had arrived at the conviction that national regeneration founded upon a better education for all was the only means of turning the late changes in the social system to some permanently good account." [1] Encouraged by his support, Pestalozzi drew up a plan for a school on the lines he favoured, that is to say, a school in which instruction and education centred round industrial training.

Stapfer, the Minister of Arts and Sciences in the newly constituted government, was an enlightened man,

---

[1] Cp. Biber : *Henry Pestalozzi and His Plan of Education*, 1821.

who as a professor in Berne had already shown the keenest interest in the subject of popular education. The scheme won his approval and at his instance the National Executive adopted it and voted money for the purpose. Delay, however, ensued owing to the difficulties in providing a suitable site, and in the meantime Pestalozzi was asked to take charge of a government newspaper, the *Helvetisches Volksblatt*, by means of which it was hoped that the new constitution might win the goodwill of the people, who in many districts looked upon it rather as a tyrannous infliction than as the guardian of a newly acquired freedom.

They were born and bred in a democracy which found expression in the annual meeting of all the free men of the district, and they were in no mind to change over to the bureaucratic methods of an executive, however it might be chosen. Pestalozzi accepted the office of editor with joy. He secured promises of help from the best men of the time—Füssli, Lavater, and others. The first number appeared on September 8th, 1798, and 3000 copies were printed. Ministers of religion, teachers, and government officials received copies gratis on the understanding that they were to explain its message to the people. The venture was not successful. Pestalozzi himself was in control until another undertaking was placed in his charge, and the journal ceased to appear at the end of the following February. The early numbers were the best, but the paper was suspect from the outset, and circumstances were not likely to remove the suspicion.[1]

The unrest was strongest in the Nidwald canton, where it was fanned by the Capucin monks. It became serious enough to call for action on the part of the French, who

[1] One may, perhaps, compare the position and object of the Swiss Government with that of our own in its efforts to popularise the recent Insurance Act.

had called the new government into being. The province was invaded by French troops, the little town of Stanz was reduced to ashes, and the unhappy villagers were treated with ruthless harshness.

This dreadful calamity happened the day after the appearance of the first number of the new journal (September 18th, 1798), which was to bring peaceful persuasion to bear upon the stubborn people. Although the government was in sympathy with the purpose of the troops, there were so many destitute children that they were compelled to take action on their behalf. They decided to erect an orphanage, and on December 5th, 1798, they asked Pestalozzi to take charge of it under the general oversight of two specially appointed commissioners. On the 7th he went to Stanz. He says, " I went gladly, for I hoped to offer these innocent little ones some compensation for the loss they had sustained, and to find in their wretchedness a basis for their gratitude. In my zeal to put my hands to the task which had been the great dream of my life, I should have been ready to begin even in the highest Alps and without fire and water, so to speak, had I only been allowed."

The outbuildings of the Ursuline Convent at Stanz were to be transformed for his purposes, but little had been done when Pestalozzi arrived. The need, however, was pressing. In spite of unspeakable difficulties he decided to receive a number of the now importunate little ones on January 14th. They were in a dreadful condition both of body and mind. For more than four months they had lived as homeless beggars. Only a genuine Christian love such as glowed in Pestalozzi's heart, a love which saw a brother in the most abandoned of men, could have devoted itself to the task of raising them out of the slough of their existence under such circumstances as Pestalozzi did. He was all in all to the children: master, servant, father, guardian, sick-nurse, and teacher. There was only one room available. His only assistant was a housekeeper.

His exertions were almost superhuman. He was the first to rise and the last to go to bed, and even in bed he would continue to teach his children. He had no school materials. Nature and the children's daily needs were the only " tools " available. His difficulties were increased by the attitude of the surrounding people, who looked on him as the instrument of a hated government and a heretic to boot who was endangering the souls of the children. All his old Neuhof troubles were repeated. His neighbours hindered and slandered him ; some of his pupils betrayed him, though most of these were quick to find out the friend they had in him. But the story of his work is best told in his own words.

After describing the circumstances which led to the opening of the orphanage, and his preliminary difficulties, Pestalozzi continues : " My convictions were at one with my aim. I wished to prove through my experiment that the advantages which home education has over public education are such that the latter has no value for the human race, except in so far as it makes home education its model. All good education requires that a mother's eye should read daily and hourly, as she lives with her children, every change in the mental life of her child as it is expressed in his eye, in his speech, and upon his brow. The power of the teacher must be that of the father in the purity of its exercise at home.

Difficulties of the Situation.

" On these principles I built my procedure. I wished my children to realise at every moment that my heart was theirs, that I was sharing their fortune, and that their joy was my joy. I wished above all to win my children's trust and to make them feel their dependence upon me.

" In this respect, however, my difficulties were really favourable to my object. I had to be all in all to my children. I was practically alone with them from morning till evening. Everything they received, whether for body or mind, came through my hands. Every offer of help, every lesson came from me. My hands were in their hands, and my eyes rested on their eyes. I laughed and cried with them. They were out of the world, they were out of Stanz, they lived entirely with me and I with them. I ate and drank with them. When they were ill I nursed them. I slept in their midst. I was the last to go to bed at night and the first to get up in the morning. At their wish I prayed with them, and even taught them in bed till they fell asleep.

" My success was not immediate. The children were not easily convinced of my love. Their habits were too strongly fixed and many were disappointed by the necessary rigour of our lives. Sickness and even disease invaded us, and people attributed them to defective arrangements and improper food. However, not one died, and when the spring came everything went well. People were surprised at the change in the physique of the children. They hardly knew them again. Parents were especially difficult and constantly enticed their children away, but their places were filled again at once. Many of them misunderstood my position altogether : one would imagine me possessed of abundant means ; another would take me for a beggar earning his livelihood by looking after their children. Months went by before a single one thanked me, though the children for the most part learned to know me sooner.

" I soon had about eighty children. Most of them had excellent abilities, but they were woefully ignorant. Yet when they realised that learning would be useful they were untiring in their zeal, and in a few weeks children who had never had a book in their hands worked almost unceasingly.

"My circumstances made it impossible for me to start with a definite plan either in matters pertaining to the household or in the instruction. The very bases of such an organised plan were wanting and were only to be found in the children themselves, and it was better so. Had I started with the discipline of rules the severity of external order would not have accomplished my purpose. This would have driven away the children whom I wished to win. I had necessarily first of all to awaken a right feeling within them in order to make them active, attentive, and obedient in matters external. In short, I tried to follow Christ's precept—"Cleanse first that which is within that the outside may be clean also," and, as always has been the case in my experience, the application of this principle brought success.

"My point of view led me first of all to make the children feel like so many brothers and sisters, and to regard the house as a real home. On the basis of such a relationship I endeavoured to stimulate moral feeling. I was fairly successful in my object, and it was surprising to see over seventy children of the wildest kind living together in such peace and love, mutual attention and cheeriness, as is rare even in small households.

Family Feeling aimed at.

"To bring this about I sought to broaden the children's sympathies, to bring love and kindness into their daily experience and actions, hoping thereby to fix these feelings firmly in their hearts, and finally to make them the habitual motives of their daily conduct. With regard to words, these dangerous signs of good and evil, I attached them to the daily events of the household and the neighbourhood in such a way as to enable the children to view rightly the circumstances amongst which they lived. But brevity is particularly important, and if I lost a night's sleep in trying to put in two words what others might perhaps have put in twenty, I never regretted it.

"I explained very little to my children; I taught them neither morality nor religion; but when they were particularly quiet, I would ask them whether it was not really better and more reasonable to be like that than to be noisy. When they fell on my neck and called me "father," I would say, "Children, would it be right to deceive your father? Is it right to kiss me now and behind my back to do what would vex me?" Or if we talked of the misery of the country, and they were happy at the thought of their own lot, I might remark on the goodness of God in having given men compassionate hearts. At other times I used to ask them whether it was not better that authorities should educate the poor to help themselves than to keep them in workhouses or give them alms without really helping them out of their misery and putting an end to the burdensome idleness of their lives.

"Above all, I held before them the idea of not always remaining in poverty, but rather of appearing amongst other men as intelligent and capable, of being useful citizens and enjoying the respect of their fellows. They began to feel that I would carry them further than other children, to recognise the inner relation of my efforts to their future life, and to picture to themselves a happy future as actually within their reach. Effort was now easier to them. Their wishes and their hopes were in harmony with my aim. Friendliness and virtue flourished in the midst of this harmony as young plants thrive when the soil suits their nature and the needs of their tenderest shoots. I saw an inner power awake in the children, the universality of which far exceeded my expectations, and the particular expressions of which often both astonished and touched me.

"I told them that the neighbouring town of Altdorf had been burnt down and suggested the probability of there being a hundred homeless children there. How readily they agreed to my proposal that twenty of them should come and live with us! I pointed out that it meant some hardships for them; there would probably be no more money than at present for food and clothes; they would have to work harder and eat less. I made them repeat this to be quite sure they understood, but they persisted in their wish to help.

"In the same way I always tried to awaken the feeling of each virtue before talking about it, for it would have been unwise to talk about things of that kind unless they thoroughly understood what they were saying. Such talks were followed up by exercises intended to teach them self-control, that what was good in them might be put to practical use.

"Under the circumstances, organised discipline was practically impossible. Such discipline as there was grew up step by step out of our needs. I always insisted upon quietness when I was teaching, and I took pains also in respect of the way the children sat. Both points were helpful. I found in particular that merely to accustom the children to proper bodily attitudes has considerable moral effect.

"By following out these principles, the dispositions of my children grew quieter and more readily inclined to good action than anyone acquainted with their general ignorance could have thought possible. But as a matter of fact this ignorance scarcely ever stood in my way, and I found it much easier to treat the absolutely ignorant children than those who had already acquired wrong ideas. The latter were incomparably less accessible to pure feeling than those who were merely ignorant.

"When children were persistently obstinate and rude severity was necessary, and I had to use **Punishment.** corporal punishment. When conditions are favourable, it is possible to rely altogether on the pedagogical principle which says that we should win the hearts and minds of a crowd of children by words alone; but in a mixture of dissimilar beggar children such as I had to deal with, differing in age and in their deeply rooted habits, when forced, too, by the needs of the situation to accomplish my aims rapidly, corporal punishment was a necessity, but I did not thereby lose the confidence of my children. It is not the rare and isolated actions which determine children's dispositions and ways of thought, but it is the whole mass of your daily and hourly dealings with them. This fixes their attitude towards you and in the light of it they form their impressions of solitary actions. That is why the punishment of parents rarely makes a bad impression. Quite different is the position of schoolmasters who are not always with the children, night and day members of the same household. They have not the advantage of that basis of intimate relationship. They are relatively strangers to their children.

"My punishments never produced obstinacy in the children, on the contrary they were quite happy if I gave them my hand and kissed them a moment afterwards. This came from the fact that I was with them all day long and constantly giving them proofs of my affection. They did not misjudge my actions because they could not mistake my heart. Others misunderstood me, but I did not mind so long as my children understood.

"I always did my utmost to make them understand clearly the motives of my action in all matters likely to excite their attention or their passions. This brings us back to the whole question of the moral means to be employed in a truly domestic education.

"Moral education, generally speaking, rests upon three points, (1) the attainment of a moral disposition through pure feeling, (2) moral exercises, that is to say, exercises in self-control and effort in matters of right and good action, and (3) the working out of a moral purpose through reflection and the comparison of right and wrong in the actual circumstances of life.

Steps in Moral Education.

"I have already described my procedure in respect of the first two of these steps. My procedure in regard to the production of ideas of right and duty was just as simple and direct. It was still based upon the daily events in their own lives. When, for example, there was a great noise, I appealed to their judgment as to whether it was possible to teach under such circumstances. I shall never forget how free and strong I found their feeling for right and justice and how this feeling increased and established the kindness of their general attitude.

"To this feeling I appealed in every event that concerned the household. A report is current in the village that they have not enough to eat. I ask the children whether they are not better fed than they were at home. I ask them to think carefully and tell me truly whether it would be wise to accustom them to things in the house that it would be impossible for them to get when they leave it. 'Do you lack anything that is really necessary? Would it be right to spend the money I get upon thirty or forty of you instead of seventy or eighty?'

"Similarly, when I heard from outside complaints of my severity, I asked the children what they thought. My friend, you were there and heard them beg me not to spare them when they did wrong.

" I tried to make them set up standards of conduct, to decide what could and what could not be tolerated. I did not talk of freedom or equality to them, but in every possible way I tried to make them feel completely at their ease in my presence, treatment which produced that frank and happy look in their eyes which experience has shown me to be the result of a truly liberal education. I did all in my power to be equal to the trust which these eyes expressed in me; every day I tried to make them stronger in independence, and to keep everything from troubling those angel eyes in which I found the great joy of my life. I could not bear wrinkled brows; I myself often smoothed them; then the children laughed and avoided frowns in the future even amongst themselves.

"Among so many children I found daily opportunities of pointing out the difference between the beautiful and the ugly, between good and evil. Good and evil are equally contagious, and the greater the numbers the greater the possibility alike of evil and of good. I spoke to them quite frankly about this and I shall never forget the impression my words made upon them when on one occasion I had to reprove them for unruly behaviour. 'Children,' I said, 'it is the same with us as with any other household. When there are many children disturbance causes so much trouble that the weakest of mothers is compelled to treat her children sensibly and to force them to submit to order and justice. That is just what I must do.

" ' In a large household there are many things one cannot allow which might not be very serious in a small one. But you must help to maintain the necessary order, or the house cannot go on and you must go back to your old miseries. Think what that will mean. Children, in the world man

Home Education the Pattern.

learns either through necessity or conviction. If neither can teach him, then he is despicable. Think what it would mean if you were placed out of the reach of want and at the same time you cared nothing more for what is good and right. At home when you were quite small you always had somebody to look after you, and, besides, your poverty at times compelled you to do right, as it often may even against our will. But to do right on principle is far better and will carry you much further than what you did at home under compulsion. If you of your own accord will strive after the good in which your highest interest always lies, you will receive much encouragement from the seventy examples in the midst of which you live.'

"I often talked to them like this without troubling whether they understood every word, but I made quite sure that the general impression was properly conveyed to them all.

"I used also to impress upon them concrete pictures of situations into which faults of various kinds might lead them later. For example, I would ask them whether they did not know people whom everybody disliked on account of their wicked tongues. On the other hand, I would paint delightful pictures of the effects of the good, in particular the difference between a good and a neglected education. 'Don't you know men who are unfortunate because they were not accustomed as children to think and reflect?' 'Don't you know men who could increase their earnings three or four times if they could only read and write, and can't you imagine what may happen to you if you neglect your present opportunities?' 'Do you know anything more beautiful than to give help and counsel to the poor and suffering?' 'But if you remain ignorant, with the best will in the world this will be beyond your power.' Such talks impressed them very deeply and in general I have found that great ideas are essential even to the first steps in the development of wisdom and decisiveness of character.

"Great ideas which cover our whole capacity and circumstances, if they are brought forward in the right spirit, that is to say, simply, lovingly, quietly, but forcefully, necessarily lead to a kindly attitude of mind and a ready sense of the true and the good. In this way hundreds of subordinate truths are promptly seized and assimilated even though they are never expressed in words.

"I am above all convinced that wordy teaching and instruction unsuited to the intellectual condition and external circumstances of the children often merely confuse their early thoughts. Success depends on whether the teaching appeals to the children themselves as true—not in any vague sense, but from the intuitive recognition of its connection with their own experience. Without a background of this kind, truth is merely an unsuitable toy which bores them.

"As to my course of general instruction I knew no order, no method, which did not rest upon the children's conviction of my love for them. I did not care to know any other. Thus I subordinated the children's learning to a higher point of view. I wished to stimulate their better sense, and to let our mutual relations have the fullest possible influence upon them.

General Instruction.

"I had a reading-book, but I used it very little. I could not proceed on the same lines as a completely equipped and well-organised school; my children were too mixed to make that possible. It was necessary to treat them as a whole. Besides, I attached little importance to the learning of words even when I explained the ideas they stood for.

"I started with the idea of connecting their learning with their manual work, of making them run together, but I could not carry out my idea fully because I had neither the staff nor the equipment. Not until a short time before we gave up was it possible for a few children to begin at the spinning-wheel. Further, I was now quite convinced that, before there could be any talk of such an intimate union of intellectual training and manual work, there must be a separate general elementary preparation in both directions, and the special nature and requirements of each must first be made clear.

Manual Work.

"I had also come to the conclusion in respect of manual work in school, that its value lay in accustoming the children to work, and in making them capable of earning their livings in the future rather than in any immediate profit it might bring. In the same way I regarded the so-called learning as exercise for the mental powers, and to that end I considered it specially important that attention, observation and memory should be exercised and firmly established before the art of judgment and reasoning was called into play. Only in this way can judgment be preserved from the superficiality which goes with the facile fluency induced by the premature exercise of judgment, a fluency which is always more fatal to the progress of humanity than the ignorance of simple people of good sense.

"I was, therefore, less anxious to teach my children to read and spell and write than to use these exercises to develop their minds in as all-round and effective a way as possible. I made them spell words by heart before they knew their A B C, and the whole room could spell most difficult words without knowing the form of a single letter. At first I followed this up by letting them read the words they had learned to spell, but later I found it a more useful exercise to arrange the

Reading and Writing.

alphabet in combinations of two, three, four, and five letters, introducing all the sounds. Such a series of syllables I intend to have printed as an introductory primer of reading and writing. The consonants were put before and after the vowels, first in two's as *ab, ba, ed, de*; then in three's as *bud, dub, tap, pat, gum, mug*. Afterwards more difficult combinations of sounds as *ig, igm, ep, ept*.[1]

" Each set of combinations was learnt perfectly before going on to the next, and at the end whole words were built up out of these elements: *eph, ephra, ephraim*; *mu, muni, munici, municipal*, etc. Each series was learned by ear before the children saw it. Then they learned to write the series, and afterwards they saw it in print. The writing served, of course, to double the impression of the spelling.

" As to writing, I spent a long time over three or four letters which contained the elementary forms of many others; they also learned to put these together as words in all possible ways before passing on to new ones. Thus, when they could write *m* and *a*, they had to write *man* and continue writing that word until they could do it perfectly.

" I had hastily gone through the sections in the reading-book dealing with history and geography. But **History and Geography.** without knowing a single letter, they could pronounce accurately by heart whole rows of names of countries, and they showed such readiness in attaching what they knew from experience of the animal and vegetable kingdom to the technical terms which embodied the general notions covering those experiences, that I was quite convinced that in my simple way I had

[1] It is to be remembered that Pestalozzi was dealing with German, which is practically phonetically written.

succeeded in rapidly drawing out of them what they had been able to acquire of these subjects in the course of their experience, and that I was on the way to completing a definite course with them, which, on the one hand, would have embraced the whole of that knowledge which is useful to everybody, and, on the other hand, would have provided any child possessing special talent in one or another direction with sufficient previous knowledge to make further pursuit of the subject on his own account easy. I had done this without in any way going beyond the limits of their own daily lives. I consider that holding fast to a principle of this sort is the best means of discovering talent and helping it forward effectively.

" I always insisted upon the children learning everything perfectly, even that which was quite unimportant, and I never allowed them to forget what they had once learned or to fall below the best work they had once done. I was patient with the slowest, but if a boy did anything worse than he had done it before, I was severe.

" The number and the inequality of the children really made my course easy. Just as the older **Inequalities** children take pleasure in teaching what they **among the** know to the younger members of their family **Children.** and feel proud at taking their mother's place, so my children delighted in teaching what they knew to the others. The feeling of honour awoke and they learned themselves twice as much through making others repeat after them what they had learned. I soon had helpers among my children who were really more useful, and useful in a greater variety of ways under the special circumstances of the institution, than specially appointed teachers would have been. I, myself, was learning with them. Our whole procedure was so artless in its simplicity, that I could not have found a man who would not have thought it unworthy to teach and learn as I was doing.

"My aim all through was to push the simplification of all means of instruction to such a point that **When should** any common man might easily be put in a **Children go** position to teach his children, thereby making **to School.** it possible to dispense almost entirely with the need of schools for the first elements. Just as the mother is the child's first physical nurse, so should he receive his first intellectual nourishment from her; and I look upon the tendency to send children too early to school, and to substitute outside artifice for the home in the early education of children, as a very serious evil. My experience quite confirmed these views. I am also more than ever convinced that the sooner we unite, firmly and psychologically, instruction with manual work, the sooner a race will arise which will discover that what has been hitherto called learning need not take up one-tenth part of the time or the energy which it has done in the past. My experience has certainly established two facts which will contribute to this end—first, that it is possible to teach a large number of children even of different ages at one and the same time; and second, that this large number may in many cases be taught when they are actually engaged in manual work. . . ."

This long letter of Pestalozzi's was not published until 1807, when it appeared in the *Wochenschrift*, a weekly journal published in connection with Pestalozzi's school at Yverdun. (*Vide* Ch. VI., p. 106.) It was partly written during the time he was recuperating at Gurnigel, but, according to Niederer, his colleague and chief assistant at the time, it was not finished until he chanced to discover the MS. and asked Pestalozzi to agree to its publication. The letter is important, not only because of the authentic account which it offers of the establishment and conduct of the orphan school, but because, at least in Niederer's eyes, it presents an outline of the system of moral education which ruled in Yverdun itself. It might, wrote Niederer, be regarded as the ground-work upon which their whole system of moral education had been built. Niederer published it in the earnest hope "that it might contribute to the right and certain use of such means as are available to the teacher, whether in the home or in the school." "Although it contains no direct practical guidance, yet it is full of principles, examples, and types, the application of which does not appear to be difficult." [1]

In passing the chief points of the letter in review, we note that, as at Neuhof, his aim had been to combine instruction and industry, but he no longer looked on the produce of the children's labours as a possible source of revenue. School handwork was now rather a means of training physical dexterity, of promoting bodily efficiency and mutual helpfulness. He had not in any case the equipment for giving instruction in manual work; but there seems also to have been a change in his point of view. His pedagogy was broadening.

On the intellectual side, he had tried chiefly to cultivate the fundamental activities of the mind—"the powers of attention, observation, and memory, which must precede the art of judgment and must be well established before the latter is exercised. Only in this way can the judgment be preserved from the superficiality which comes from the facile fluency induced by its premature exercise—a facility which is always more fatal to the progress of humanity than the ignorance of simple people of good sense."

Whatever the children learned they had to learn

---

[1] Vide Niederer's Introduction, M., iii., p. 66.

thoroughly, and we see that the cleverer children were employed in teaching the rest. In circumstances of this sort, there arose in his mind the idea that there must be a simple and universal method of instruction, by means of which any mother might teach her own children effectively, and that if this could be found the schools would no longer need to trouble about the earliest elements.

His greatest anxiety had been to win the hearts of the children; he felt that it was only by gaining their loyal and loving goodwill that he could ever hope to transform his wild pupils into attentive, well-disposed, and obedient children. He tried to make them feel like brothers and sisters, each one of whom had an interest in and duties towards the others. In the family atmosphere the feelings of love, gratitude, and unselfish regard for others might develop, thereby constituting the bedrock of the higher life to which he wished to lead his children. He trusted to this much more than to lessons in morality, for he felt that abstract generalisations were quite unsuited to his purpose.

Incidentally we find that the unpractical Pestalozzi discovered the "school slate" during his five months at Stanz.

The work at Stanz, however, was soon over. In June the French army, having been severely defeated by the Austrians, once again approached Stanz. They needed every available building for their exhausted troops. The school had to be broken up. Short as the time had been, Pestalozzi's success had been almost miraculous. "Even before the spring sun had melted the snows from our mountains, my children were no longer recognisable." The men deputed to watch his work had at first generously acknowledged its value, though at a later stage, misunderstanding its nature, they were estranged because Pestalozzi had been unable to accept the advice and suggestions which they offered.   Troubles of this kind, the continued hostility of the people, and the unremitting exertions the work itself had entailed, were proving too much for Pestalozzi. He was breaking down under the strain.   For him the needs of the French army proved a blessing in disguise. He left Stanz to recruit in Gurnigel, a favourite Alpine health resort, hoping to return to his work restored in health when the buildings were free.   He was not permitted to go back.

Of course his giving up furnished fresh opportunity for criticism and calumny.   Even his friends said " Yes, for five months he may pose as a worker, but in the sixth it is no go."   Or they would tell him frankly, " It would be ridiculous to expect a man to do something reasonable at fifty because he wrote something sensible at thirty."   Yet in those five months Pestalozzi had done work which can never be forgotten, for his orphan school at Stanz is " the cradle of the modern elementary school.   Over it rises the silent glory of a martyrdom which needs no legendary adornment for its exaltation." [1]

[1] Schenkel, *Pestalozzi und dessen Bedeutung für seine und unsere Zeit*, p. 29.   Mann, I., p. lxxii.

CHAPTER V.

The Schoolmaster of Burgdorf.

Pestalozzi's critics had mistaken their man. As soon as his health would allow, he was impatient to begin work again. "Gurnigel was a rock in the ocean on which I was resting in order to begin swimming once more. I could not live without my work." The French had left the convent and the orphanage was opened by men who reported very unfavourably of Pestalozzi's conduct of the institution: he had been a bad housekeeper, dirty in his habits, brutal in his treatment of the children whose affections he had alienated. Slander could hardly have gone further. Stapfer, who was still Minister of Education, stood by his old friend, and he would have sent him back to his old post.

In the meantime, however, work had been found for him at Burgdorf, where an old friend of Pestalozzi (Fischer) had already gone to set up one of the cantonal training colleges for teachers which Stapfer had planned as an essential part of his scheme of educational reform.

From the point of view of Pestalozzi's own development and of his constructive work, this, his third period of educational activity, is perhaps the most important. He was to receive a small quarterly salary, to have apartments in the castle, and to teach in the lowest-grade school in the town—the school to which the children of non-burgesses were sent—conducted by one Dysli, a shoemaker, in his

89

own house. Pestalozzi's influential friends were not powerful enough to overcome local prejudice against him sufficiently to give him a post in one of the schools of the upper town to which the burgesses sent their own children.

Pestalozzi had now a very definite aim before him. As already suggested, his experiences in Stanz had somewhat changed the direction of his outlook and effort. At Neuhof he was living with beggar children in order to teach them to live like men. They were all the poorest of the poor, and would probably remain so. Yet they were human, and might be taught to lead independent, self-respecting lives, *if properly trained for poverty.* A poor man need not be degraded by his want of means to the level of a beast.

To prove the truth of this conviction may be said to have been Pestalozzi's prime motive. At Stanz the children were poor indeed, but not all of them had always been so, and some might reasonably expect to return to the comfortable standard of life into which they were born. The type of pupil was, therefore, much more varied. The children's powers were not all deadened by bad discipline at home and at school.

He allowed this variety of capacity and of individuality to find free expression, and as he watched his children he saw the truth as he had never seen it before, that *human powers develop of themselves and in accordance with law.* The problem of the teacher, therefore, was to understand the nature of this development in order to know how to guide and further it. This was the problem he set himself to solve. He was especially concerned to find the point from which development begins.

He was now interested in a wider question than that of the education of poor children, and although he was not long enough in Stanz to advance far towards its solution, he learned some definite practical lessons there which bore fruit at Burgdorf. He tells us that "he learned the importance of stopping over the beginnings . . . and, as never before, the relation of the first steps in every kind of knowledge to its complete outline." He saw in the unschooled ignorance of his pupils "a power of sensory apprehension and a firm grasp of that which reached them through their senses, such as our A B C puppets had never dreamt of." He learned the natural relation of book knowledge to real knowledge, and the drawbacks of a one-sided adherence to the former, which means absolute reliance upon words which are only sound and noise unless experience is behind them. "I saw how this may actually hinder observation and prevent a real understanding of the objects immediately about us." [1]

In the matter of practical teaching skill, he tells us that through having to instruct the children entirely by himself he learned the art of teaching many together, and since his voice was his only means of teaching, the idea of making the children draw, write, or spin, at the same time as they learned, occurred to him. The confusion of the repeating crowd led him to feel the need of rhythmic utterance, a practice which seemed to him greatly to increase the force of the impression made by repeating the lesson.

He therefore began his work at Burgdorf possessed of greater technical skill, and having a clearer idea of what he wanted to do than he had ever had before; but his novelties were not pleasing to the cobbler schoolmaster. Instead of learning the catechism the children were repeating some A B C rubbish after their new

Successful work in Burgdorf School.

---

[1] *How Gertrude Teaches her Children*, Letter I. He had, of course, remarked this before in his diary, probably long since forgotten. Cp. also *Diary*, p. 31 of this book.

teacher, and were frivolously wasting time over drawing. If this man was to experiment with the children, let him do it in the burghers' school. The parents could not fail to be attracted by this last argument and they declined to allow their little ones to be experimented upon.

But this check did not prove serious. One or two faithful and influential friends obtained leave for him to teach in the lower school of the upper town. The children were from five to eight years old. "I felt that I was really most fortunate, yet I was at first very shy. Every moment I feared they would turn me out of my school-room. I was, therefore, more nervous than usual, and when I think of the fire and the life of my first hours at Stanz, by means of which I built, as it were, a magic temple, and then of the nervousness with which at Burgdorf I bowed myself under the yoke as a matter of business, I can hardly understand how the same man could do both."

In spite of his trepidation and the irksomeness of the school discipline, "not free from pedantry and pretension," he continued his investigations and experiments with the same untiring enthusiasm and the same want of method as in Stanz. He was seeking the highways of education and instruction, and in the midst of dusty school duties, which began at eight in the morning and ended at seven in the evening, he was constantly lighting upon facts which indicated the existence of law in the processes by which our minds pick up and retain impressions from the outer world.

A chance suggestion from an interested friend, "*Vous voulez mécaniser l'éducation*," revealed to Pestalozzi the true nature of his purpose. As he did not know much French, he understood the words to mean that he was "seeking the means of bringing education and instruction into psychologically ordered sequence; and taking the words in this sense, they threw a flood of light upon his whole endeavour." Hitherto, "vague but vivid feeling" had been his guide ; now for the first time he saw clearly the true nature of the path which he was trying to follow.

Although in the course of his school work he could not always be true to the principles he was gradually formulating, we know that he did his duty faithfully from the point of view of the school authorities, for after a special enquiry and a careful examination his little pupils were found to have made extraordinary progress under the novel treatment. The report stated that " in eight months he had not only taught children of five and six years of age to read perfectly, but that the best among them could already write and draw well, and had made progress in arithmetic. He had also succeeded in awaking amongst them all a taste for history, natural history, geography, and geometry, and future masters would be greatly assisted by the foundations he had laid." Comments were also passed upon the simplicity of his methods, which were such as " even an intelligent servant might apply in the midst of her household duties." The " School Board " congratulated their new teacher, and showed their confidence in him by promoting him to a mastership in the second boys' school of the town, where, with renewed zeal, he continued his pedagogical experiments (May 1800).

One of the men most interested in Pestalozzi's work at this time was, of course, Fischer, who not only proved himself a wise and sympathetic critic, but was the means of introducing to him the man who became his first fellow-worker.

Krusi Taken into Partnership.

A number of orphans from the distressed province of Appenzell were, at Fischer's instance, to be provided for by charitable Burgdorf people. Fischer wanted a young man to bring the children to Burgdorf. He looked for one who wished to become a schoolmaster and to be trained for the work. Krusi was recommended to him. He had already had some practical teaching experience, and although almost wholly uneducated, he had an open mind, and considerable insight into child nature. In January (1800) the children arrived, and with them Krusi.

Fischer did not remain long in Burgdorf after Krusi's arrival. His plans for a training college had not prospered. A month or two later he died from typhoid fever, but not before he had consented to a suggestion that Pestalozzi and Krusi should unite their forces. The former could hardly have found a better partner. Krusi had in a high degree what Pestalozzi had not, the art of the practical schoolmaster. He was also intelligent and modest enough to submit himself entirely to the intellectual lead of Pestalozzi.

In some respects, however, the combination added to Pestalozzi's difficulties. It brought a new element into the school in which differences of age had already proved a hindrance both to collective work and to the continuance of his researches. The worrying demands of anxious parents naturally increased when these pupils, for the most part of a very different type, were brought into the school.

As freedom was absolutely essential to the work he had at heart, he approached the State authorities with a plan for an independent institute, in which he might follow his own course without external interference. With the help of Stapfer, his idea was approved by the National Executive, and a grant-in-aid was voted. Not satisfied with this, Stapfer founded, in June 1800, a Society of the Friends of Education, for the express purpose of winning support for Pestalozzi in the country. In order further to justify themselves the Society sent a commission to Burgdorf to enquire into Pestalozzi's work. In anticipation of their visit he prepared an account of his principles and processes, that they might know what exactly to look for.[1] The visitors were delighted, and transmitted a most favourable report to the government.

Encouraged by this double success, Pestalozzi decided to open his "Educational Institute for the Children of the Middle Classes" at once (October 1800). In the following summer, through the good offices of Krusi, further assistance was forthcoming.

Two men, Tobler and Buss, joined their fortunes to that of the Institute. "With these three colleagues Pestalozzi set himself to the task of establishing the practical consequences of his fundamental doctrines and of systematising his methods. At the same time he was working at a more elaborate statement of the ideas which were now taking definite form within him." The book *How Gertrude Teaches her Children* appeared in 1801, and for the second time Pestalozzi succeeded in attracting the attention of a wide circle of readers.

"How Gertrude Teaches her Children."

The book, which has profoundly affected subsequent opinion and practice in education, takes the form of fourteen letters to Pestalozzi's friend Gessner, a bookseller in Berne. In the first three he sketches the circumstances which brought himself, Krusi, Tobler, and Buss to the work : in letters four to eleven he states the results of his reflections and of his experience in the sphere of instruction on the purely intellectual side. The twelfth letter discusses practical education, that is to say, the education of the physical rather than intellectual powers, whilst the

---

[1] A translation is given in Part III., Ch. XVII.

last two are concerned with the questions of moral and religious training.

As we shall treat in detail of its contents later, it will suffice now to say that Pestalozzi's purpose was to show that by reducing knowledge to its elements, and by constructing a series of psychologically ordered exercises, even an uneducated mother might be put in a position to fulfil the duty which nature intended should be hers—the education of her children. This was his reason for adopting the somewhat curious title which pointed back to Gertrude, the model mother of Pestalozzi's creation. Educationally, it is by far the most important of his writings. " It will remain for all time a corner-stone in the vast educational structure which the nineteenth century has raised," not because it fulfilled its purpose in respect of the mothers, but because it laid down principles of education applicable equally to the school and the family.

Once again Pestalozzi had achieved a literary success, and visitors from all parts of Switzerland and Germany came to see the school in which his ideas were being worked out, though there had been a steady stream for some time before the book appeared.

In 1799, whilst Pestalozzi was still in the A B C school of Fräulein Stahli, a young German who was then a private tutor in a Swiss family had been to see what it was in Pestalozzi's practice that made the higher Swiss educational authorities put so much faith in him. This was Herbart,[1] who some years later succeeded to the Professorship of Philosophy at Königsberg, and who was to become the most philosophical of all the exponents of educational theory. He has himself expressed his indebtedness to Pestalozzi, whose subsequent career he followed with close attention,

---

[1] *Vide* also pp. 269-70.

taking a leading part in spreading Pestalozzian principles throughout Germany.

The number of pupils in the Institute increased, but in one important sense this was not pleasing to Pestalozzi. He had secured his independence, but he was a step farther away from the great desire of his heart—that of doing something for the children of the poor. He took as many poor children as he could manage to keep, but he saw no means of reaching the masses except that of training teachers for the work.

He had of course already students, philanthropically-minded men, who saw the national need and were eager to find the remedy, but this was not enough. He approached members of the Government who had shown interest in the work, and at their instance a special commission was sent to examine into the affairs and conduct of the Institution, and to report upon the best means of utilising its services in the interests of the public. The report of the two commissioners, of whom Dean Ith was the chief, gives an interesting picture of Pestalozzi's work.

After explaining Pestalozzi's principles, the report says of the actual work: "There is no trace of **Dean Ith's Report.** memory drill. Everything which the child learns is the result of his own observation, of his own experience. He learns nothing which he does not understand, he understands everything he learns. In the lower classes the chief exercises deal with observation and naming. The boys are led to notice first the objects in the room, then they go over the whole house, observing and naming everything.

" When this source is exhausted they are taken into the garden, into the fields and the woods, gradually accumulating a large stock of mental pictures and names. The children are then led to notice the objects in greater detail, their situation and the relations of their parts, their permanent and changeable qualities, the qualities that are general and those that are peculiar to them, their influence, their function, and their destiny. Thus they pass from simple to complex ideas, from mental images and names to judgments, descriptions, conclusions—in one word, to the definite and intelligent use of language. They understand what they say, and they say what they understand.

" For dogmatic religious instruction in the upper classes Pestalozzi employs a Protestant and a Roman Catholic clergyman who give instruction to the children of their own communion; in the lower classes child religion, not theology, is aimed at. The object is to stimulate and educate the moral feelings.

" To that end the whole life of the school as well as the instruction is religiously organised. Morning and evening prayers are specially adapted to the events of the day, and private talks with the boys do much to strengthen the impressions made by experience. Corporal punishment is rare. It must not be thought that this moral atmosphere comes from fear or from the strictness of discipline. The rod is almost unknown. It is only used in the solitary cases where sensory excesses must be frightened away by sensory pains."

Many visitors had been struck by the uncleanliness of the institute and its general appearance of poverty. The report says: " As to the latter, I am not exactly in a position to deny it. But one must remember that the Institute is essentially organised for the children of the poor, that it is not yet two years old, that it was started with absolutely no help or credit, and that nearly one-sixth of the pupils live at the cost of the Institute. To make matters still more difficult, school fees are always three months in arrear. They must, therefore, live from hand to mouth in the truest sense of the words, and this credit system, combined with frequent short payments at the end of the quarter, is one of the reasons why the Institution has already several times been nearly ruined. At least 10 per cent. of the income is lost in this way. Surely the head of the foundation ought to be praised rather than reproached in respect of this poverty.

"As to cleanliness, I have noticed nothing which, under the circumstances of the Institute, could be easily avoided. My arrival at eight o'clock in the morning was quite unexpected, but I found everything in order; the dormitories and beds were clean and well-aired, the children were combed and washed; their clothes varied, of course, according to their circumstances; the table was abundantly provided in respect of quantity; as to quality there was obvious frugality, but teachers and children shared alike. For breakfast they have soup, for supper soup and vegetables, for dinner, besides soup and vegetables, a small portion of meat and wine, and between dinner and supper a little fruit."

Accepting the report of the commissioners, the Government decided to transform Pestalozzi's foundation into a national institution. The staff were to receive fixed salaries, provision was made for twelve "students of the method," and sums of money were voted for the publication of the various school exercises which Dean Ith had remarked upon, as text-books for wider use.

By this means Pestalozzi was enabled to issue the three elementary books: (1) *The A B C of Sense-Perception, or Lessons in the Observation of Form*, (2) *Lessons in the Apprehension of Number Relations*, and (3) *The Mother's Book*. They were the work of the whole school staff under the general superintendence of Pestalozzi. The last of the three was received with special hostility, but the most objectional parts were really the work of his colleague Krusi.[1]

It was about this time that two notable additions were made to Pestalozzi's staff:—Schmid and Niederer, men destined to play the chief part in his future career. Schmid came as a poor pupil, but his abilities were so conspicuous that he was invited later to become a member of the staff. Niederer had been a minister. He was well educated, and naturally philosophical in his interests. He joined the Institute at Pestalozzi's invitation in May 1803.

Political changes inspired by Napoleon were again immi-

Deputation to Paris. nent in the little Swiss Republic. A great national deputation was sent to Paris to interview the First Consul on behalf of the nation. Pestalozzi, whose political interests had always been keen and strong, was elected a member. Before going he published a tract containing his views upon the general principles which should guide political effort.

It is an interesting document, which exhibits in brief the interconnection of his political, social, and educational work. Summing up his argument he says, " Our legislature should have its attention chiefly directed to the four following objects : (1) A suitable scheme of popular education, with an organised system of higher and professional schools based thereon, (2) a sound judiciary, (3) a good military system, (4) sound finance." [2] His visit to Paris gave him no pleasure. He may have had hopes of drawing attention to his own particular objects, but Napoleon was too busy to trouble about his A B C.

---

[1] An account of the contents of these books will be found in Part III., p. 378.

[2] *Ansichten über die Gegenstande auf welche die Gesetzgebung Helvetiens ihr Augenmerk zu richten hat,* von Heinrich Pestalozzi, Vorsteher des Erziehungsinstituts zu Burgdorf, 1802. (S., Bd. viii.)

The deputation was ineffective, and the political changes brought disaster to Pestalozzi's Burgdorf foundation. The new Government located in Berne had no interest in it. They questioned his right to the tenancy of the castle and finally gave him notice to quit on the plea that the rooms were wanted for their own officials. To save themselves in the eyes of their critics the authorities offered him the disused buildings of an old monastery at Münchenbuchsee. Although he received numerous offers of hospitality for his Institute from other towns, he elected to accept the Government's offer, and in June 1804 Pestalozzi's connection with Burgdorf came to an end.

The change cut him to the heart, for the place was endeared to him both by the friendships he **Pedagogical** had formed and the work he had accomplished **Development** there. As already pointed out, he began to **at Burgdorf.** teach in the Burgdorf schools with a more clearly defined aim than he had had either at Neuhof or at Stanz. His motives were no less philanthropic, but whilst his interests had broadened, his experiments had been concentrated upon the solution of a particular problem.

His object was the simplification of the means of early instruction, the reduction of the teaching process to a psychologically ordered form which should be so perfect, so simple, and so certain that, whilst it might be regarded as an instrument of precision, it might also be successfully operated even by ignorant teachers. It was to be useful especially to mothers, whose work would dispense with the necessity of schools for the very young, which were wrong in principle, because they tended to break up the most natural and therefore the most effective of all educational institutions—family life.

At Burgdorf Pestalozzi established the principle that observation is the absolute base of all our knowledge, that the child should therefore first be exercised in the sensory examination of objects ; next he should be told their names and the names of their qualities.

Prior to this second step, however, he should be trained in the accurate articulation of sounds which would make the pronunciation of words easy to him. Practice in the use of speech should proceed step by step with observation. These steps should be graduated on the principle of un-interrupted continuity, and each word as it is learned should be put into a sentence and repeated after the teacher. This is the principle of *The Mother's Book*,[1] and the famous " Hole in the curtain " lessons, which Ramsauer describes, are another example of the principle in practice.

" The best lessons he gave us were the combined obser-vation and speech exercises, especially those which centred in the curtains which were hung round the schoolroom walls. The curtains were very old and torn, and in front of these we often had to stand for two or three hours together and say what we could of the shape, number, and position of the holes and of the figured pattern. What we saw and mentioned had then to be gathered up into longer and longer sentences. Thus he would ask one of the children, mentioning him by name, ' What do you see ? ' Answer : ' A hole in the wall,' ' a tear in the curtain,' etc. Pestalozzi : ' Good, now say after me

I see a hole in the curtain.
I see a long hole in the curtain.
Behind the hole I see the wall.
Behind the long narrow hole I see the wall, etc., or
I see figures on the curtain.
I see black figures on the curtain.
I see round black figures on the curtain.

[1] *Vide* p. 177.

I see a rectangular yellow figure on the curtain.

Near the rectangular yellow figure I see a round black one, etc.' " [1]

In working at the " elementarising " of observation he conceived the idea of an " observation alphabet " (*A B C der Anschauung*), by the use of which children should be enabled to compare, measure, and reproduce form accurately, and in endeavouring to " elementarise " arithmetic he saw its intimate connection with form, and alongside the " alphabet of observation " he worked at an " alphabet of number relations." Along with *The Mother's Book*, these exercises constituted the three elementary books which have already been mentioned, and of which a more detailed account is given in Chapter X. Sound, form, and number were in his view established as the " three elementary means " of instruction.

At Burgdorf, too, Pestalozzi definitely severed himself from the improved catechetical methods to which Campe, Salzmann, and other Philanthropinists pinned their faith— Socratic instruction as they called it. It was on this point that he differed most from Fischer, who, as a pupil of Salzmann, endeavoured to train Krusi on the Socratic lines. Of course, Pestalozzi was dealing with young children, and, as he said, " a child cannot give out what he has not yet taken in," " the time for learning is not the time for judgment." Krusi, an ignorant but earnest student, had stumbled absolutely before the methods which Fischer tried to teach him; he welcomed with great relief Pestalozzi's outspoken criticism of this Philanthropinistic development.[2]

---

[1] *Raumer*, Vol. II., p. 336.
[2] *How Gertrude Teaches her Children*, Letter II. (G., p. 94 ff.)

CHAPTER VI.

The Institute at Yverdun.

(1805-1827.)

Not without some feelings of bitterness, Pestalozzi

München-buchsee. arranged for the last of his furniture wagons to leave the castle of Burgdorf on June 22nd, 1804. Tobler and Krusi followed immediately with their pupils. One thing cheered him. He left the seat of his four years' labours entirely free from debt. His success in this respect was due to others rather than to himself however, and his colleagues hoped that he would take the opportunity offered by their change to new quarters of handing over the business management of the establishment to one of them.

They had urged something of this kind as early as 1801 on the ground that the petty details of household management were a waste of his time and energy. They pointed out that whilst other men could do these things, none could take his place in the researches on which he was so keen. "Every expenditure of energy, every minute which you give to other things is an irreparable loss to our cause," wrote Tobler in 1801.

In Buchsee the need was more pressing than ever, for all government subsidies had been withdrawn, notwithstanding which they knew their master would wish to keep open house for any child whose parents were too poor to pay fees. It was not, however, petty self-interest that moved them. They were thinking of the loss to educational progress if the institution should go under.

They succeeded finally in persuading Pestalozzi to enter into an agreement with Fellenberg, a young man of thirty-three. He was the son of an old friend of Pestalozzi and he himself had been for years on friendly terms with Pestalozzi. At that time Fellenberg was the head of a great industrial school (at Hofwyl) less than a mile away from Buchsee, and he agreed to take over the business management of Pestalozzi's school, on terms which the latter very soon found intolerable. Fellenberg was to approve any new members of staff, to have the absolute disposition of the income of the school, to appoint a housekeeper and a household staff—all this without any thought of personal profit but in the interest of the school and of the cause it stood for. The reorganised staff drew up a prospectus of the school which after many corrections and many compromises was sent to Fellenberg for his final approval.[1] He returned it with so many emendations that it caused the final breach. In October Pestalozzi left for Yverdun, where two old teachers of his had already established a school. The time at Münchenbuchsee had been mainly spent in drawing up a great prospectus of the Pestalozzi-Fellenberg institution. It is a long document of fifty pages which was very largely the work of Niederer. It is the first sign of his growing influence over Pestalozzi.

Thanks to a timely present from the King of Denmark, in return for kindness shown to two Danish students at Burgdorf, Pestalozzi was enabled to spend the next few months at Yverdun in quiet literary work. He wrote his

---

[1] A translation of this Prospectus is given in Part III., Ch. XVIII.

Views and Experiences relating to the idea of Elementary Education, and entered into controversies with the Philanthropinists, who claimed priority in respect of all Pestalozzi's teachings. After long and frequently unpleasant negotiations with Fellenberg, it was finally decided to remove the whole establishment from Münchenbuchsee to Yverdun, the authorities of the latter place having expressed their readiness to house it in the castle.

Although Pestalozzi was now on the point of entering upon the most brilliant of his practical successes, as a matter of fact his work as an investigator was practically finished at Burgdorf. His later writings are in the main based upon his experimental work there and his experiences at Stanz. In some respects these later writings, influenced as they were by Niederer, are less trustworthy accounts of his views than the Gessner Letters. Niederer became the mouthpiece of his master to such a degree that some not unimportant misunderstandings have arisen in respect of Pestalozzi's opinions.

The household was reunited in July 1805. A period of astonishing prosperity began. Pupils came to the lakeside village from all parts of Europe, and many governments, attracted by the social aspects of Pestalozzianism, sent young men to study "the method," with a view to its introduction into their own schools.

Yverdun Institute.

In May 1807 a weekly newspaper, *Die Wochenschrift für Menschenbildung*, was started under Niederer's editorship. The most notable contents were: (1) Niederer's scheme of physical education[1]; (2) The text of an address by Pestalozzi to the Society of Friends of Education at Lenzburg in 1809, "Concerning the Idea of Elementary

[1] *Vide* p. 237.

Education." The text is both edited and annotated by Niederer, who often philosophises his master's principles almost out of recognition[1]; (3) Pestalozzi's Letter concerning his work in Stanz (*vide* Chap. IV.); and (4) Report to Parents and to the Public upon the present work and condition of the Institute at Yverdun.[2]

The Report to parents is a valuable document, inasmuch as it lays down the ideals which Pestalozzi and his staff held before them, and gives an authoritative account of the actual organisation of the school. Besides this, it expressly denies the equally damaging statements that the school was only for young boys of eight or ten, or that it was meant only for children of the higher classes who could afford to wait for the results of an exceedingly slow rate of progress. It tells us also that German and French were taught, and that boys who wished might learn Latin and Greek. The other subjects of the school were geography, natural history (experimental and descriptive), history, literature, arithmetic, geometry, surveying, drawing, writing, and singing. The Report deals also in great detail with such questions as the moral and physical well-being of the boys, and the special pains taken to study the individuality of the pupils and to adapt the instruction thereto.

This Report was written in 1807, at the moment when Yverdun was at the height of its fame. Pestalozzi's fame had now spread over two continents. The man who had never been able to spell correctly, and who always readily owned to his friends that he spoiled whatever he put his hands to, had become the prophet of instruction and of education ; the man who lived always in the present, and whose intellectual life, if we may accept Niederer's striking

---

[1] *Vide* pp. 379-80.   [2] *Vide* p. 320.

expression, had no history, was the inspiring personality of a movement of vast significance in the history of culture. The man who had scarcely been outside his own country had drawn to himself the astonished attention of the whole world, and the man who always complained of his absolute unfitness for a position of authority was the dominating force in a great movement and the object of a devotion which for his sake sought to make the "impossible possible."

The only explanation of such a series of contradictions is perhaps to be found in Pestalozzi's own expression : " I was taught as a child the holiness of meek and humble service, but now I have found out that even a grey-haired man may perform miracles if he too will minister to the lowly."

His devotion to the details of the work which he loved involved almost incredible hard work. With rare exceptions he was writing at two o'clock in the morning, and Ramsauer, who spent many years in the school, first as a pupil and later as a teacher, tells us that for years no member of the staff was in bed after three o'clock. The spirit of unity and brotherhood which reigned at Yverdun during the first four years was so perfect that, although the whole of the staff had free access to the school purse, nobody abused the trust. But even at the moment when their reputation was at its height, when their numbers were greatest and their material success was most striking, Pestalozzi's New Year address was most pessimistic in tone.

This was in 1808. He felt that the canker of disunion was silently growing amongst his colleagues. Although there was not yet an open conflict, different views as to policy were represented by Niederer and Schmid, and their differences of temperament were not such as made compromise possible.

Canker of Disunion.

In the struggle for influence over Pestalozzi, Niederer gradually gained ground, and as his authority increased the Institution took a character further and further removed from the pattern of Burgdorf. The idea of making it a great international school naturally grew out of the fact that from the outset they had tried to serve two different linguistic areas—French and German. Whilst this increased the number of their pupils it tended to destroy the unity of the educational arrangements. The curriculum was broadened by the introduction of the classic and other subjects which the teachers were not really competent to undertake on Pestalozzian principles, and in regard to the treatment of which the master himself could not exercise an efficient oversight.

Pestalozzi felt that dangerous rocks were ahead, but Niederer's influence was too strong. Schmid, on the other hand, warmly opposed Niederer's policy, and outside critics were quick to see what looked like pretentiousness in the educational programme. Even the visitors who came from all parts of Europe, and who were the outward and visible sign of the glory of the Institution, were a source of difficulty. They took up valuable time and exposed the teachers to the temptation to work primarily for show.

In 1809 and 1810 criticism was so vigorous that Niederer suggested the advisability of inviting the Government itself to appoint an impartial commission to examine into and report upon the conduct and efficiency of the Institution. Against the urgent remonstrances of Schmid Pestalozzi adopted the suggestion, and in 1810 the State commissioners were appointed. Their report did full justice to the nobility of Pestalozzi's purpose and character, but while much was found worthy of praise in the teaching of individual members of the staff, the general tone adopted by the commissioners was unfriendly. On the whole, they took the view that what was good in the work was not new, and what was new was far from good. The effect of the report was that, although the National Assembly expressed by resolution the thanks of the father-land to Pestalozzi, all hope of Yverdun becoming a State institution for the training of teachers was completely cut off.

Pestalozzi felt strongly that justice had not been done to his Institute. A long-drawn-out literary feud followed, and Schmid resigned his post.

Schmid's departure was a great blow to Pestalozzi. His addresses to the school at this time reflect his pain and his fears for the future. In his Christmas oration of 1810 he made a great appeal for unity. " The hour is come to separate the wheat from the chaff. The time is come when our dis-union must cease to afford food for the wicked. . . . We must either part and follow each his own appointed way, or else we must stand together before God and man, with one heart and one soul, resolved to follow one common calling. Let us be faithful to that calling. I am the weakest among you, but I am ready to make any sacrifice that may be required for our holy purpose. Friends and brothers ! Be ye also ready to make such sacrifices. They will not be small, for the cause is great. . . .

"I have been labouring under a great mistake. I thought the way to my end was shorter than it is; while the praise which has been showered upon us and the un-expected success of some unripe experiments confirmed me in my mistake, and prejudiced our unity. The seeds of corruption began to germinate among us. We con-tradicted each other in dogmatic arrogance, and ills began to spring up which, when it was no longer fashionable to praise us, gave the chance to the enemy. Our time of

Address of 1810.

trial has come. . . . The voice of censure is severe. . . . My poor house! Thy very lovers have become thy accusers."

But in the long run these appeals were of little service, and neither the literary polemic nor the loss of Schmid proved advantageous to Pestalozzi's cause. Schmid, although not a highly educated man, was an excellent teacher of mathematics, an organiser and a man of business. Neither Niederer nor Pestalozzi had capacity in these directions, as they showed shortly after when they added to their responsibilities by opening a printing and bookselling business, which soon proved a source of serious loss. Financial embarrassment ensued, but with the help of friends the foundation held together without Schmid until 1815, when he consented to return.

During Schmid's absence Pestalozzi's literary activity had not slackened, in spite of the business worries which crippled finances entailed. He wrote his *Swansong* and his *Life's Destiny*—the former a restatement of his educational doctrines, the latter a review of his life-work. These writings were not published until 1826, when they appeared as one book under the title *Pestalozzi's Swansong*. In 1814 he also wrote a long article addressed " To the Innocent, Serious, and Magnanimous of my Fatherland." It is an interesting testimony to Pestalozzi's ceaseless care for the people whom his school could not then touch. He complains bitterly that Switzerland is lagging behind Prussia in this matter. The foundations of national welfare are everywhere alike ; salvation lies only in the education of the children, but the children belong to the parents and not to the State.

" The imperial greatness of England rests on the inviolable sanctity of the home. Napoleon's worst act was that of handing over the machinery of the schools of the poor and of the localities to the rough management of the

State. May all the noble and the good unite against this tendency to forget that the home is the chief agency in the education of the moral, intellectual, and physical powers." Of course, Pestalozzi is not protesting against the establishment of universal schools, but he did object to purely central control, which by making the schools mere cogs in the wheel of a great machine, destroyed their individuality, and cut off their connection with the home life of the children.

Schmid's vigorous measures of reorganisation did not bring peace. After the death, in 1815, of Pestalozzi's wife, whose influence had done much to prevent an open breach, the oldest of Pestalozzi's fellow-workers, Krusi, resigned. Niederer followed him in 1817. Completely overcome by all these troubles, Pestalozzi threw himself entirely into the hands of Schmid, who was successful in raising a sum of money for a collected edition of Pestalozzi's writings which yielded a net profit of £2,500.

Last Years of the Institute.

The New Year's address of 1818 was naturally pitched in a triumphant key, and in his new ardour Pestalozzi made a further appeal for funds to establish an Institute in which his old work at Burgdorf should be continued. He wished to see educational research resumed on a more settled plan. There should be an Institute devoted to the further simplification of the means of instruction, the compilation of text-books in the various subjects of instruction suited to popular education, and the training of men and women teachers in the spirit of home education; alongside such an Institution he wished to establish one or more schools in which the results of the research might be put to the test of carefully supervised practical experience.

The money already raised he decided to devote to the education of the poor. He had twice previously made an

attempt to open such a school at Yverdun, but circumstances
prevented the successful accomplishment of his purpose.
Schmid at first objected, but as Pestalozzi held to his purpose he gave way. The new school was opened at Clendy
in the same year (1818), and once again sunshine came into
Pestalozzi's life. He had already in the *Wochenschrift* described his ideal school for poor children, and Clendy was
to be of this type ; but Pestalozzi had lost his grip, and
gave way to the request of the Englishman Greaves, who
knew neither French nor German very well, that he should
be allowed to try "the method" in giving English lessons
to the Clendy children. Then French and Latin were
added. There was reason, therefore, in Schmid's proposal
that the work should be done at Yverdun. Pestalozzi
agreed, and in 1819 the reunion took place.

Some objections were taken by the town authorities to
the children of rich and poor, both boys and girls, being
collected under one roof. This provoked Pestalozzi's " A
word concerning the present position of my pedagogical
work and the organisation of my Institute," in which one
finds the dominant interest in his mind then was the
training of teachers,[1] a subject to which he returned in
an address, " Views upon industry, education, and politics,
with especial reference to our position in these matters
before and after the Revolution" (1822). The people
possess powers given to them by God ; Christ teaches that
it is the duty of the rich to devote their property to the
poor ; they cannot do this better than by helping to found
Institutions in which men and women shall study the development of human nature and human powers and the
means of assisting in that development, with especial
regard to the circumstances of the children.

---

[1] *Vide* Part II., Chapter XIV.

If one might attribute any special development of Pestalozzi's pedagogy to his work at Yverdun, it would be the idea of a liberal professional training for teachers; liberal, that is to say, as opposed to a merely mechanical training in the employment of particular means, liberal as differentiated from mastering a particular technique. He conceived the idea of a science of education, applicable as such to the education of all classes, and he is chiefly concerned to establish institutions of a threefold character. In one branch the science of education should be the subject of research, in another the results of this research should be put to the test of prolonged practical experience, and in the third branch men and women who are to become teachers should be taught the principles of their profession and, at the same time, associated with the research and the practical applications carried out in the associated branches. One hardly need say that Pestalozzi's ideal has scarcely been realised even at the present day.

All this time he was doing his utmost to effect a reconciliation with Niederer and Krusi; but Schmid was the stumbling-block, and, instead of reconciliation, long and painful litigation embittered Pestalozzi's last years at Yverdun.

The affairs of the Institute were going from bad to worse, and finally in 1825 it had to be closed. Pestalozzi returned to his old home at Neuhof, and although all his hopes had been shattered, he took up his literary work again with great vigour. He published the *Swansong*, in which he passes in review the whole sum of his endeavour, and a new *Life's Destiny*, in which he describes with some acerbity the circumstances which led to the destruction of his Institution at Burgdorf and Yverdun. He was very proud at this time of being elected president of a local national society for the year 1826, and delivered an address to the society on "The Fatherland and Education," in which he describes the services education might render to a non-industrial country like their own.

But troubles were crowding in upon him. His *Life's Destiny* provoked many bitter responses. Fellenberg and Niederer in particular wrote angrily about it, but worst of all was a lampoon by Biber, who had been one year at Yverdun—*Contribution to Pestalozzi's Biography.* The old man suffered terribly from these attacks, not so much on his own account, but because men were pouring scorn upon his work, upon things which to him were holy. He fell ill on the 15th of February, 1827, and died at Brugg two days later. His last words were: "I forgive my enemies. May they now find peace to which I am going for ever." He was buried in the churchyard at Birr. In 1846 a monument was erected over his grave. One sentence thereon fittingly sums up Pestalozzi's life-long struggles—

Alles für andere; für sich nichts.

PART II.

CRITICAL ACCOUNT OF HIS EDUCATIONAL DOCTRINES.

CHAPTER VII.

PESTALOZZI'S FUNDAMENTAL PRINCIPLES.

In an important passage in the third part of *Leonard and Gertrude* [1] Pestalozzi discusses the many proposals for educational reform which reached the authorities who had now begun to take a genuine interest in the well-being of the people. Most of the proposals, he says, came from people with special axes to grind. They were interested in the development of this or that type of institution, or they were specialists in this or that subject. The great majority of the would-be reformers had no conception of education in the proper sense of the word. They failed altogether to look at the problem as a whole, whether from the point of view of the *fundamental necessity of providing an education which should be in intimate agreement with the course which Nature uniformly follows in the development of men's powers in their entirety, or from the point of view of the actual needs of the individuals concerned.* [2]

Education according to Nature.

---

[1] S., Vol. XI., p. 395. 　　[2] Natorp, *Pestalozzi*, p. 40.

The passage is remarkable in many ways, not least for its warning against the teacher whose interest is primarily in his subject; but the sentence in italics is quoted by Natorp as containing the germ, so to speak, of the whole Pestalozzian system, if one may speak of system in a writer who thought much more of his message than of the form which it took. Education must be "according to Nature." The phrase has, however, been so variously used that, unless the quotation will yield a richer harvest, it is hardly worth attention. But directly or indirectly we may arrive at a much clearer notion of its significance by a closer study of the words.

In the first place, of course, Nature here means Human Nature. It is not the Nature which Comenius had chiefly in mind, but all those qualities and capacities in man which at once distinguish him from the lower animals and make all men brothers. "What is man in essence? Apart from the differences of station which divide the king from the cottager, what is the nature of their common manhood? To answer this question should be the chief concern of those who call themselves the shepherds of the people, but do they, in point of fact, care as much about it as the farmer cares to know about the nature of his cattle?"[1] We are thus concerned with the course which our common human nature follows, when circumstances are not too strong for it, in the development of a moral personality. The possibility of such a development is what constitutes the humanity of a man, whatever station in life he may occupy. In other places Pestalozzi often uses the word Nature in Rousseau's sense. This is specifically so in the *Enquiries*, where he describes in detail the qualities which belonged

What does Nature mean?

---

[1] Cp. *Evening Hours of a Hermit* (G., p. 15).

"by Nature" to man before his degradation began and before he had entered into a social organisation.[1]

And now, going back to our quotation, we find the course which Nature takes is not an arbitrary one; it is uniform, methodical. We see further that men's powers are not contributed from without, they are latent and in due course "unfold"; that these powers are not abstract capacities; on the contrary, they are revealed in action, be it intellectual, artistic, or emotional; they do not exist *in vacuo*. Further, we note, though not so clearly here as elsewhere perhaps, that man's powers are to be developed in their entirety; there is no partiality or one-sidedness in Nature's scheme as Pestalozzi saw it; the complex of powers represented in the individual is to be completely and harmoniously unfolded. Lastly, we should not overlook the succeeding sentence in which Pestalozzi suggests the necessity of looking at the problem from the practical point of view—the actual calls which real life makes upon the individual. He never forgot that man is by nature a social animal.

The idea that education should follow Nature runs through all his work. He actually wrote a book on *Natural Education (Naturgemässheit der Erziehung)*, which was ultimately merged in the *Swansong*, in the course of which he develops more fully all that is implicit in the sentences we have discussed. Indeed, as we have already said, they furnish the keynote to all his writings. We may sum up their implications in a sentence or two. Development is spontaneous in its origin and in its continuance; it is in accordance with law, orderly and methodical; it depends on personal contact with reality, on concrete experiences; it is in a social *milieu* that the development of a social being with social instincts and a social destiny takes place;

[1] *Vide* p. 207.

and when that development is perfect, it is free from all one-sided specialism ; balance and harmony of powers characterise it. Here are five principles which lie at the root of Pestalozzian doctrine. To take them one by one:—

I. THE PRINCIPLE OF SPONTANEITY.

It is characteristic of all organic life that the forces which alone can initiate the changes in form, structure, and function which we call development, are not communicable. They are given, and they are unchangeable. This is the principle of life itself, and the human mind is no exception to the general rule. Mental development is as much a process of Nature as is the development of the acorn into the oak.

Impulse to develop lies within.
1. Moral Impulses.

" Our native powers unfold by reason of an inner indestructible impulse towards development," and the art of the teacher is like that of the gardener under whose care a thousand trees blossom and bring forth fruit. The principle of growth lies in the trees themselves ; the gardener contributes nothing to it. He plants and waters, but God alone gives the increase. . . . He only watches that no external force should injure the roots, the trunk or the branches of the tree, or in any way disturb the order of Nature in accordance with which the various parts of the tree grow side by side, working together to ensure the final success of the organism as a whole.[1]

But just as the seed left to itself may fall upon ground unsuited to its healthy development, so may the infant be born in surroundings which are unfavourable. He may grow up lazy, ignorant, imprudent, and regardless of others. His animal nature, his sensuous appetites may

[1] Address, 1818, par. 13 (G., p. 195).

determine his behaviour. He may become useless, even dangerous to society. But he has it in him to rise above his primitive animal nature, in which condition he is the slave of instinct and the victim of circumstance. Instead of the man given up to the pleasure of the moment, the child may become the man " who distinguishes, chooses and directs, the man who changes the momentary into the permanent."

But man does not make the jump from slavery of this kind to freedom, from the condition in which he is the victim of circumstance to the position in which he is the master of circumstance, directly. He passes through a stage in which he is under the rule of others; in which his conduct is regulated for him by others, in which he acts as the law directs. This is not, however, the end of things. It is only an essential stage in the forward movement. " The discipline of society is the condition under which man's higher nature unfolds; the development from rule by others to self-rule is the education of the human in man." This principle underlies all the social work described in *Leonard and Gertrude*. Its object was to make man free, the belief that the stability of the State depends on its success in furnishing the stimulus and the opportunity for men to take care of themselves. " The best thing men can do for their fellows is to teach them to help themselves," to help them to realise their freedom and to become worthy of it. It is in this native impulse to make his own law, this power of letting thought triumph over instinct, that man is distinguished amongst God's creatures. Even his religion is his own work. Man knows God only in so far as he knows himself, and man's relationship to God is the nearest of all his relationships.[1]

Human Freedom.

---

[1] *Evening Hours of a Hermit* (G., p. 24).

But it is not only in his moral development that the determining force lies within; it is equally so on the intellectual and practical side of man's nature. "I wish to psychologise instruction; but that is not possible except we succeed in bringing it into line with those eternal laws in accordance with which mind works up its miscellaneous sensory experience into clearly defined general notions."[1]

2. Intellectual Impulses.

This is the text also of a large part of *How Gertrude Teaches her Children* and of the *Swansong*. Just as the "natural man" has it in him to become a moral personality, and just as, in so far as he attains that level, he realises his "humanity," so, under suitable conditions, man rises above the condition in which the constantly changing experiences of the moment demand his whole attention and furnish his whole delight, to the higher thought-level in which he sees uniformities behind the sensuous variety, thereby fulfilling on the intellectual side his human possibilities. Again, all this has its starting-point in himself; and it proceeds in accordance with the inner law of his being, and not as others would have it. The art of the educator cannot alter by a hair's-breadth the nature of the process by which our race rises from the confusion of sense-impression to the condition of definite ideas. It fulfils its function in one way only. As soon as it attempts to fashion men in any other way, it throws them just as far back into the inhuman condition from which it was appointed by the Creator to raise them.[2]

Every parent knows the joy that comes from watching his child's first forward movements. The child's first step, his first word bring untold pleasure. Why does this tender sympathy with the inner life and development of

---

[1] Cp. Ch. XVII., pp. 291-2.
[2] Cp. *How Gertrude Teaches her Children*, X.

the child, which we find in the humblest cottage, not go on ? Why do parents later on repress his bodily restlessness and his ceaseless enquiries, often with angry words ? It comes from misunderstanding the meaning of it all. They miss the relation of these spontaneous activities to the development of their child.[1]

Yet the good mother, Gertrude for example, is the model Pestalozzi holds up to the teacher, just because the latter ordinarily starts from the standpoint of his subject, whilst the mother starts from the standpoint of the child. The teacher arranges his subject-matter in an orderly way in accordance with his own knowledge of it ; the mother thinks nothing of subjects, but only of her child's impulses and activities. The teacher puts his pupils through a course ; the mother suits her teaching to the occasion and the need. The teacher is guided by his misunderstanding; the mother is guided by her love. She gives free play to the child's self-activity, and she is the prototype of right method in education.[2] Gertrude's children seemed to learn everything as if they knew it before.

The principle of spontaneity applies equally to the development and therefore to the education of man's practical powers. This is nowhere more clearly expressed than in the *Swansong*. "The natural foundation for the elementary training of practical power lies in our native impulses, just as is the case in the education of character and intellect. We are constitutionally inclined to put our perceptual powers and our powers of movement to practical use.[3] The child, impelled by an innate feeling of power, begins with the

3. Practical Capacity.

[1] Cp. *Introduction to ABC of Mathematical Experience* (S., Vol. X., pp. 143-145).

[2] *Ibid.*

[3] Cp. *Swansong*, § 30 (G., p. 280).

many-sided use of his senses and of his limbs. This love of independent activity is precedent to outside guidance, which must accept a second place. At this stage guidance must take the form of stimulus only. It should give the child a pencil or a piece of chalk, and let him make lines crooked or straight at his will, without attempting to interfere. Presently he will realise that he cannot accomplish what he has set his hand to, and that his mother might help him; that is the moment when her assistance will be at once natural and welcome. The principle should obtain in every form of practical training which is based on spontaneity and freedom of expression.[1]

"In all respects, therefore, the secret of man's development lies within him, and if we would help in the process, we must study its natural course. Misery and failure are the common lot of men. Everywhere men are making painful and spasmodic efforts to improve things. But where is the truth which is essential to this improvement? Driven by necessity, he will find the way to this truth in the study of himself. Man's capacity for happiness is not dependent on the skill of others or upon fortuitous circumstance. It lies within himself. It is man himself, his inner sense of power, that is the concern of natural education."

II. THE PRINCIPLE OF METHOD.

In explaining the principle of spontaneity, we have repeatedly emphasised Pestalozzi's view that human powers develop in a certain order; it follows as a corollary that the methods of the educator must correspond to this order. Method, in other words, must in principle rest on the principle of spontaneity.

---

[1] Cp. *Swansong*, § 77 (G., p. 312).

In his Stanz letter Pestalozzi wrote : " I knew no order,
no method, no art—except such as came from

**Order—
Thorough-
ness—
Complete-
ness.**

my love for my children. I did not wish to
know any." It was later at Burgdorf that
he became a conscious student of Method.
Long before his Stanz days, however, when
he was teaching his small boy, Jacqueli, we
find him striving after effective and orderly procedure.
His man-servant, Klaus, warns him against over-pressure.
His friend Füssli advised him to advance slowly and
thoroughly. " Do not pass from a to b till a is thoroughly
known, and so on ; thus you will avoid the distracting
effects of superficiality." [1]   Order, accuracy, thoroughness,
and completeness became his watchwords.

We have the same ideas in the *Evening Hours of a
Hermit,* though this time he speaks of progress as concentric instead of linear. " The range of knowledge which
makes man efficient in his daily life is narrow, and in
early life it is narrower still, centred always about himself
and his immediate neighbourhood. Gradually the range
is widened, but every extension derives its usefulness from
its connections with those intimate beginnings from which
the feeling for reality is derived. Capacity for dealing
adequately with a familiar environment is the bedrock of
true human wisdom." [2]   " Parents, do not hurry your
children into working with things far removed from their
minds before they have got all the strength that comes
from dealing effectively with matters nearer to them. Be
fearful of all sternness and strain. By anticipating the
ordinary course you diminish their powers and disturb
profoundly the equilibrium of their nature." [3]

[1] Cp. Chap. II., pp. 35-6.
[2] *Evening Hours of a Hermit* (G., p. 20).
[3] *Ibid.*

But at Burgdorf he set himself to find out, by observation and experiment, what were the ultimate elements upon which methodical procedure should build. The Philanthropinists had written much about Method and about the beginnings of education (*Elementarbildung*), but they did not succeed in reaching the ultimate bases. His contemporaries often jeered at him and called him a plagiarist, but he knew better. He had to establish his own ground and work out his own procedure. The fundamentals must first be determined ; no organisation of instruction was possible otherwise ; these he sought in the child himself. He sought, that is to say, the absolute foundations on which knowledge and wisdom rest. To find these would be to understand the true nature of the problem of elementary education.

But these elements are not to be mistaken for the logical elements of which we speak when we have the beginnings of a subject of study in mind—they are not like the first principles of Euclidian geometry, for example. They are not definitions upon which deductive systems of knowledge are to be built. They are rather the fundamental factors involved in knowing, they concern the very origin of knowing itself, and they are therefore to be found only *in* the child, *i.e.* not in the subject of instruction. These, as we shall see later, he reduced to three innate and elementary modes of knowing : Sound, Form, and Number.

His first demand was that Method should be based upon them ; his second was concerned with the material of instruction. This needed careful graduation and it was the business of Method to effect this. Advance in knowledge should be unbroken ; the course should move forward in continuous and scarcely perceptible steps from easy to more difficult, keeping pace with the increase in power in the child,[1] and, thirdly, it should be thorough, each forward step should be definitely accomplished, and furnish a sure foothold for the next upward movement. "Before we pass from one step to another, we must make quite sure of the first, so that the teacher can say definitely just how far his pupil has advanced." It was in furtherance of these two ideals that his elementary books were pro-

His A B C's. jected, his various *A B C*'s, as he called them.

His problem in this respect was a twofold one. He had, on the one hand, to consider the particular subject of instruction (Reading, Writing, Mathematics, or whatever it might be) and to reduce it to its elements, and, on the other hand, to determine the order of their presentation, so that it should be in consonance with the stage of development the child had reached.

Once this is accomplished, everything will go with ease and certainty, for we shall have given to the pupil the power to go forward in the subject himself.[2] The method is as easy as a game, once we have got the fundamentals right. "The forces of Nature show no stiffness in their working, though they lead inevitably to the end for which they were designed." "Any method of ensuring the development of men's powers which claims to be natural, must be open and easy,"[3] for it must correspond to the necessary spontaneity of the child's own efforts.

In an essay written in 1800 for the guidance of friends who, at the instance of Stapfer, were interesting themselves in Pestalozzi's work, he gives the first account of his method,[4] in the course of which he makes it clear that it is based on

---

[1] Cp. *Swansong*, pp. 283, 311 (G.); also *How Gertrude Teaches her Children*, p. 101 f.

[2] Cp. *How Gertrude Teaches her Children*, Letter XI. (G., p. 135).

[3] *Evening Hours of a Hermit* (G., p. 19).

[4] *Die Methode. Eine Denkschrift Pestalozzi's*, 1800. A translation is given in Chapter XVII.

the laws which govern the development of the understanding. "The essential principle of method in instruction is that it should assist and be in harmony with the natural forces at work in the development of the understanding."

It is this which he has in mind when he says that there is only one method,[1] though he never claimed to have finally determined its character. So when a visitor suggested that he wished to mechanise education, he accepted that word as just hitting off his intention, but all he meant was that he wished so to methodise instruction that the internal mechanism of the learner worked smoothly. He speaks, for example, of the *"mechanism of nature's march* from confused sense impressions to definite ideas" in *How Gertrude Teaches her Children* (Letter VII.).

What is the one Method?

Similarly, in the introduction to his *Exercises in the Apprehension of Number Relations* (*Anschauungslehre der Zahlenverhaltnisse*) he says that they offer a contribution to the method of teaching arithmetic in accordance with the nature of mind and the development of the powers of thought. The observations are arranged in series in such a way that each set helped all the rest, as *the parts of a machine help the whole to accomplish its task*. And again, when he speaks of the teacher becoming a tool in the hands of the method, at least so far as elementary work was concerned, he means no more than that the results will be due to the method itself, and not to the particular skill of the teacher. Thus he would so simplify the whole matter that "any ordinary man could teach his children, and make the school superfluous for the elements at any rate."[2]

Although, as we shall see, Pestalozzi attempted a psychological analysis of the process by which our minds make

[1] Cp. *How Gertrude Teaches her Children*, Letter XI. (G., p. 129).
[2] *Ibid.*

the advance from vague sense-impressions to definite ideas, he did not attempt to reduce method to a definite scheme, as Herbart and Ziller did later. He felt it was capable of infinite development in the direction of the ideal, that it was moreover adaptable to subject, to pupil, and to teacher. He was concerned only with an *inner* likeness, not with a common external form into which all lessons might be forced.

III. The Principle of Harmony.

The distinction between intellectual and moral power was familiar to psychologists from the earliest times, but it is Pestalozzi's distinction to have recognised the signifi-cance of what he variously calls physical or technical capacity, and the capacity for work. These are for him the three fundamental potentialities of human nature, and a "natural" education must provide equally for the com-plete development of all these, not, however, in isolation simply, nor in such a way that one did not interfere with the other, but in mutual support of each other. One-sidedness in any direction is to be avoided at all costs.

The relation between them which he regards as the true one is that which looks on the intellectual and moral powers (inner powers as he calls them) in intimate con-nection with each other, as preceding the capacity by means of which they are made effective in life. But that is not the whole story, for practical efficiency is essential to the development alike of moral and intellectual power. "Doing" is not merely the test of insight and of good-will, but the essential condition of their growth, for, in general, power grows through being put to lively use.

But of the two inner powers again, moral power takes precedence because it expresses in the deepest and most direct way the principle of spontaneity. The feelings which are at the root of true morality are intimate, personal, spontaneous in a sense which our ideas never can rival. As the development of intellect corresponds most closely to the principle of Method, and that of the capacity for action to the principle of concreteness, so does the development of morality touch most closely the inmost of human characteristics.

In his earliest educational writings, and in *Leonard and Gertrude*, he tends to over-emphasise the practical aspect of education. He writes : " Knowledge is only necessary for the sake of efficiency in action." This is the main consideration ; knowledge and understanding are the means to this end. What we teach should, therefore, be determined by what the boy will have to do in life. Yet, with apparent inconsistency, he will not substitute a narrow vocational training to the general education of what is characteristically human. As he tells us in the *Evening Hours*, man does not work at his calling for its own sake, " but that he may enjoy the quiet blessings of home life," and " the education of men for this or that occupation, or for this or that particular social position, must be subordinate to the education which aims primarily at the purity and blessedness of family life." This is the true end of man.[1]

In the Stanz letter Pestalozzi was chiefly concerned with the moral aspect of education, as in the Gessner letters he addressed himself in the main to the question of intellectual training, though he did not in either case forget his principle of Harmony. Any one-sidedness of treatment is more than made up for in the *Views and Experiences* (*Ansichten und Erfahrungen*), the keynote of which is given in the picture of the man of whom friends and neighbours testified that he was one whose *intelligence, good feeling,* and *professional skill* could always be relied on.[2]

[1] G., p. 23.   [2] Vide *Views and Experiences*, Letter IV. (G., p. 159).

Still more emphatically and clearly is his position defined in the last edition of *Leonard and Gertrude* and in the *Swansong*. In the former he writes: "Each of man's powers develops in accordance with its own laws, independently and spontaneously." But these laws are united in a holy bond to a common end. They are not mutually destructive; their inner unity belongs to their very nature, though it is conditional on the due subordination of intellect and action to the higher demands of our moral and religious natures. The aim of education is to raise man from the sensuous appetites of his animal nature to the enjoyment of all the blessings of which he is capable, when heart, mind and conduct are in harmonious union. And in the *Swansong*: "The principles of education are based on the unity of human nature." "Only that is truly and naturally educative which appeals to the whole of our being, heart, head, and hand alike." [1] "Whatever is specially designed to develop this, that or the other power undermines the natural harmony of human nature as a whole, and leads ultimately to perverse artificiality of life." [2]

That this was an ideal unattainable in practice, Pestalozzi recognised, but it was nevertheless, as a principle, fundamental, and under its influence, at any rate, the worst features of much that passed (and passes) for education in the schools would be done away with.

IV. The Principle of Concreteness (Anschauung).

Nothing is more difficult to grasp in Pestalozzi's doctrine than what exactly it is that is meant by the untranslateable word *Anschauung*. Intuition, as suggested by Quick, does not express the idea satisfactorily, for it does not

---

[1] *Swansong*, § 6 (G., p. 269).   [2] *Swansong*, § 3 (G., p. 268).

mean the mere acceptance of an inner revelation, nor does it mean sense-receptivity as it does, for example, in Kant's writings. Observation, rightly understood,[1] comes near to it in a limited field of mind activity, because Pestalozzi uses the word to cover the contributions which mind itself makes in what we call experience. It approaches very nearly to what Kant called the synthetic function of thought, as opposed to the analytic. It is the creative power of the understanding, though Pestalozzi uses it also of our feelings (*innere Anschauungen*).[2] Much of what is implied by us when we speak of *learning by experience*, all that is involved in getting a sensory acquaintance with things, is covered by the word.

With the insight of a genuine philosopher Pestalozzi saw that the whole mind of the child was present even in its simplest sensory activity. Such activity is not merely receptive. The child's instructor may begin with sensory elements, but the result in the mind of the child is not a sensation, it is an *object* that is sensed, it is located in space and given a " now." Here is the mental contribution to the experience which psychologists call Perception. Our adult perception is so largely a matter of routine that it is only on relatively rare occasions that the feeling of having accomplished something follows the perceptual act. Children probably experience the pleasure of such activity frequently, and the keenest pleasure comes with the consciousness of the personal share in the experience. This is the type of activity which is characteristic of immaturity, but it is not partial activity. It occupies the attention of the child completely, and his

Whole Mind Concerned in Simplest Perceptual Act.

---

[1] Vide *Primer of Teaching Practice*, Chap. VIII. (Longmans, Green, & Co.).   [2] *Vide* p. 210.

conduct is determined very largely by it. Sometimes, indeed, Pestalozzi uses the word to mean experience (in the Stanz letter, for example), and it always implies that inner sense of reality which is the proper meaning of our word concrete. Thus a child who is faced with the question of how much he must draw out of the bank in order to make his sevenpence into a shilling is dealing with the concrete, though the sevenpence may be locked up in his money-box as the rest of his money lies in the bank, whilst another who has counters or even real coins may be busied with abstract unrealities.

Already in the education of his son, experience taught Pestalozzi valuable lessons in this direction.

Lessons of Experience. " Let him see and hear and find ; let him fall down and get up again ; let him make mistakes; let him avoid words wherever action is possible; what he can do himself, he ought to do." [1] So in the *Evening Hours of a Hermit* (G., p. 21) we find that " a mind formed by actual contact with uncompromising realities is adaptable and effective in future situations." Confidence and strength come from such training. Again, in the *Schweizerblatt*, he prefers the mind of the common man who, of necessity, learns the truth in his daily work to that of the teacher who gets it from books. "Personal experience so rarely misleads, and books so often." [2] Education is the result of continuous and well-organised experience. The point comes out still more emphatically in the *Denkschrift* of 1800.[3] " My starting-point is this : Personal experience (*Die Anschauung der Natur selber*) is the only true foundation of human instruction, as it is the only foundation of human knowledge. Whatever goes beyond

---

[1] *Vide* Chapter II., p. 41.   [2] Cp. *Schweizerblatt*, S., Vol. VI., p. 6.
[3] *Vide* Chapter XVII.

that is merely abstracted from experience, and in consequence, when experience is incomplete or partial, it leads to uncertain and untrustworthy results. Whenever experience is at fault, illusion follows.

"And now I ask myself: How does it come about that the world around me is rightly represented in my mind? Through what means does my experience of the most essential parts of my environment become ripe enough for my own satisfaction? I find that everything depends on three factors: my general surroundings, my necessities, and my responsibilities (*meine Lage, meine Bedürfnisse und meine Verhältnisse*).

"My general surroundings determine the manner of my experience of the world, my necessities drive me to effort, and my responsibilities direct my attention and make me prudent and careful. In this way the foundations of my general knowledge, of my professional knowledge, and of my morality are laid in concrete realities, instead of in the shifting sand of words." [1]

It is important to understand that when Pestalozzi speaks of the laws of instruction whereby the mind develops from vague sensory impressions (*dunkle Anschauungen*) to definite ideas, he is not thinking of a subsequent operation of the intellect which transforms the things of sense; the intellect is active from the first. An object has neither number nor measurement, nor points, nor lines, nor shape before the mind gives them to it. Even the vague awareness which Pestalozzi calls *dunkle Anschauung* is a mental process. What, for example, is *one*? The twig, or the whole tree, or the forest, or the universe itself? They are, of course, each one, because our minds make them so. This and all the synthetic

---

[1] Cp. also *Denkschrift* of 1802, S., Vol. VIII., p. 467.

operations of the mind are included under Pestalozzi's term.

V. The Social Principle.

So far at any rate as the individual as such is concerned, we seem to have covered the ground sufficiently as a foundation for educational practice. The point of view has been so entirely individual that we have described education as nothing more than a process of helping men to help themselves. But the description of a helping process raises the question of the nature and source of the help that is required. It cannot be dispensed with, and it is social in character. In fact, man in isolation is a mere abstraction. The individual in such a position would not become a man. The fact that man's moral powers lie at the very centre of this personality points to the social constitution of human nature, and the process of education is as much a social process as it is an individual. Modern pedagogy emphasises very strongly the social aspect of the problem, and we are to see how clearly Pestalozzi recognised this.

It is a common error to regard Pestalozzi as having in principle departed from Rousseau more perhaps **Pestalozzi and Rousseau.** in this respect than in any other, and to oppose the social education of the former to the individual education of the latter. This is based on a complete misunderstanding of Rousseau, in whose "educational dream" (*Traumbuch* Pestalozzi called the *Emile*) the hero is removed from his home and educated by a tutor in entire isolation. But that Rousseau means seriously to advocate the education of separate units as the ideal is disproved by his social philosophy, which is founded on the idea of a "general will" and a "general ego" in which the individual is entirely lost. Communities organised to such perfection did not, however, exist. Disunion, the strife of parties, and the self-seeking of the individual were the dominant characteristics of society as he saw it. This was not as the Author of Nature would have it. Everything is good as it comes from His hand, but everything degenerates in the hand of man! In his notes on the government of Poland he writes approvingly of the patriot sucking in the love of country with his mother's milk. This love is his whole existence. . . . Take him by himself, and he counts for nothing. If his country ceases to exist, so does he. If not dead, he is worse than dead! " Children should not be allowed to play separately at their own fancy, but made to play all together and in public, so that there may be always a common end to which they aspire." "The State will expect and get much from a carefully-thought-out system of education." [1]

It was not, therefore, in a spirit of anarchy or of anti-patriotism that Rousseau wrote, but he could not see in the social institutions and customs of his own country the right basis. The very idea of a common fatherland was wanting. He could see no basis for sound social education. Even family life was not "the thing"—there were neither fathers nor mothers in the old-fashioned sense of those words. It was not possible, therefore, to trust the education of his hero to them, and he took refuge in the tutor, and withdrew the boy from the vicious influences of home, putting him through a course of education which was not natural, in order to bring him back to Nature once again.

Rousseau was fully impressed with the social importance

[1] Vide *Rousseau's Minor Educational Writings*, tr. W. Boyd, pp. 139-149.

of education, and Pestalozzi, alike in his writings and in
his practice, showed how greatly he was influenced by him.
That social conditions set limits to educational possibilities,
that social well-being is the true object of education, that
education should be intimately connected with the life and
occupation of the family, that education is the first duty
of parents—all these are teachings common to both.
Pestalozzi's chief difference from his master was that he
tried to be practical.   Instead of writing dream-books, he
opened industrial schools, worked amongst the orphans,
and for twenty years conducted a school of world-wide
reputation.   His first undertakings were unsuccessful from
the business man's standpoint, but they deepened his
earliest convictions.

The writings which followed his disastrous experiment
in Neuhof—the *Evening Hours of a Hermit, Leonard
and Gertrude*, and the *Enquiries*—are the chief sources of
our knowledge of this side of Pestalozzi's doctrine, though
it is restated with added force in some of his revolutionary
tracts,[1] and in the book addressed in 1815 to the thoughtful
amongst his contemporaries.[2]

The most important question raised in the *Evening
Hours* is that of the relation between man and
his environment.   Pestalozzi knew to what
depths of degradation untoward environment
often reduced man, but experience had also
taught him that the germ of humanity was never completely
destroyed, and that differences in external circumstances
were not absolutely decisive in their effect upon development.   Simplicity of life, even narrowness of circumstances, were not unfavorable ; indeed, in some respects

Evening
Hours of a
Hermit.

---

[1] Notably in *Ja oder Nein* (S., Vol. VIII.).
[2] *An die Unschuld, den Ernst und den Edelmut meines Zeitaltes
und meines Vaterlandes* (S., Vol. XI.).

they were advantageous. At times, nevertheless, men's surroundings were so oppressive as to make it almost impossible for them to escape from crime and all its attendant miseries, and the problem of how to bring environment and man into the right relationship was of first importance and of the utmost difficulty. That such an ideal relationship could be found was an article of faith for him. He saw the ideal in the capacity man had for adapting his environment to his needs. He puts it clearest of all in the *Researches*. " So much I saw very quickly : Man is the creature of his circumstances ; that at the same moment I perceived : Man makes his own circumstances. He has within him the power to bend them to his will. In so far as he does this, he himself takes charge of his education and assumes control of his environment."

Man lives not for himself alone on the earth. Nature trains him to deal with external affairs, and, indeed, through their actual agency. These external affairs are in the main other people, and the closer his connections with them the more powerful their influence on his training. The experience that comes from the more intimate of our relationships is the chief source of power in dealing with remote matters. Thus the experience of a father makes a good ruler, the feeling of brotherhood makes for good citizenship; in combination they produce order in the home and in the State. Family relationships are the first and the chief of natural relationships, and thus the household is the prototype of natural education. From family to village life, and from village life to the life of the State, were natural steps in the enlargement of the environment, which were met, if followed in their proper order and without undue haste, by the corresponding enlargement of the individual. School life helped in the transition.[1]

[1] Cp. *Evening Hours of a Hermit* (G., p. 26 f.).

The social principle in education is expressly defined in a passage in *Leonard and Gertrude.* " Educa-

Leonard and Gertrude.

tion," he says, " is nothing else than the forging of the individual links in the great chain which binds men into one great whole, and educational failures come chiefly from treating the links separately, without regard to the chain to which they properly belong, when everything depends on securely attaching one link to the next, and making each strong enough and pliant enough to follow the daily movements of the whole." We may find fault with the particular metaphor on various grounds, but it emphasises the general position taken up in the story that man is very largely a creature of circumstance. "How very much alike men are! How easily the best might become what the worst are, and the worst what the best are." Recognising this, " we must begin to treat the poor folk whom we call criminals in a new way, and look upon their rescue and their betterment as our first duty." [1] It is not so much the man as his unhappy circumstances which are responsible for his position.

In all his educational schemes he feels that life far outweighs school in educational importance. " Life's duties are the only real sources of true wisdom," and repeatedly in the *Swansong* he reminds us that " life educates." So in the later volumes of *Leonard and Gertrude* all legislation is conceived as a great educational instrument. It is a powerful means whereby men may be elevated to true freedom. His social projects foreshadow much of the spirit and doctrine of the modern reformer. Property, he says, has its duties as well as its rights. It exists for the sake of the public, and not *vice versa*, but in his

---

[1] *Leonard and Gertrude*, Book II., Chapter LII. (S., Vol. IV.).

land reforms he will not have the landlord thrust aside merely to make room for the capitalist.   " The manufacturer and merchant shall not carry in his pocket-book the people's means of livelihood, as the feudal lord of old times carried it in his boots."   That the people should be economically and legally free is an essential condition of their moral and intellectual development.   The particular form of the State did not matter.   He anticipates the continuance of princely government, but only on condition that princes do their duty.   Failing that, he is wholly on the side of the people.

In the book of 1815 already referred to, he distinguishes between a *Kultur-staat* and a *Civilisations-staat*.[1]   In the former men are free and independent.   " We must first be men in order that we may be citizens, and so become States."   In the latter form of state no regard is paid to individual freedom.   The people are held together by external forces, economic or other; they cohere as aggregates of men through the exercise of outside pressure, they are not communities.   He pleads for the humanising of the State as opposed to the subordination of men to its requirements.   The State exists for the education of the individual citizen, and it is necessary to that end.

[1] *An die Unschuld, den Ernst und den Edelmut meines Zeitaltes und meines Vaterlandes* (S., Vol. XI.).

CHAPTER VIII.

THE AIM OF EDUCATION.

We may now consider in greater detail the more special aspects of Pestalozzi's doctrines.

Pestalozzi's whole life was spent, directly or indirectly, in the furtherance of one object—social amelioration. He was over fifty when serfdom was abolished in his native country, and he was one of the most ardent supporters of the new order of things inaugurated by the short-lived Swiss Directory (1798-1803). From his early youth he had felt that the condition of things which made the peasant of free Republican Switzerland as much a bondman as his brethren in Russia was intolerable. He welcomed heartily the constitutional changes which redressed this wrong. Philanthropic efforts which are usually directed to the relief of the wants of the very poor had always seemed to him rather to increase than to reduce the evils they were designed to meet. To his mind the fatal flaw in social work of this kind lay in the fact that it did not teach men to help themselves, but left them more dependent than ever. "The best service man can render to man is to teach him to help himself." "Man as a whole in his inner nature must be improved if the external circumstances of the poor are to be bettered." [1]

Social Reform.

---

[1] Introduction to *Views and Experiences*, M., III. 324.

This sentence contains the eternal secret of the Pestalozzian spirit. "The rich man in his superfluity does not think of YOU; at best he could only give you bread, nothing more; he is himself in truth a poor man whose sole possession is gold." [1]

In an eloquent passage in the *Swansong* he points out the fundamentally selfish character of man's care for the material well-being of others. Even parental love commonly means little more than the readiness to make great sacrifices that children may "get on." It is not in love of this type that the bases of religion are to be found. It means no more than that we love those who shall love us in return, and do good to those who shall do good to us again.

Such benevolence blesses neither him that gives nor him that takes.[2] It touches only the outer man, in most cases leaving him actually feebler than he was before. In the last resort " we can only improve the external circumstances of the poor by improving their inner nature." The strength of a people lies in their character, not in their possessions.[3]

Dawning political freedom was a move in the right direction, but it could not do more than remove obstacles to a general improvement in human nature. Mankind as a whole, however, has no virtue; virtue is essentially an individual quality. The State is not virtuous; it can only make use of the virtue of its individual members. This must first be established. " Those who wish to make the community virtuous and strong, before virtue and strength

---

[1] Quoted by Leser: *Johann H. Pestalozzi*, p. 14, after Seyffarth in his *Biography of Pestalozzi*.

[2] Cp. *Swansong*, § 139.

[3] The student may with advantage in this connection read Mrs. Bosanquet's *The Strength of the People*.

are developed in the individual, may frequently lead the State into wrong action, because they try to fix the external forms of virtue and strength upon men without making sure that the essence of the thing is theirs." [1]

Legal reforms at best only clear the way· Years before he decided to make teaching his profession he had realised that the true sources of human well-being lie within the individual man, and that to develop these is one of the prime needs of mankind.[2] So in his view a single educational undertaking is more valuable than a charitable gift of £50,000, even though the former should only result in the making of one real man.

Experience taught him how little was to be expected from politicians. Keenly disappointed with the selfishness and nepotism of the political leaders of the time, whose clamour for change culminated somewhat unexpectedly in the revolution, men to whom "the purer doctrine of his early days was only noise and words," he ceased to expect a good issue from "the tinkling cymbals of a civil truth," as beaten by his contemporaries, and decided to become a schoolmaster.

In his pedagogy, as in his politics, social reform was the prime motive of Pestalozzi's work. It is only in the light of this fact that we can obtain a true idea of his educational theories. Around him he saw, on the one hand, ignorance, poverty, and degradation; on the other, a crowd of insincere politicians whose rhetoric was empty and inconsequent, because it did not spring from a first-hand acquaintance with facts. Words void of real meaning were bandied about from man to man as if they were true coin.

---

[1] Letter to Nicolovius, 1809.
[2] *Evening Hours of a Hermit* (G., pp. 15-29).

For the moment the position seemed hopeless. Here was wretchedness and misery in plenty, and in the face of it abundance of talk concerning "the rights of man" and other formulae current at the time, high-sounding, but in their use hollow and unreal. What else could be expected when education, from top to bottom, dealt with nothing but words, grammatical or ecclesiastical formulae which did not touch in any way the real lives of those who learned them? Education wrongly conceived was the source of much social mischief; education rightly understood and rightly carried out was the only radical cure.

In this spirit, and "with full faith in the possibility of improving the human race," he turned his attention to educational reform. In so doing he was acting in strict conformity with the whole intellectual movement of the time. If the intellectual freedom which the "Enlightenment" had won was to be preserved, it must become the property of all classes. As we have already seen, education was in the air. In 1770 Iselin had written: "The problem of education is to teach men to be men, and this is the greatest service one generation can perform for another."

"We have spelling schools, writing schools, catechism schools, but we need *men's* schools,"[1] wrote Pestalozzi. The elevation of humanity, the making of men, was the aim he set before himself. *Humanity* inspired his labours at Neuhof and Stanz, the same philanthropic motive gave zest and meaning to his indefatigable experiments at Burgdorf; never entirely obscured even during the brilliance of his Yverdun success, it reappeared almost in its original form at Clendy, and the last utterances of the old man on the brink of the grave testify to his undying interest in the social aspect of his work.

[1] *How Gertrude Teaches her Children*, Letter XII., § 9 (G., p. 139).

But society is a great aggregate of individuals and the elevation of the individual is the only means of elevating the whole. Pestalozzi saw the elements of humanity in every man, latent human powers instinct with life, awaiting the opportunity to unfold. The inner impulse is already there, education has merely to furnish the opportunity and to offer guidance.[1] It is its business to bring out these latent powers, to watch over the process of development, to guide them towards that sum of qualities we usually call manliness, of which perhaps the chief characteristic is strength, moral and social efficiency. "The development of human nature, the harmonious cultivation of its powers and talents, and the promotion of manliness of life : this is the aim of instruction." "One may have produced a good tailor, a good shoemaker, or a good soldier, and yet not have produced a man in the highest sense of the word."[2] "He is not a man whose inner powers are undeveloped."[3]

Development of the Powers of the Individual.

We must finally rid ourselves of the idea that Pestalozzi strove merely to improve by education the material lot of the majority of men, if we would grasp clearly his point of view. It was not so much the poverty of those around him that filled him with pity, but their spiritual degradation.

With Ruskin, Pestalozzi would have had no sympathy for an educational ambition which was mainly inspired by the "goddess of getting-on." That men should be enabled to lead lives worthy of themselves as human beings, each intellectually directed, each sharing, however modestly, in the great process of human thought, was rather his ideal.

[1] Cp. Address of 1818, § 13 (G., p. 195).
[2] *How Gertrude Teaches her Children*, Letter X., § 22 (G., p. 130).
[3] Cp. *Evening Hours of a Hermit* (G., pp. 16-19).

Only when that ideal is achieved can men be men in the right sense of that word, and like Kant he believed that "men only become men through education."

Again, however, we must be clear as to what this process means. It was not the medieval idea of it that Pestalozzi stood for. Education did not mean the process of imparting to men something external to them—the dogmas of the Church, for example. A like idea is latent in Locke, who compared the initial condition of mind to a sheet of white paper upon which impressions from without were to be made. Pestalozzi, and Froebel after him, introduced a new element into the concept of education—that of self-activity. Healthy human life was not for them made up of soundness of wind and limb; it meant playing a part in the world, making as it were an original contribution to the sum of human endeavour, and they conceived education as the process of waking up this capacity actually latent in all men.

To work on lines of this kind was not the way to win a reputation as a successful schoolmaster. At Burgdorf Pestalozzi's results did not please parents accustomed to measure their children's progress by the usual tests. Where he strove to awaken capacity, they found ignorance of the A B C; where he tried to teach his pupils to think, feel, and act rightly, they found them unacquainted with the catechism. The standpoint of these critics is not difficult to comprehend. Most people still apply criteria of this sort to the work of the school. Within limits it is not unreasonable that they should, but more enlightened folk look deeper, and that there were such to befriend Pestalozzi we know from the opinions of Krusi and Fischer, which are quoted in the first two letters of *How Gertrude Teaches her Children*. "He wishes to increase intensively the mental powers of the children, not merely to enrich their minds by the addition of ideas" (Fischer). "He (Krusi) now saw that in everything I rather tried to develop the inner powers of the child than merely to produce detached results for each of my several activities."

Pestalozzi was quite conscious that he was departing from the traditional paths. "The schoolmaster of the past," he wrote, "had regard to the external rather than to the inner life, to the superficial rather than to the essential, to the immediate requirements of daily life rather than to those of the man himself." "The teacher usually finds his starting-point in his subject; you, mother, will find it in your child. The teacher has a fixed form of instruction through which he puts the child; you will subordinate the course to the child's needs, adapting it to him as you adapt yourself to his physical demands."[1] The difference is clear. One is education by addition from without; the other is education from within, an endeavour to bring to full maturity the child's own nature in its original God-given purity. Parental complaints did not disturb his plans; he continued his efforts to find the one and only way—"the way of Nature"—to the goal he had set before him, the development of the inner powers of the children.

Although in the Gessner letters (*How Gertrude Teaches her Children*) Pestalozzi does not explicitly state what those "inner powers" are of which he speaks, it is still obvious that he had the classification in mind which is expressly given in the opening sentences of the *Swansong* as *intellectual* capacity (*Geisteskraft*), *practical* capacity (*Kunstkraft*), and *moral* capacity (*Herzenskraft*), using the term moral to include *religious*, connoting, that is to say,

---

[1] Preface to *A B C der math. Ansch. für Mütter*. (Vide *Wochenschrift, S.*, Vol. X., 145.)

the attitude towards God which, in Pestalozzi's view, is the only true basis of right living. He treats of intellectual education in Letters IV.-XI., of practical training in Letter XII., and of ethical and religious training in Letters XIII. and XIV. These three sides of human nature, he tells us, develop each according to its own unchangeable laws. That is why he deals separately in this book with three sides of education, (1) intellectual, (2) physical and technical, (3) moral.

Character (Morality) the Final Aim. Has the teacher, then, three independent processes to watch over? This was not Pestalozzi's view. He fully recognised the necessity of some unifying principle. To define education as the process of developing the "inner powers" of the child, and to follow this up by an enumeration of those powers without explaining their mutual relationships, could give no guidance to the teacher. If he is to pursue three independent aims, what is to ensure his maintaining the proportions which will secure the "harmony of the powers," which is at the same time desired? Although the point is not explicitly met in *How Gertrude Teaches her Children*, it is clear in his later writings that Pestalozzi felt the truth as put by Herbart.

"We might assume as many problems for education as there are possible aims for men. If it is to be possible to think over thoroughly and accurately and to carry out systematically the *business* of education as a single whole, it must be previously possible to comprehend the work of education likewise as a whole,"[1] *i.e.* to regard it as pursuing a single aim. Even in the Gessner letters, however, Pestalozzi tells us there is a "keystone to his system," and in the thirteenth letter he gives more than a glimpse

[1] Herbart, *On the Aesthetic Revelation of the World as the Chief Work of Education*, Felkin's Translation, p. 57.

of its relation to the intellectual and practical sides of our nature, with the development of which he has been previously concerned. " Education and instruction must be brought into harmony with the feeling of my inner nature, through the gradual development of which my mind rises to the recognition and veneration of the moral law."

Indeed, one cannot read *How Gertrude Teaches her Children* without realising that Pestalozzi might have defined the whole sum of his endeavour as seeking to establish in the child a Christian disposition, resting on the broad basis of a cultivation of the powers which are essential to practical life. The point, however, does not really arise in the book, chiefly because it is concerned primarily with intellectual education—that was Pestalozzi's chief interest at the time of its publication—and not with a general discussion of educational aims.

In his later writings he approaches the question over and over again. The most exhaustive discussion is in the *Swan-song*, but the point is taken up with more or less fulness in almost all his later utterances, probably in answer to contemporary criticism, which was often pointed and substantial enough to need attention.

"The whole work of education and its *only* work may be summed up in the concept Morality." " Morality is universally acknowledged as the highest aim of humanity, and consequently of education." These are Herbart's words. He follows them up by an examination of the concept of morality, expanding its usual acceptation, and demonstrating its real possibility. This is an orderly and a scientific procedure, but it is not Pestalozzi's method. Instead of defining morality, he gives us the plain man's answer to the question, " What is that man like who is as all men should be ? " This ideal man shows in all his judgments, in all his counsel, in all his undertakings, a

sound and trained intelligence; a steadfast, strong, benevolent heart that is capable of any exaltation and effort;
and such skill and patience in his actions as ensure a
successful issue to whatever he takes up.

One-sidedness in any direction is fatal. The man of
cultivated intelligence who has no sympathy
with suffering, the philanthropist who is ever
ready to sacrifice himself in pursuit of good
work but is wanting in tact, the artist who is
pre-eminent in his own sphere but is unfriendly
and self-seeking—all alike fall below the plain
man's ideal.[1] To sum up this whole idea one may perhaps
say that Pestalozzi's ideal man is one whose benevolent
disposition is guided by intellectual insight and made
effective by practical acquaintance with affairs. *Disposition and Efficiency* are the determining factors.

*Education
seeks to
establish
Disposition
and
Efficiency.*

To look more closely at what is here called Disposition,
we find that Pestalozzi is quite definite in his view as to
the elements which determine its nature aright. They are
Faith and Love. "I regard all the powers of the intellect,
all the practical skill and insight which belong to my
nature, only as a means for the divine exaltation of my
heart to love. Man's improvement is for me only the
advance of the race towards Humanity, and the sole
eternal basis for such an advance is Love." Instruction in
itself no more develops love than it develops hate; it cannot, therefore, be the essence of education. "Education
proper to our nature leads to love, *not a blind, but a seeing
love*, in which our moral, intellectual, and practical powers
unite, thereby constituting our humanity." [2] "But true
Love can only come from true Faith." [3] "In Faith and

[1] *Views and Experiences*, Letter IV. (G., pp. 159-61).

[2] Address, 1809 (M., Vol. IV., p. 15 f.).

[3] Cp. *Evening Hours of a Hermit* (G., pp. 26-32).

Love alone our powers begin, continue, and end the process of their development. They are thus the Alpha and
Omega of a natural education to humanity."[1] In the atmosphere of family love, the love of God and of our fellow
man develops. This gives the tone and direction to disposition, which, combined with efficiency, constitutes character.

Granted, however, that human nature is capable of
modification by the atmosphere in which it
Environment and Freedom. matures, the question naturally arises as to
whether or not human nature is entirely a
creature of its environment, whether the individual man is no more responsible for his ultimate form than
the plant which the gardener tends or neglects as suits his
purpose, whether man is pre-determined or self-determined,
whether or not the will is free. Pestalozzi takes up the
question at some length in his New Year's Address, 1818.

He uses his favourite simile of a tree developing from
its tiny seed. The seed is planted in a particular soil, and
if conditions are favourable, the tree completes its destiny by
bringing forth fruit, an end towards which its whole energy
is directed, in spite of, nay, with the help of its differently
organised parts, which find their unity in this ultimate
end. But the seed is at the mercy of its environment. It
will wither and die in a dry or rocky soil; the plethora of
good things in an over-watered or over-manured soil is
irresistible to the consequent destruction of the tree.

Man's case is very different. Like the tree, he has a
great variety of separately functioning parts; all, however,
are (or may be) united in the service of the lofty end
which is the kernel of the humanity of men. But unlike
the tree, and unlike all other natural forms animate and
inanimate, man is not at the mercy of his environment.

" This environment is made up of his sensuous bodily

[1] *Swansong,* xiv. 136.

nature, his specific hereditary tendencies, together with the physical and spiritual forces which are external to him. This is the soil, so to speak, in which the human germ is planted, but that germ is of a higher order than that of the tree. It has within it the power to reject and to choose. Freedom is the characteristic mark of the human element in man. He absorbs the good or the evil as he will. Man has a conscience. God's voice speaks to him and tells him what is good and what is evil, and invites him to choose the good and thus become one with God. But man can open or close his ear to the divine voice as he will. He is free even to deny his own freedom and yield himself completely to external influences." [1] In a later passage he says, " Love and Faith, as the basis of education, presuppose the lofty freedom of the Will as the organic centre of all man's powers, and this presupposition makes it absolutely essential to recognise the duty of exalting the Will, through Faith and Love, to unselfish devotion to the cause of truth and right, to the truth of God and to the rights of our brethren."

Freedom of will and a sense of duty are not incompatibles. " The child must be prepared for the ready and active performance of the whole circle of his duties towards God, towards his neighbours, and towards himself. He must be vigorously trained to such sustained effort and prolonged endurance as the performance of duty may in the future demand." [2] " The educator must aim at the unification of all human powers for the purpose of their final determination in the freedom of the human will, through Faith and Love." [3] " The education of our intellectual powers must be subordinated to the higher laws of our will; in this way we shall rather confirm and increase the

---

[1] Address to his House, 1818, § 7 (G., p. 191).   [2] Cp. *Leonard and Gertrude*, Bk. IV., Chs. LXXI., LXXII.   [3] Address, 1818.

strength, perfection, and independence of those powers than endanger their justice and truth." [1]

We may, perhaps, now put Pestalozzi's position in the following way. Whilst he was always moved by philanthropic motives, and by the great social benefits he expected education to bring about, he regarded the problem of education as primarily an individual one. He saw in each individual the germ of that which we call humanity. Its distinguishing factors involve, on the one hand, a personality which is free and self-determined, yet susceptible to external influence and guidance, and on the other a complex of powers, physical, mental, and moral, which are capable of indefinite and progressive advance. Whilst these powers are co-equal in a quantitative sense and demand an equal amount of attention from the teacher, who must above all things avoid one-sidedness, in a qualitative sense it is always the ethical element, touching as it does the personality, that is of first importance. Intellectual, moral, and physical education are not to stand side by side in isolated detachment, they are to react one upon the other, with a due subordination of the intellectual and physical to the moral, which through faith and love is the basis of human personality.

Position Summed up.

The individual character of the problem of education as viewed by Pestalozzi comes out again in a matter upon which much discussion has been raised, viz. as to whether or not all children should have the same initial education, no matter what their position and prospects may be. Pestalozzi's own views have been frequently misunderstood, largely through the influence of Niederer, who acted for so long as his interpreter, and frequently edited his writings before they went to the press.

The Aim of Education is throughout Individual and Concrete.

[1] Preface to Lenzburg Address (M., Vol. III., p. 370).

There can be no doubt of Pestalozzi's views on this subject before he came under the influence of Niederer, as we see from the fact that the twelfth letter in *How Gertrude Teaches her Children* is written from the point of view of the children of the poorer classes. In the concrete, education must take into account the conditions of life from which the child springs, and in the midst of which the child will in all probability spend his whole life. This is another reason why the home should be his first school, and why later on "the teacher must weave his accessory work into that of the parents', as a weaver works a flower into a whole piece of cloth." His *Letters concerning the Education of Poor Country Children*, his *Evening Hours of a Hermit* urge the same point. *Pestalozzi will have every child educated, but his education shall be suited to the life he will probably lead.*

As we have previously pointed out in this chapter, he was not interested in education as a means of getting on; his concern was that men should live intelligent manly lives in whatever station they might occupy. He would enable men to find resources in themselves which would make them superior even to adverse fortune.

Writing from Paris, he says: "The one great essential in elementary education is the harmonious development of the powers, but in their use subordinated to the demands of the actual circumstances of man. The child of my method feels his power only in surroundings that are real to him. He is not puffed out with empty learned words which have no background in his experience."[1] And again in 1803, to Countess Schimmelmann: "No one brings our universal aims into discredit as the *dreamy* universalists. . . . We must, therefore, always attach popular education firmly to the actual needs of the people.

[1] Cp. Morf, ii. 147 ff.

. . . Every real elementary school in every place must be suited to the particular circumstance of its situation if it is to fulfil its mission."[1] In the Lenzburg address he says: "All the exercises, the whole complex of means which are employed in elementary education must aim at establishing connections between the child and the realities of his actual life."

To the end of his life he held this view. In the *Swansong* he writes: "Education in its very earliest stages . . . must never stand in the way of life's needs; it must never aim at furthering the knowledge of things or of words unsuited to the child's position in life or likely to set up differences between home and school—two institutions which should always be in harmony. Education should never make the child discontented with or unfitted for his station; it should never create discord between the child and his life."[2]

Education and Actual Needs of Life.

Later in the same work he proceeds to consider the types of school suited to the farm labourer, the artisan, and the merchant or man of letters.[3] The kind of education suited to each grade of society must be determined by the circumstances, powers, and necessities that are common to it. As a matter of fact, he was mainly interested in the first two—the country school and the town school, the school for the peasant and the school for the artisan, who together constitute the great bulk of the people.

In the education suited to particular walks of life, the universal aim of all education is not, however, to be forgotten. To be happy and useful in his own sphere is the particular aim of every man, and the attainment of this aim should be furthered by his education. "Nevertheless,

[1] Rein, Art. *Pestalozzi*.   [2] *Swansong*, § 47 (G., p. 293).
[3] Cp. *Swansong*, §§ 54 and 119 (G.).

education for particular walks in life must be subordinated to the general aim of man's education." [1]

Without neglecting in any way what human nature demands for the unfolding of a child's divine powers, he must be so trained that he will feel himself happy and blessed within the limitations of his home surroundings, and that he will eagerly seek to acquire such knowledge and skill as will enable him to make his position satisfactory and prosperous, in spite of its peculiar difficulties and worries.[2] "The neglect of this principle, and the removal of the children from the educative influences of the home and of their father's calling, are the chief sources of ever-increasing family unhappiness in the world. All systems of education which favour this are radically mistaken. They constitute a serious danger of our time." And again : " To live happily in his own station, to be useful in his own circle is man's destiny and the object to be attained in the bringing up of children." [3]

Pestalozzi did not regard class divisions as being absolutely fixed, nor did he believe that a child

Individuality. should necessarily pass his life in the circle within which he was born. On the contrary, he recognised that compound of inborn and acquired peculiarities which we call individuality. The schoolmaster in *Leonard and Gertrude* observes the children carefully to find out their special aptitudes, and he would have the way of escape from its surroundings always open to talent. " What an inexpressible pleasure it is to the teacher to find talent—perhaps where least expected, even in the pitiably neglected son of the poorest day-labourer— to come across genius and greatness and to rescue it."

---

[1] *Evening Hours of a Hermit*, G., p. 17.
[2] Cp. *Leonard and Gertrude*, IV., § 68.
[3] *Schweizerblatt*, xxviii., i.   (Seyffarth, Vol. VI.)

CHAPTER IX.

INTELLECTUAL EDUCATION.

I. SENSORY FOUNDATIONS.

Pestalozzi's division of man's powers into those of "the head, the hand, and the heart," each developing in accordance with its own laws, necessitates the separate treatment of the educational problem according as it is regarded from each one of these points of view. At the same time the unity of the problem as a whole is not to be lost sight of. The master himself is always insisting upon the intimate relations of the intellectual, moral, and physical sides of human nature.

Before considering in greater detail his views on intellectual education, we may once again emphasise the importance of two axiomatic principles which underly all his educational thought: (1) that the impulse to development lies within. It is a spontaneous force, the existence of which is at once a help and a warning to the teacher. (2) That development follows exercise. "The natural and, indeed, the only means of development our powers possess is their use." Morality, love, and faith develop in the practice of right action and in the atmosphere of love and faith; thought-power comes with thinking, and practical skill is acquired by doing.

"Nature impels the eye to see, the ear to hear, the feet to walk, the hand to grasp, the heart to love, and the mind to think." [1] Rightly managed, "the child thinks as gladly as he walks, and learns as gladly as he eats." The teacher's business is to furnish opportunities for exercise which will foster development in a direction for the determination of which he is responsible. What the child *has* done, he feels he *can* do. He begins to be conscious of power, and to seek opportunity for its exercise. "The feeling of power is for every young child a greater reward and a greater joy than any of those rewards and decorations which men devise for his encouragement in learning. Yet in the schools no use is made of it; we find instead the most pitiable and unnatural substitutes employed. At best they only make the child tolerate that which their teachers wish to cram into them." [2]

These axioms apply of course throughout, and not merely to intellectual education, with which we are particularly concerned in this chapter.

The object of intellectual education is the acquisition of definite ideas, and the greater part of *How Gertrude Teaches her Children* is devoted to explaining the psychological steps which lead to this ultimate goal, and to an exposition of methods of instruction based upon them. In the tenth letter Pestalozzi tells us what he means by definite ideas. *Definiteness (Deutlichkeit)* for him means simply *capable of being*

Definite Ideas.

---

[1] *Christopher and Elizabeth*, 23rd Evening (Seyffarth, v., p. 173). The passage is also interesting as emphasising the importance of the unity of our powers. "Man is only rightly at work when he is using all his powers side by side as they are in his person. None of our powers should disturb the rest . . . all should work together in the common cause. . . ." When this is not so, a man is like a wound-up watch. He goes on in one direction until the spring runs down. He has no resources in himself. "When a man does not use his brain his handwork suffers," etc.

[2] Cp. *ibid.*, 14th Evening (G., p. 41).

defined. "An idea is definite when I can express its essence in words with the greatest possible accuracy and brevity." When he says, therefore, that intellectual training is to lead to definite ideas, he is thinking of their expression in words.

But for all practical purposes I may know the meaning of such words as "horse," "leaf," and yet I may be quite unable to express the ideas in any form of words which would be at the same time "accurate and brief." Possibly they take the form of vague mental pictures which refuse to be expressed within the limits of a definition. They are not therefore *definite*, and from the point of view of Pestalozzi they could not be looked upon as satisfactory results of instruction.

In this insistence upon the definition Pestalozzi is in agreement with the teaching practice of his day. He rails against the verbalism of the schools, not because the children learn definitions by heart, but because they reach them in the wrong way. The definition was not, in current school practice, the coping-stone of a solidly-constructed arch having foundations deep down in the pupil's sensory experience; it was rather the beginning, the middle, and the end of the whole matter. Education was a matter of words all through. At the same time, it was obvious that a view which made the definition the final goal of all teaching processes, even though proper foundations were ensured in the careful accumulation of sensory data, might easily lead to errors in practice. There are many ideas which do not admit of definition at all, and others which, within school age at least, cannot be reduced to fixed formulae without falling into the mistake which Pestalozzi very severely and quite properly criticised. That it led the master himself into error is quite beyond question.

Ideas of objects which are familiar to our senses, as for example those of a horse, a leaf, a house, have **Clear Ideas.** of course a place in Pestalozzi's system. They are a necessary preliminary to the definition, and as such they are called *clear* ideas. "The power of *describing* usually precedes that of *definition*. I can describe what is clear to me, but I cannot on that account define it. I only know the object, the individual. *I cannot yet refer it to its genus or its species.*" [1] The more complete my knowledge of the sensory qualities of an object is, the better I can describe it, that is to say, the clearer is my idea.

Prior to the stage of *clearness* (*Klarheit*) is the stage of *distinctness* (*Bestimmtheit*). Here is the actual **Distinct Ideas.** germ of all our knowledge. It consists in the separate apprehension of an object, the recognition of a sensation-complex, as standing apart, so to speak, from the relatively unbroken sensory background. To the new-born infant this sensory background is absolutely unbroken; it is an "undifferentiated sensory continuum," in which sensations of sound, light, contact, etc., are in no way distinguished from each other. The breaking up of this continuum is shown by the child's response to sensory stimuli—other than those which merely excite instinctive activity—as when his eyes follow a moving object, when his crying ceases as the sound of his mother's voice strikes his ear, when he looks about as if to see what he can see. [2]

The world is still "a swimming sea of confused sense-perceptions," and Pestalozzi, in the true spirit of psychological research, undertook to investigate the processes

[1] *How Gertrude Teaches her Children*, X. 26 (G., p. 132).
[2] *Vide* Stout: *Groundwork of Psychology*, p. 14. Cp. also Loveday and Green's *Introduction to Psychology*, Ch. III.

whereby single perceptions have gradually been separated
from other sensations simultaneously presented, whereby
the mind has severed that which formerly appeared to
be united, and to trace the progress from these vague
beginnings to the definite idea.

Although his statement of the problem is admirable, he
is not so successful in his method of investigation. He makes the initial mistake of sup-
posing that an adult's proceeding in a conscious
effort to disentangle a confused mass of presentations would be a suitable guide to the
mental processes of a child unconsciously pursuing the
same end. " In a rambling reverie upon my whole purpose, I happened to think of the way a cultivated man
must act when he wishes carefully to separate out the
details of an object which appears confused and dark
before him, and thus gradually to make it clear to himself." [1] In this purely purposive act Pestalozzi distinguishes three steps. The man, he says, will attend to
three things : he will try to discover

(*a*) How many and how many kinds of objects hover
before him.

(*b*) What they look like in respect of form and outline.

(*c*) What they are called, that is, what sound or word
will serve to bring the idea back to his mind.[2]

The word serves to secure the idea, to bring it back into
consciousness at any future time, and the qualities of
number and form are instinctively sought out because of
their universality. *Number, shape* and *sound* (word) must,
therefore, he argued, be those starting-points of knowledge
which he had set out to discover.

As already suggested, Pestalozzi's reasoning from the

---

[1] *How Gertrude Teaches her Children*, VI. 9 (G., p. 109).   [2] *Ibid.*

adult to the child is vitiated by the factor of conscious purpose, which is present in the one case and not in the other. There can be no analogy between the directness of purposeful action and the indirect roundaboutness of action determined by what is called "subjective selection." In this respect Pestalozzi makes the mistake he himself cautions us against in other places, that of presupposing in children powers which adults possess.

He says in effect, when you or I have made out the shape of a curious object, and found out whether it is a single thing or a group, and when we have learned its name, we have then made a start so to speak in acquiring knowledge of the thing. This is the "natural" way of beginning. We ask: (1) granted that this were so, does it follow that children would proceed in this way? May not our procedure be due to acquired habit? and (2) Is it true that either *we* or children would note these things first? What of colour, for example? Does knowledge of things begin with their mathematical qualities?

Pestalozzi feels the difficulty in respect of the choice of form and number as the elements in which knowledge begins. Why should these sensory data be more fundamental than any other—as *e.g.* colour? His answer is that number and form are common to all objects, a distinction which no other qualities possess. He might further have added that they differ from colour because we cannot in any way escape them. We may be colour blind, but normally sane people cannot be unaware of shape and relative quantity. These qualities must therefore be primary, and it is for that reason they "strike us at the first moment and enable us to distinguish one object from another."

He might have said that it belonged to the nature of mind to work in that way, that sensations are interpreted spatially by mind because it can do no other. Space in other words is the form which mind gives to its visual and tactual experiences. To find out these *necessary* starting-points was precisely Pestalozzi's object. There were, he thought, three of them, and he called these the *three elementary means.* That the analysis was not very successful we shall see presently.

In the meantime a further reference to the passage in question [1] will show that upon the three elementary means he bases three didactic principles :—

Three Didactic Principles.

(*a*) Children must be taught to regard each object which is presented to them as a unit, *i.e.* as separated from those objects with which it seems to be united.

(*b*) They must be impressed with the shape of each object, *i.e.* its size and its proportions.

(*c*) They must be taught the names of all objects known to them at the earliest possible moment.

Clearly the teacher who works on these lines is at least outwardly conforming to the "spatial nature" of mental process, so far at least as (*a*) and (*b*) are concerned. These three didactic *principles* are of course directly parallel to the three *steps* (*a*), (*b*), and (*c*) above, but if we compare (*a*) in each of the two series, it is clear that there is a confusion between psychical and arithmetical unity. In the principle (*a*), Pestalozzi has in mind the disintegration of the sensory continuum—the misty sea of sense-perceptions, as he calls it—which takes place when the infant begins to recognise separate sensory complexes as standing forward, so to speak, from the rest.

Psychical and Arithmetical Unity, Number and Form.

---

[1] *How Gertrude Teaches her Children*, VI. (G., p. 110).

These sensory complexes are psychical wholes, but they do not involve any idea of number, "which is a rational, not a sense, fact."[1] Of course a young child has vague notions of magnitude—he knows when he has a big piece of cake for example—long before he has reached the number idea. Similarly he has an idea of "ball," he may recognise and use the name long before he thinks of *one* ball. What indeed is *one*? The twig, or the whole tree, or the forest, or the universe itself? They are, of course, each one, if and when our minds make them so. But this is beyond the infant playing with the ball. When the "cultivated man" resolves the confused presentation into its elements and *counts* them, he is applying powers of abstraction which the young child does not possess, and which the race itself only acquired at a comparatively late period in its history. Number in other words is not given *a priori*. It is derived from experience or from instruction, or from a combination of the two.[2] From a theoretical point of view, therefore, the first of Pestalozzi's "three elementary means" rests upon an unsound basis, and Pestalozzi never arrived at a true explanation of the first steps in mental development, viz. those which have their origin in "the movement, disappearance, and reappearance of a sensation complex upon a relatively motionless background."[3]

As we have seen already, there is something to be said for regarding form as a primary quality of objects, though this does not mean that children perceive spatial differences with any precision, or that form is the first

[1] Cf. McLellan and Dewey, *Psychology of Number*, Ch. III.

[2] The student might read with advantage the chapters dealing with Number in Tyler's *Anthropology* or Avebury's *Origin of Civilisation*.

[3] Wiget, *Pestalozzi and Herbart*.

quality to strike the mind of the child. It is the brightness of objects which seems first to attract his attention.
Now although we cannot see brightness without seeing
it extended in space, we are not necessarily attending
to the extension. Spatial qualities may be implicit in
our perceptions without our being explicitly aware of
them.

Pestalozzi's view that "form" is the quality in objects
which first strikes the child-mind helped to bring about
the confusion between a psychical and an arithmetical unit.
We cannot treat form in teaching unless comparison and
measurement are involved, and these lead at once to number, or to the more explicit analysis of the child's ideas of
"more or less," which Pestalozzi, in the eighth letter of
How Gertrude Teaches her Children, refers to as the basis
of numerical relations.

It is obvious that the third elementary means—*sound*—
Sound.   is essentially different from those of *magnitude*
                    (*number*) and *form* in respect of their relation
to an object. Whilst the latter are qualities of the object
itself, *sound* is an arbitrary symbol selected by the race
and associated with the object as a convenient substitute
for the presence of the object when we are speaking or
thinking about it. As Pestalozzi says in Letter VI., 9
(3), the word "serves for the representation of objects and
for their permanent retention." He is thus careful to distinguish it from the sensory content which experience of
the object itself gives to the idea. But in a paragraph
or two later on (VI. 13), number, form, and sound are
spoken of as "*qualities of objects*, differing from all other
qualities in respect of their universality." Here the error
and confusion are obvious. [1]

----

[1] *Vide* G., pp. 109, 110.

Stripped of this confusion, the first step in the progress
Steps from Vague to Definite Ideas. from vague to definite ideas according to Pestalozzi may be represented as follows :—

(1) The idea of an object begins with the *isolation* of a sensation complex—its *one-ness*.

(2) It is at first a vague whole, in which *form* is chiefly recognised.

(3) It is held fast by a *word*.

Such a perception is neither *definite* nor *clear*, but in comparison with the chaos from which it arises it is *distinct*. The infant playing with the coloured ball on the floor or table perceives the object just in this way. His idea of it is *distinct*. But in defining a distinct idea, Pestalozzi introduces the mistakes we have already discussed. It is one which includes the properties (number and form) of an object and its name. " I saw now that awareness of the unity, form, and name of an object make my knowledge distinct." He does not, you see, include the sensory qualities of colour, smell, etc. If we try to estimate the infant's idea of that ball which he rolls about so joyfully, we shall best realise how wide of the facts Pestalozzi strayed. Colour, movement, life, are all lost. His *distinct* idea is already an abstraction, having no basis in actual child experience ; it is the first link in the chain which leads to definitions.

Pestalozzi's next step is interesting. He finds that these three elementary means correspond to three spheres of knowledge—sound to language, form to drawing (writing), and number to arithmetic.[1] No doubt the fact that he had tried at Stanz to solve the problem of teaching these subjects by resolving them into their elements explains why, in the psychological analysis already described, he

[1] Cp. *How Gertrude Teaches her Children*, Letter VI., §§ 13-15 (G., pp. 111, 112).

fixed his attention on number, form, and sound rather than on the qualities of things which first appeal to the child. Instead of discovering that arithmetic, etc., corresponded to his " elementary means," the " means " were probably the result of his thinking too exclusively of these elementary subjects of school instruction : Reading, Writing, and Arithmetic.

In either case there is an important distinction between the relations of number to arithmetic, sound to reading, and form to writing which Pestalozzi did not see clearly. The apprehension of number relations leads quite directly to arithmetic ; the discovery of meaning in sounds and the imitative purposeful use of sounds leads to language. Reading is a stage beyond, in which the recognition of form enters.

In the case of writing, Pestalozzi makes it a special case of drawing, but except in so far as drawing depends partly on fine muscular control, there is very little analogy. In learning to write we learn to use a number of apparently arbitrary but meaningful signs as we do when we learn to talk, but in one case the signs are made by finger movements and in the other by movements of the vocal organs. The written symbols do not represent the forms of the objects. The form of the letters has no connection with the meanings of the words, and it is this meaning that we emphasise. There is a muscular connection between drawing and writing, but not an intellectual connection, except at the very outset.

We are now in a position to examine Pestalozzi's whole analysis of mental development from vague to **Pestalozzi's** definite ideas in reference to the " whole art of **Analysis** methodical teaching." In Letter VI. 5 there **of Mental** **Progress.** are three consecutive rules, each with three clauses. The object of instruction, he says, is attained in three steps :—

I. (a) *Separating* the objects, thereby removing the confusion in the sense-impressions.

   (b) Bringing together again, in representation, the objects which are alike, thereby making them *clear*.

   (c) Raising these perfectly clear ideas to definite conceptions.

And he adds that these steps are attained by—

II. (a) Presenting the confused sense-perceptions *separately*

   (b) Changing the conditions under which the observations are separately made.

   (c) Bringing them finally into connection with the remaining content of our knowledge.

Thus, he says, our knowledge grows—

III. (a) From vagueness to *distinctness* (*Bestimmtheit*).

   (b) From distinctness to *clearness* (*Klarheit*).

   (c) From clearness to *definiteness* (*Deutlichkeit*).

We may, with Wiget, adduce the parallel of Letter VI. 13—

IV. (a) Through the consciousness of the unity, form, and name of an object we attain to *distinct* knowledge.

   (b) Through the gradual extension of our knowledge to all its remaining qualities it becomes *clear*.

   (c) Through the knowledge of the connection of its distinguishing characteristics it becomes *definite*.

and of VI. 15. Progress in all three elementary subjects (reading, writing, and arithmetic) advances from—

V. (a) Vague to distinct observation.

   (b) Distinct observation to clear representation.

   (c) Clear representation to definite conception.

By bringing Pestalozzi's various statements into line in
this way it is possible to determine exactly what he means.
Although worded differently, the final clause (c) in each
case is intended to present the same fact viewed either as
process or result. The definition, it will be remembered,
is the crowning point of instruction, and the definition is
the statement of the relation of the thing defined to the
whole content of our knowledge. It gathers up the distinguishing features of a class of objects and expresses
them as belonging to a system. This is the stage to which
(c) in each of these parallel statements refers. The first
clauses (a) are similarly in harmony, and obviously all
refer to that step in the forward movement which he has
called *distinctness*.

Comparing now the clauses marked (b) there are some
important differences. By analogy we should
Abstraction.   expect them all to refer to the step which Pestalozzi calls *clearness*, that stage in our knowledge of a
thing which enables us to describe it, and this is clearly
meant in IV. *b*, but how we are to pass from IV. *b* to IV. *c*
is not obvious until we look at I. *b* and II *b*, where a stage
beyond that of mere " clearness " is hinted at, or rather a
process is suggested which to some extent presupposes
" clearness." Although the word " clear" occurs in I. *b*,
the process of comparison invited by calling to mind
similar objects, and the process of changing the conditions
under which the objects are separately observed (II. *b*),
obviously point to a process of abstraction by means of
which the casual qualities may be separated from the
essential—a process which is brought to a head in (*c*), *i.e.*
in the definition.

It is interesting to compare the results of this analysis
with Pestalozzi's statements in Letter V. The point of
view is reversed. He begins, " Everything which touches

my senses is for me only so far a means of arriving at a correct judgment as its appearance makes me sensible of its unchanging and unchangeable essence " (§ 2, *a*); we attain to this by putting together objects which are alike in essence, thereby weakening the one-sided, preponderating impression made by the striking qualities of single objects (§ 2, *d*), but first of all we must be clear about the qualities of single objects, employing as many senses as possible to that end (§ 2, *c, f*; *vide* G., pp. 103, 104). This amounts to saying that we reach *definite* ideas by means of abstraction, the materials for which are furnished by *clear* ideas of single objects. Going over similar ground in the *Swansong* (70), he explicitly refers to abstraction as the means whereby man passes from the stage of sense-perception to the stage of thought proper.

That he understood the nature of this process and its place in the course of development is shown by his remarks in the preface to *Lessons in the Apprehension of Number-relations*, Part II. "When the mother lays peas, leaves, pebbles, sticks, and whatever else it may be, upon the table for the child to count, she must not say,—that is *one*, but that is *one stick*, that is *one stone*; and again when she points to two, she must not say, that is twice one, but that is twice one stone, or that is two stones, two leaves. . . . If the mother shows the child different kinds of objects, such as peas, stones, etc., and teaches him to recognise and name them as one pea, two peas, three peas, etc., repeated in this manner the words one, two, three remain always unchanged, whilst the words peas, pebbles, etc., change according to the object shown; this combination of stability and change gives rise to the abstract notion of number in the mind of the child, that is to say the definite consciousness of more or less, independently of the objects themselves. Yet the consciousness of the real relations is never lost." This "inextinguishable consciousness of reality" gives life to the definition, and so preserves it from the reproach of mere verbalism which marked the education current in Pestalozzi's day.

Bringing together the various steps in the process of advance from "the misty sea of sense-perceptions to definite ideas," we get—

(1) The apprehension and naming of separate objects.
(2) The apprehension of the qualities of those objects in detail.
(3) The comparison of objects alike in essence, but dissimilar in certain features or in the conditions of their presentation.
(4) The abstraction of the essential qualities, *i.e.* of the permanent from the casual and changing.
(5) The definition.

These are all expressed or implied in Pestalozzi's analysis. It will be noted that throughout he is dealing only with sensory presentations, the whole content of which is given by the sensory activities (1) and (2) above. Comparison can, of course, add nothing to this content. It may clarify and deepen, but it cannot add to what we have learned through the senses. Hence the fundamental importance of sensory activity for all knowledge. "The final ripening of each and every general notion is essentially dependent on the perfected force of its first inception. Everything that is imperfect in the germ will be crippled in its growth." [1]

"Life educates," says Pestalozzi in the *Swansong* (70), **The** actual contact with sensory circumstance gives **Principle of** impulse and nourishment to development. **Concreteness** Ideas are *definite* when experience has exhausted **(*Anschauung*).** its powers of adding to their clearness, *i.e.* when further observation can bring to light no additional

[1] *How Gertrude Teaches her Children*, Letter X., §§ 27, 28 (G., p. 132).

qualities, when the work of our sensory activities has been completed, and the necessary abstraction has been thought out.

This principle, viz. that *actual sensory experience, carefully organised and systematically worked out*, is the only sound basis of instruction, was not only the first to come out in the historical development of Pestalozzi's pedagogy, it was also, for him, the most important of all his contributions to educational science, the centre of his whole system. His earliest teaching practice was, of course, connected with his little son Jacqueli. His diary reveals his method. Paternally directed observation leads the child to see that water flows down hill, that some things float and others sink in water. In trying to teach him the conception of number he discovered *how a knowledge of words, which are mere sounds to a child, may become a real obstacle to his obtaining a knowledge of truth.*[1]

Throughout his career he held fast to this principle. In the *Schweizerblatt* we read "that the man who in his youth has not caught butterflies, nor wandered over hill and dale hunting for plants, etc., in spite of all desk work, will not get far in his subject. He will always be exposed to blunders which otherwise he would never have made." In rainy weather toadstools grow fast on every dung-heap; and in the same way definitions, not founded on sense impression, produce, just as quickly, a fungus-like wisdom, which dies rapidly in the sunlight.[2] In his last pedagogic utterances he returned to the subject, treating it with especial fulness in the *Swansong*.[3]

The child must learn to know and express himself clearly about the things around him. However humble his cir-

---

[1] *Vide* Chap. II., p. 30.
[2] *Vide How Gertrude Teaches her Children*, X. (G., p. 131).
[3] Cp. *Swansong*, § 97 (G., p. 316).

cumstances, round about his house there are objects which
he should learn to know from his cradle upwards. It is
not the slight acquaintance with many objects that is
wanted, but the clear and accurate knowledge of the few.
Of animals, for example, he may learn some of the mammals,
the birds, the fishes, which are in his immediate neighbourhood, but these few thoroughly; he should be led to observe
with elementary exactness the various forms of water and
its transitions from one form to the other in nature (dew,
rain, vapour, frost, hail, snow, ice), and the influence it
exerts in these various forms upon other natural objects;
in the kitchen he should see the dissolving of sugar and
salt and their recovery by evaporation and crystallisation.
Similarly he may watch the fermentation of the wine in
the cellar, the changing of marble into lime.[1]

Pestalozzi has in mind very much what the better
advocates of Nature Study in these days are urging upon
teachers. His view was sounder, however, than the practice
of those who under the guise of Nature Study present
botanical abstractions to their pupils—so often nothing
but words, in spite of much illustrative material that is
brought into the class-room.

Brought up in the way Pestalozzi describes, a boy will
be ready in the future for the scientific pursuit of any
branch of knowledge. His work will be sound because it
will be guided by the habit of looking at facts, which he
has acquired in the earliest stages of his education. In
the school at Yverdun a special point was made of outside
work. The school journey was a regular institution, as we
gather from Pestalozzi's legitimate boast in the Lenzburg
Address [2]—that although from 120 to 130 boys in different
divisions had made journeys on foot lasting two or three

[1] Cp. *Leonard and Gertrude* as summarised, p. 54 ff.
[2] M., iii. 498.

weeks, and including the ascent of formidable mountains, except for a cold or two, they all came back none the worse for their exposure to the very changeable weather. Contemporary independent accounts of the method of teaching geography [1]—the walks, the measuring and judging of distance, and actual observations in the neighbourhood of Yverdun, and the exercises thereon—all show how Pestalozzi emphasised concrete experience in intellectual education. He particularly combats the substitution of pictures for objects. In most cases they either put before the child what he cannot see in Nature, or they are pictures of things which he might see every day. "Comenius and Basedow substituted a painted world for the real one."

[1] Cp. Part III., Ch. XX., *Report to Parents,* and also p. 367.

CHAPTER X.

INTELLECTUAL EDUCATION.

II. SOME GENERAL FEATURES OF INTELLECTUAL DE-
VELOPMENT AND THEIR RELATION TO TEACHING
PRACTICE.

Pestalozzi frequently compares the development of the mind to that of a plant or a tree. In *How* **The** *Gertrude Teaches her Children* (IV. 10) we are **"Elementary** **Method."** asked to consider how Nature produces the largest tree from a tiny seed: "first she produces a scarcely perceptible shoot, then just as imperceptibly, daily and hourly, by gradual stages, she unfolds first the beginnings of the stem, then the bough, then the branch, then the extreme twig on which hangs the perishable leaf." As a picture of the growth of a tree there is a good deal wanting in this sketch, but the "gradual imperceptible advance" struck him forcibly as "Nature's way," and as he "*knew* that the mechanism of human nature is essentially subject to the same laws as those by which physical nature unfolds her powers," he arrived at a most important practical principle which is the essence of his "Elementary Method." "Try to make, in every act, graduated steps of knowledge, in which each new idea is only a small, scarcely perceptible addition to that which is already known."

Pestalozzi's special concern is, of course, that instruction is to be adapted to the powers of the pupil. "Everything which the child has to learn must be proportioned to his strength, getting more complicated and difficult in the same degree as his powers of attention, of judgment, and thought increase."[1] But the psychology of attention teaches us the inappropriateness of the "scarcely perceptible additions" which are to govern the teacher's graduation of his subject-matter.

Again, Pestalozzi fails to see just how far his principles —especially those derived from analogy with the life of the organic world—apply, and the development of the doctrine of "scarcely perceptible additions" into that of "uninterrupted continuity" produced the absurdities in *The Mother's Book* (see p. 179) which drew upon him the scorn of many critics. "Elementary" for Pestalozzi—in the Lenzburg Address, for example—means "without gaps," "unbroken continuity," and as the *Report to Parents* informs us, the great problem of the Institute was to accomplish a graduation of all the subjects of instruction in accordance with the demands of this principle.[2]

Psychical progress is unbroken, and its daily advance, like that of the plant, is imperceptible; the course of education must be similarly unbroken, accompanying step by step, the increase of power with suitably graduated stimuli. A course of education organised on these lines and embracing the intellectual, physical (practical), and moral sides of human nature, Pestalozzi calls "Elementary," and the whole method he calls the "Elementary Method." Its nature is discussed in the Lenzburg Address,[3] though it is not always easy to distinguish the vague

[1] Cp. *Report to Parents* (1807), p. 346 f.
[2] *Vide* Part III., Ch. XIX.
[3] Cp. references to the *Elementary Method* in the *Swansong* (G.).

generalities of Niederer from the more directly practical views of Pestalozzi. In the *Swansong*, too, the idea is carefully, though less philosophically, worked out. There it is Pestalozzi and not Niederer who is speaking.[1]

The search for the " elements " which lie at the base of such an " elementary " scheme of instruction led Pestalozzi to a point of view which has received a good deal of attention in recent years. In the *Report to Parents* we read : " The Institute recognises only one course of instruction for each subject, viz. that which, in perfect harmony with the course of development of human nature, follows the nature and the development of the subject itself." " We put our children on the road which the discoverer of the subject himself took, and had to take. We put into his hand the thread of its extension, and the steps of its development, as they have been pursued by the race, in order that he may himself independently seize and put to use in the same direction the materials to hand, going as far as his powers will allow." Although this report bears the mark of Niederer's editorship, the same idea is involved in Pestalozzi's treatment of language in *How Gertrude Teaches her Children*, which is described in detail in the next chapter.

The ideal was, of course, impossible in practice : men of science had not at that time worked at the history of their respective subjects ; but the suggestion is interesting, and although it cannot be crudely applied to any subject, the point of view is often nowadays in evidence, especially in the teaching of science, and distinguished authorities have recommended its more frequent adoption.[2]

[1] *Vide* G., pp. 267-322.

[2] Cp. *The Heuristic Method of Teaching* (Armstrong), in which the idea of putting children at the point of view of the investigator is worked out.

We have seen, on the one hand, the steps through which
the mind advances from vague to definite
Law of
Physical
Distance.
ideas, in which the latent power of abstraction
plays the final part, and, on the other hand,
the nature of the graduation which the subject-
matter of instruction must undergo in order to come
into line with the progress of mental power. The problem
of bringing these two—the growing mind and the objects
which contribute to its nourishment—into effective relation is yet to be faced. Pestalozzi found its solution in
the *Law of Physical Distance*, which he enunciates in the
sixth letter of *How Gertrude Teaches her Children.*

Here we read "that clearness of knowledge varies
according to the nearness and remoteness of the objects
which are in touch with my senses." All that surrounds
us reaches our senses in impressions which are confused,
and difficult to make clear and definite, in proportion to its
distance from us; and on the contrary everything is distinct and easy to make clear and definite in proportion as
it lies near to our five senses. "As a physical being you
are nothing but your five senses; consequently the clearness or mistiness of your ideas must absolutely rest upon
the nearness or remoteness with which all external objects
touch these five senses, that is, yourself." And as the
nearest object for the exercise of the senses is one's self,
one's knowledge of one's self must be the starting-point
of one's knowledge of truth.

This law, literally understood and applied in the
"elementary" sense, produced the first six
The
Mother's
Book.
exercises of *The Mother's Book.* This famous
manual was published in 1803. Only the
introduction and the greater part of the
seventh exercise were written by Pestalozzi. Everything
else was the work of Krusi. It is such a perfect practical

application of the two principles we have just been discussing, viz. the law of physical distance and the principle of uninterrupted continuity of progress in scarcely perceptible steps, that its arrangement should be studied carefully. The mother is teaching her child to see and to name objects—producing thereby *distinct* ideas. The object physically nearest to the child, and therefore the object which will produce the earliest and strongest impression upon his senses, is his own body. The mother is supposed to point out the object to the child and to say the name which he repeats after her. The first exercise begins as follows :—

Exercise I.

The body.	The back part of the head.	The nose—
The head.		The nose bone.
The face—	The parting of the hair.	The partition between the nostrils.
The right side of the face.	The forehead.	The nostrils—right and left.
The left side of the face.	etc.	etc.
etc.		

The whole of the body is examined on this principle—down to the nail on the middle toe of the left foot.

In the second exercise the spatial relations of the parts of the body are observed and expressed in sentences as—The head stands on the neck. The face is at the front of the head. The eyes are under the forehead. The nail of the middle finger lies on the upper side of the third bone of the middle finger.

The third exercise draws attention to the relations of whole and part amongst these things—as "the nose is a part of the face," and so on.

The fourth exercise enumerates the parts of the body which occur singly, in pairs, fours, eights, tens, etc.

The fifth exercise deals with the shape and other physical properties of parts of the body, each treated separately; *e.g.* the lips are soft, mobile, and elastic, inside they are red, smooth and damp.

The sixth exercise classifies the parts of the body according as they are marked by particular qualities; *e.g.* those which are round, pointed, black, white, red, elastic, etc.

The seventh exercise deals with the most characteristic function of the various parts of the body, the most striking differences in these functions, and the ordinary occasions which call them into use.

Up to this point the exercises have followed the principle of " uninterrupted continuity " in the most literal sense of the word. The seventh exercise, which deals with the part of the body in action, is by Pestalozzi himself. The subject-matter clearly offers opportunity for more lively treatment, and the author rises to the occasion. To take one example—that of the eye. The section is prefaced by a characteristic appeal to mothers to observe how their infants use their eyes, the delight they take in seeing things, first in the room, then through the window, at the door, and again outside; how they will creep on all fours and crow with delight when they reach the object that has caught their attention. This is the prompting of God in the nature of the child, and mothers should follow up the clue this offers to the child's mental needs. Then come twenty pages of suggestive examples. The child is first told what it sees, and, in sentences which are to be repeated by him, he is told what he is doing: he sees, looks at, towards, upon, and through an object, he sees it often or rarely, gladly or unwillingly, clearly or confusedly; " one sees it in a boy when he has been naughty; one sees in the fields whether the farmer is lazy or diligent; everybody looks chiefly at that which is his business—the smith at the iron which is on the anvil, the maid at the milk which is on the fire." "One can see through water, glass, thin horn, amber, crystal, and many other things," etc., etc.

The object of course is that the free exercise of his senses should be combined with progress. The child is to be provided with a wealth of vocabulary and turns of speech, such as formal instruction in language could never give.

In judging of the merits of *The Mother's Book* it is always to be remembered that Pestalozzi regarded it as indicating what might be done, as showing mothers how to give their children language lessons; he did not mean it to be used as a text-book. This point many of his critics overlooked. It was a piece of pioneer work in the organisation of the teaching of the Mother Tongue, and as such it deserves respect. Like so much of what was done by the Burgdorf pioneers, it went wrong through the mechanical interpretation of guiding principles. Had they looked at them in the light of the greatest principle of all : *Life educates*, neither Pestalozzi nor his disciples would have missed their imperfections.

That Pestalozzi himself did not mean the law of physical distance to be taken in its literal sense is clear **Physical v. Psychical Distance.** from other passages in *How Gertrude Teaches her Children.* We read, for example, in Letter V. (§ 4), "Man can only learn the truth about the world in its physical aspects in proportion to his familiarity with his immediate environment." It is clear from this that Pestalozzi does not mean by his " law of physical distance " that we really cannot know anything which has not reached us through observation, but rather that what has so reached us is the means by which our knowledge actually may transcend our experience. That which actual experience teaches is *psychically* nearest, it is liveliest, the most intimate portion of our mental content, and by its means we are able to comprehend that which is physically remote.[1]

And this is exactly what Pestalozzi says later in the same book (Letter VII., § 51).[2] "Lastly," he writes, "knowledge derived through our senses has an analogical value ; by its means I learn the characteristics of things which have never come within the range of my observation. My knowledge is thus greatly advanced ; it is no longer dependent entirely upon my senses, but the whole range of my mind's powers may work up the materials my senses provide." Whilst the " physical distance law " is approximately true of very early life, so soon as a stock of well-established sensory knowledge is acquired, analogical tendencies set the child free to the extent that he may learn of things far removed from his own experience—of things which never even happened or existed at all—provided that he is in possession of images which will serve to build up the new picture. His existing knowledge only fixes limits to what we may teach him, because it furnishes the materials for its proper apprehension.

The most striking effect of Pestalozzi's *Law of Physical Distance,* as enunciated in the sixth letter, was that it led

---

[1] Students will compare with this the doctrine of apperception as enunciated by the Herbartians—a truer statement of what Pestalozzi *felt,* but could not express. Locke had put the point in another way : " Knowing is seeing ; and if it be so it is madness to persuade ourselves we do so by another man's eyes, let him use ever so many words to tell us that what he asserts is visible. Till we ourselves see it with our own eyes and perceive it by our own understandings, we are as much in the dark and as void of knowledge as before, let us believe any learned author as much as we will" (*Conduct of Understanding,* § 24).

[2] *Vide* G., p. 118.

him, in the *Swansong*, to reject history as a subject for study in schools. "It is utter nonsense that men who have no living acquaintance with the world as it stands before their eyes, should wish to be made acquainted with the spirit of a bygone world, removed from the world of to-day by hundreds and even thousands of years. In this subject, one can do no more than to exercise the children in mnemonically memorising extended lists of names of men and places which history proper demands."[1]

It is the same principle more reasonably applied which made him regard "modern languages" as prior to dead languages. The subject-matter of the books read in modern languages is obviously more nearly related to the child's stock of ideas than that of the classical authors. "Homer, Plato, and Tacitus are not reading for younger children, their contents being beyond their power of comprehension."[2] The odd conjunction of names shows how completely the "law of distance" had taken hold of Pestalozzi.

Niederer appreciated the law much more clearly in the psychical sense than his master. He holds it as the principle which decides whether or not a subject is suitable for a child at a particular moment. In the *Report to Parents*, already quoted, we read: "Each child shall be taught that which he has to learn at the time his nature calls for it, for this is the proof that his sensibility and power are ready for it." Unlike Pestalozzi, he approved of history teaching on condition that it was brought into harmony with the development of the pupil, and he regarded Herbart's example in reading Homer with his pupil as a sound pedagogic introduction to the subject. Niederer's influence probably also accounts for the fact that history always occupied a place in the curriculum at Yverdun.

---

[1] *Swansong*, § 103 (G., p. 318).   [2] Lenzburg Address (M., iii. 512).

One may note, in concluding this chapter, a striking passage in the *Report to Parents*, which is sufficient to demonstrate the fact that in spirit at least Pestalozzi was the reverse either of a formalist or of a mechanical educator. We have already seen that in respect of the graduation of the subject-matter of instruction two principles governed the teacher's action, (1) the historical principle, *i.e.* the actual history of the subject as such, and (2) the principle of uninterrupted continuity of advance in scarcely perceptible steps. So far the children do not come specifically into account, except in so far as these principles correspond respectively to a suspected parallelism between mental development in the child and the race, and to a parallelism between the growth of a plant and the growth of the mind.

Individuality in Intellectual Education.

In practice, however, Pestalozzi found that children differed in the rapidity with which they followed the path the teacher had laid down for them, and that the same child advanced in one direction more quickly than in another. The school was therefore organised so that the same subject was taught throughout the various classes at the same time, to make it possible to transfer the children from class to class in accordance with their actual progress.

But this principle of suiting the instruction to the child was carried further. What each child was to learn and when he was to begin was determined by his particular nature. The subjects which appeal to him are thereby proved to be those particularly suited to his powers. If the psychological moment has been found, he will learn in a month what otherwise might take years. Further, continues the report, "we try to discover on which side a child is strongest, in order to make that the centre, so to speak, of his intellectual activity, or that we may use this special interest as a thread by means of which we may lead him towards a life of intellectual independence, having confidence in his own efforts and never ceasing to widen the circle of his activity. And whilst as a matter of fact there is no child who is universal in his capacity, so is there none who does not possess special talent in some one direction, and who, given the opportunity, would not excel therein.

"What is more, the time when a particular aptitude may develop is quite uncertain. A boy suddenly shows a new feeling for a subject which previously had not the smallest influence upon him. . . . Clearly then, as it seems to me, the nature of the child must determine all the details of his education, and an educational institution must be so organised as to afford room for adaptation to the inclination and needs of the individual pupil." [1]

[1] *Vide* Ch. XIX., p. 347.

CHAPTER XI.

CONCRETE INTELLECTUAL DEVELOPMENT

(With Special Reference to Language and Arithmetic).

We have now discussed Pestalozzi's analysis of intellectual development in the abstract, and the laws which govern practical procedure on the part of those who are concerned in guiding and forwarding that development. We have noted in particular the emphasis he places upon the first steps to clearness in the acquisition of ideas, the manner in which the advance from clearness to definiteness (from knowledge of the particular to knowledge of the general) is made, the unbroken continuity of the child's development to power and the relation of environmental impressions to knowledge of the world as a whole.

We may now study with advantage how he applied these fundamental doctrines to the concrete situation, how he organised the teaching of oral and written Language, and Arithmetic, in accordance with them.

In the first place we must note that Pestalozzi never confined himself to the school view of education. The child has learned much before he comes to school, as he found to his sorrow when he undertook the education of a small boy of three.

"Just as I had sought in every direction for the way in which instruction might begin, I now tried to **Language.** find out the exact time when a child begins to learn, and I soon convinced myself that this coincided with the hour of birth. From the moment when he is first sensitive to external impressions, Nature becomes his teacher." One of his chief practical objects was to enable mothers to give their children ordered instruction, and his various A B C books were meant primarily for their use. "Life educates," and education begins with the first breath.

His own work was concerned chiefly with language. It was his actual achievement in this direction that gave him most satisfaction; his linguistic method is therefore the best illustration we have of the practical carrying out of his educational theory. Yet we must again bear in mind Pestalozzi's own attitude towards his work. He indignantly denied that his conception of an elementary method was a dream, but he frankly admitted that he could not point to any completely satisfactory example of it in working. "No elementary school or institution exists which corresponds to our ideal in all its details. But educational progress, like progress in all other branches of human culture, is piecemeal. Man goes now forwards, now backwards. . . . Even the most able of men, in the midst of his efforts towards perfection in this or that direction, must say with St. Paul . . . " (*Swansong*, § 36.)

With this warning we may consider the principles and practice of Pestalozzi's language teaching. In the tenth letter of *How Gertrude Teaches her Children* he gives the grounds for the linguistic methods described in the seventh. Broadly speaking, he aims at enabling the child "to acquire speech in exactly the same gradual way in which Nature has given it to the human race." The "course of nature" in this case means the historical progress of mankind as a whole, not the psychological progress which each individual necessarily (*i.e.* because of his nature) follows, and which the phrase "according to nature" usually means for Pestalozzi. To assist him in determining the

chief steps in the development of speech and, in accordance
with them, to fix the order of speech instruction, he looked
for guidance to the course which racial development had
actually taken in the matter of language.

He there distinguishes three epochs:

I. The period of imitation and gesture.

II. The period in which special names were given to
special objects—of hieroglyphs and separate
words for objects and activities. "This," he
says, "is the stage referred to in the second
chapter of Genesis, when God brought all the
animals on the earth and all the birds in the
heavens before Adam that he might look at them
and name them." [1]

III. The period in which conspicuous differences were
observed and named, developing much later into
the power of combining words variously and of
changing their forms so that all the changes
which time and circumstances might produce in
an object could be effectively represented in
language.

Racially, the process has taken thousands of years, yet
the child must learn the art in a few months. Obviously
he must take the shortest road to the desired end. It
must be exactly the same course as Nature has followed,
but without following such a circuitous route as blind

---

[1] The inclusion of hieroglyphs (by which he means that period in
the development of the written language when visual symbols stood
for particular objects) shows that Pestalozzi was thinking of written
as well as of spoken language. But historically the system of
written signs is of very much later development, and it is noteworthy that he makes no use of the history of writing in his
treatment of that side of language.

Nature has taken. For Pestalozzi's purpose the broad epochs provide the necessary guidance.

The steps in the teaching of speech as given in Letter VII. of *How Gertrude Teaches her Children* are :—

I. The training of the organs of speech, and the regular practice of all the sounds in the language. **The Learning of Sounds.** Instead of crooning at haphazard over her infant's cradle, the mother is to repeat these phonetic elements in a systematic way. " The whole compass of them is to reach the child's consciousness before he is able to speak." As this power develops he will repeat these sounds in imitation of his mother, instead of indulging in the unanalysable prattle which is "blind Nature's" way. Exercises in single tones and sequences of tones in speech and song were provided in the *Hints on Teaching, Spelling, and Reading*, published in 1801.

The actual procedure was as follows :—(1) The mother repeated the sounds of the book instead of talking baby-talk, which is planless. The infant in this way becomes familiar with the sounds. (2) He is made to pronounce them as exercises, several times a day, but with the same ease and playfulness with which children usually are made to imitate sounds. The exercises in the book were based upon the vowels, to which the consonants were successively joined on—*ab, ad, af, at,* and so on. Then these syllables were preceded by consonants in series—*bad, bab, baf*, etc.— proceeding to more and more difficult combinations.

At some stage or other in this process (Pestalozzi does not say when), the actual printed letters of the alphabet are shown in these syllabic connections. The letters were printed separately on cardboard, the vowels being in red. The principle that the basis of every syllable is the vowel to which consonants are joined on, before and after, is observed here as in the oral exercises. A spelling tablet is suggested, hung on the wall, having a groove at top and bottom, in which the letters slide easily backwards and forwards. Whole words are built up letter by letter— *f, fe, fen, fend, fende, fender*—in both forward and backward directions—*r, er, der, nder, ender, fender*.

Progress is to be slow. No step further is to be taken until the preceding work is perfectly known. All subsequent work in reading is to be founded on this course of spelling, by small and gradual additions. With large school classes the work is to be done simultaneously until the children are old enough to have the book put into their hands. It will be their first reading-book, and they are to continue in it until they have attained perfect facility.

In defence of this syllabic method of teaching to read, which is not unfamiliar even in English schools, it should be said that its author was concerned with a language which is approximately spelled as it is sounded.

II. Keeping rigidly to his views about the origin of language, the next step in teaching the child his mother tongue is to provide him with a vocabulary. His idea was to provide a book[1] with lists of names of all the most important objects in nature, history, geography, etc. He has found in experience that the time spent in teaching the children to read these lists perfectly is enough to enable them to learn them by heart. The gain for later instruction is enormous. The lists represent the chaotic collection of materials which is to be used for the building which is presently to be erected.

The Learning of Words and Sentence Forms.

Sentence structure, grammar, and composition should

---

[1] This book never existed. It is not *The Mother's Book*, which has already been described (p. 177 f.).

follow. " The first step is to teach the child to speak correctly. This will not, however, come from the inculcation of rules, but from model sentences, which the mother is to repeat to the child and make him repeat after her, with the double object of teaching him to articulate clearly and to build his sentences in the conventional way. The two objects are to be kept distinct, though the same sentences may be employed in both cases." Examples will make this clear. The child will hear and learn :—

> Papa is kind.
> The cow is lame.
> The butterfly is pretty, etc.

He will then be asked : What else is kind ? What else is the cow ? Other exercises of a like sort will follow :—

Who or what are what ?

> Tigers are ferocious.
> Swallows are swift.
> Roots are tough.

Who wishes what ?

> The prisoner wishes to be free.
> The creditor wishes to be paid.

Who can what ?

> Tailors can stitch.
> Pigs can grunt.
> Etc., etc.

So the exercises are continued in both numbers and through all the tenses, etc. Special attention is given to verbs, and to words which change their use and meaning through change of prefixes, *e.g.* form, deform, conform, inform, reform, perform, misinform. There follow exercises in building up or extending sentences as meaning is made more precise :—

I shall,

I shall preserve,

I shall preserve my health,

I shall not preserve my health by any other means.

After all that I have suffered, I shall not, etc.

" Such exercises are always based on subjects selected entirely from juvenile life."

III. For the first time, curiously enough, we are brought to the point where word and thing are related **The Learning** in this method of Pestalozzi's. Objects or **of Language proper.** pictures of objects are brought before the child and he is taught—

(*a*) To express himself about their number and their form ;

(*b*) To express himself about the other qualities of objects, derived as they may be from further sensory acquaintance with them. "As to those properties which are known to us by the intervention of judgment and imagination, I exclude them from my plan at this period. I know that many words denoting such properties will be caught by children from the conversation of others . . . but for the express purpose of instruction we should confine ourselves to such matters as are clearly perceived by the senses, with a view to cultivating clear and precise expression."

He takes the names of suitable objects from the dictionary, and writes them with their properties (as given by the children), thus :—

> Acorn—oval, green, bitter.
> Amber—yellow, transparent, bright.
> Ale—strong, sparkling, brown.

Then the exercise is inverted.   Adjectives are given and

the names of objects to which they apply are placed alongside :—

> Round—ball, plate, moon.
> Light—feather, down, air.
> Deep—sea, pits, lake.

Without attempting to be exhaustive, " the children acquire a facility and accuracy of expression which no Socratic conversations, unless conducted with untold skill and labour, can ever produce."

Finally, Pestalozzi proposes to elicit from the pupils descriptions or definitions of different objects and actions :—

"A bell is a hollow round vessel of cast metal, open at the bottom, mostly with a brim bent outwards; towards the top it grows narrower, approaching the oval in shape, etc."

This is an exercise calculated to test clearness—with which indeed all description is concerned. As exercises in definition these are typical :—

To walk is to move on step by step.

To sit is to rest the body on a chair, etc., in a position in which it forms two angles.

Lastly he learns (c) to express himself about the connections of objects with each other in their varying conditions of time, number and proportion.

The relation of these three steps in the process of language teaching to the steps which Pestalozzi lays down as those through which the race has passed in the acquisition of speech is obvious. We may also note in both cases the correspondence to the order of development of ideas. The period of imitation and of the practising of sounds is that of *vague* ideas; the period of word making and word learning (*i.e.* the apprehension of single objects and naming them) is that of *distinct* ideas; whilst in the period of language proper we have first of all *clear* ideas leading finally up to *definite* ones.

It is to be noted that number and form fall into the third (language) period. Knowledge and linguistic power develop together, and the periods of development in the child correspond to the periods of development in the race. In the Lenzburg Address Pestalozzi distinctly speaks of two such periods : (1) the period of sensory experience (*Anschauungsepoche*), and (2) the period of the general notion (*Begriffsepoche*).[1] During the former period the child is chiefly occupied in acquiring distinct and clear ideas. Distinctness and clearness are both the result of sense experience helped out by appropriate language training. Clearness of course includes distinctness, and the efficiency of the work done at this time determines the character of that accomplished in the period of greater maturity.

Let us now see how he applies his method to the teaching of arithmetic. As in the teaching of language and form, so here the work is based upon sensory experience. He describes how mothers should endeavour to give numerical notions to their children in the introduction to the *A B C of Number Relations*. They are advised to let their children count peas, leaves, pebbles, sticks, etc., and each time to say, That is (not *one*, but) *one stick*, etc., until through the constant change of object the abstract notion of number is awakened in consciousness.

Arithmetic.

" From the moment when the child begins to use his senses, Nature never ceases to put objects before him from which men have abstracted the ideas of the one and the many-fold. The object of the book is to put mothers into the position to work in harmony with Nature in this respect, to draw the attention of the child to what may be

---

[1] Pestalozzi is emphasising the distinction between the perceptual and conceptual levels of consciousness, but he is not very clear about their relations one to the other in the process of development.

counted in the various objects and groups of objects he comes across. It teaches the mother to point out to the child that ' he has *one* nose and *one* mouth; that he has *one* eye and yet *one more* eye, etc.' Once she has put him on this line she will draw his attention to his fingers in larger and smaller groups. Nature has indeed provided the hand for this purpose. But Nature's device stops at ten and our aim is to provide another on the same plan." [1]

This new device consisted of three tables, called respectively the Table of Unity, the Table of Simple Fractions, and the Table of Complex Fractions. (See Figs. I., II., III., below.)

By means of Table I. the children were to obtain a visual picture of the unit as such and as an element in a sum of units; and again, a picture of a group of units as themselves constituting a unit or as an element in a more complex group. Clear pictures of these groups and their combinations are obtained by means of eight exercises.

Exercise I.—The teacher points to the right-hand square of the top line and says *One*. The children repeat. He passes to the next square and says *Twice One* and so on. *Three Times One.* . . . The children repeat each time. He then proceeds to the second row. Pointing to the two strokes in the first square he says, *Here are twice one* (or two ones); 2 *times* $1 = 1$ *times* 2. He passes along the square and says, Twice two, three times two, and so on, as in the first row. In like manner the whole square is completed. After this the squares are taken irregularly, and the children are asked how many threes (or whatever it may be) up to this point. This type of question is

---

[1] Introduction to the *A B C of Number Relations* (*Anschauungs-lehre der Zahlenverhältnisse*), *vide* S., Vol. IX., pp. 571-2.

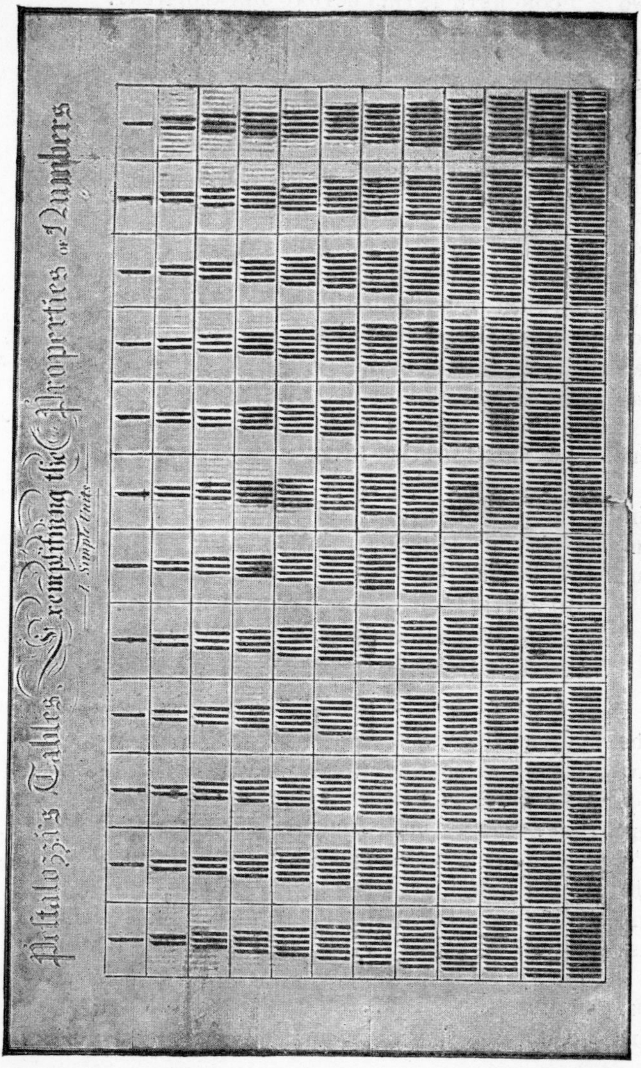

Pestalozzi's Tables. Exemplifying the Properties of Numbers
— A simple truth —

Fig. I.

repeated until the children can answer immediately for any position in the square.

Exercise II.—In this exercise each stroke in the second row is regarded as the half of two, in the third row as the third of three, and so on. Thus, pointing to the first stroke, the teacher says *One is half of two*; at the next stroke, *Twice* 1 = *Once* 2; at the third stroke, *Three times* 1 = once 2 and the half of 2, and so on across the row, when we get 20 times 1 = 10 times 2. Before going further, the point of view is reversed and the row is repeated. Instead of saying *one is half of two*, he says *the half of two is one* as he points to the first stroke; at the second, he says once 2 = twice 1; at the third, once 2 and the half of 2 = three times 1, etc.

A like procedure with thirds, fourths, and so on is continued through the square and repeated until the children answer, without hesitation, pointing to the proper squares, such questions as—

19 times 1—how many times 5 is that? Three times 5 and 4 times the fifth part of five—how many times 1 is that?

Exercise III.—The object of this exercise is to enable the children to convert a number of twos into threes, fours, fives, etc.—and so any group of one number into the equivalent group of another. How many threes are there in 8 twos? and so on. The procedure is as follows :—Pointing to the first stroke of the first two, the children say that is the half of two, and the first stroke of the first group of three is the third part of three. Then they say, as the teacher points to the succeeding strokes, twice 1 = once 2 in the second row, but twice 1 = twice the third part of 3 in the third row. Similarly three times 1 = once 2 and the half of 2 in the second row, but in the third row three times 1 = once 3. Thus they learn to convert groups of 2 into equivalent groups of 3. This is continued through all the numbers up to ten until practice makes perfect.

Exercise IV. is designed to teach children to answer (and to give from the table the grounds of the answer) such questions as—

How much is three times the half of 4? Answer: Three times the half of 4 = three times 2 = 6 times 1.

Exercise V. leads to questions as under:—

Of how many ones are two ones the half, the third, the fifth?

There are two ones—what part are they of 4, 6, 8, etc.?

Exercise VI. leads to questions like—

How many times does 4 contain the third part of 6? or the seventh of 14?

How many times does 8 contain the fourth part of 12?

Exercise VII. introduces the idea of proportion and leads to such questions as—

What is the number which is related to 4 in the same way as 2 is related to 1?

Exercise VIII. leads to questions like—

Of what number is 4 twice the third part?

The procedure throughout is on the principle of the *Elementary Method*: every step is complete and perfect before the next one is begun, and each step is so slightly different from the one before that advance is almost imperceptible. Unbroken continuity reigns supreme.

The Tables of Fractions give visual pictures of fractional relations. They were treated in similar exhaustive fashion. In the original form the squares were divided up to tenths only. In those given below, which are reprinted from an English version of Pestalozzian Arithmetic,[1] they are taken to twelfths—a much more useful subdivision.

The student who is familiar with ordinary methods of visual demonstration in the teaching of vulgar fractions will realise how these tables were used. It was not, however, for occasional demonstrations but for systematic and thorough work of the kind already described.

All these exercises were worked mentally, and the skill which Pestalozzi's boys showed in this matter astonished all his visitors.[2]

Of higher arithmetic and its applications to life some account will be found in the Prospectus of the Buchsee project and in the Report to Parents.[3]

When Steps in Development take place. Pestalozzi drew no hard and fast line between the periods of perception and conception respectively. Before the child comes to school his mother is to lead him to abstract ideas of number, and in various ways he is led to work out ordered series of sensory presentations whilst he is still at home.

Exercises in sensory apprehension over a wide field stimulate the latent power to generalise and deduce conclusions.

The child is intellectually ready for school when this capacity has been in this way awakened,[4] but the observing powers do not cease to grow at this point. In fact, as knowledge grows the powers of observation increase.

---

[1] Pestalozzi's *Intellectual or Intuitive Arithmetic*, by P. H. Pullen, 1821.

[2] *Vide* p. 364.   [3] *Vide* pp. 310 and 343.

[4] Lenzburg Address (M., Vol. III., p. 537).

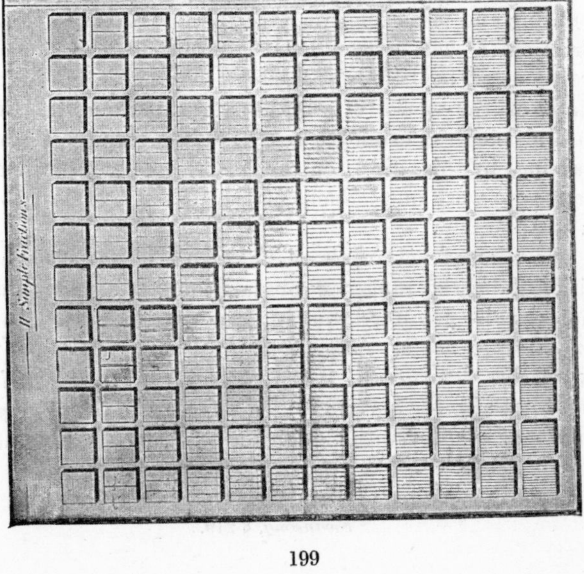

II Simple Fractures

III Compound Fractures

Fig. II.

Fig. III.

"One who is in the habit of examining the structure of plants, and is conversant with a system of botany, will discover a number of distinguishing characteristics of a flower, for instance, which remain wholly unnoticed by one who knows nothing of that science."[1]

There is of course a period in the life of every child which is inaccessible to definite ideas of every kind. Perception is logically and psychologically prior to abstraction and definition, but the power to compare and generalise appears very early, and in Pestalozzi's view is best assisted by lessons in number and form. "The Elementary Method recognises in number and form the simplest natural means of forwarding the transition from the already formed power of observation to the more perfect power of judgment, and of establishing finally the foundation of the higher power of abstraction." "In counting and measuring we have the first exercise in this direction."[2] The reason is of course that these elements are constantly being presented to the child in the shape of the world of objects amidst which he lives. But although Pestalozzi felt the importance of early training in this direction, he left it chiefly to his colleagues to work out. Some of their ideas are dealt with in Chapter XV.

The general notion, the definite idea, is absolutely conditioned by the range of observation. If the necessary material is not forthcoming in experience, *the general notion must not be formulated.* "The child's circle of experience determines, therefore, not only the *starting-point* but also the *horizon* of his thought.[3] If we regard the range of observation and conception as two concentric

---

[1] *Letters to Greaves*, G., p. 234.   [2] *Swansong*, §§ 26, 70, 98 (G.).
[3] *Swansong*, § 219.

circles, then the first may include the second, but this
second must never go beyond the first. The maxim,
'Life educates,' which fastens the observation of the
child to his own individual situation, keeps his thoughts
within the same limits."[1] Any attempt to force its exercise beyond these limits, as by hurrying on the learning of
logical rules, or by premature judgment in relation to
objects only superficially observed, will have the same
effect as forcing precocity in any other direction. The
powers of thought will " swell up, grow vague, weaken,
and finally stand still." Solid progress in thought power
can only come in one way—by practice in careful and
correct combination, separation, and comparison of objects
actually observed.

As Pestalozzi so frequently insists upon the education
of the " powers of the mind," the question has
not unnaturally been raised as to whether he
might properly be called a formalist or a realist
in his educational doctrine. Did he hold that thought
power exercised and developed in any particular direction
would be available in any sphere ? The doctrine of independent powers certainly suggests this, and his view of
the formal value of arithmetic as training in the power
of abstraction, as well as much of his practice and the
practice of his imitators, gave good ground for the
contemporary criticism which concentrated itself upon
this point.

Pestalozzi's Formalism.

Yet Pestalozzi was too keen an observer to hold such
an opinion, and every day's experience showed him that a
man with excellent judgment in one direction may be of
little use in another. He always insists that the exercise
of judgment which education provides should have direct

[1] Wiget, *op. cit.*

reference to the sphere of life from which the pupil comes
and in which he is likely to remain. "A thousand examples
show us how innumerable men, even scientifically educated,
have not been trained to think seriously and habitually in
regard to the actual circumstances of their daily life, so
that in every situation which lies outside their profession,
their judgments and opinions are hopelessly untrustworthy." As with thought, so with observation, our
powers do not develop generally, but only within a certain
sphere of habitual operations, within the limits of the
" circle of thought." [1] It is life that educates.

But certain absurdities in Pestalozzi's practice, which are
to be explained by his psychology, gave strong support to
the charge of formalism so far as his " elementary method "
was concerned, a charge which the Lenzburg Address is at
pains to refute. "I let children of three years old spell
the wildest nonsense merely because it was nonsensically
hard." [2] "I was not so much concerned that my children
should learn to spell, to read, and to write as I was anxious
that their mental powers should develop through these
exercises in as all-round and effective a way as possible.
To that end I made them spell words by heart before they
knew the alphabet, and the whole room could spell the
hardest words before they knew a single letter." [3] These
are examples of the " training of the powers " view, which,
together with the verbalism of much of Pestalozzi's teaching, are the stock examples of the contradiction between
Pestalozzi's theory and practice. As a matter of fact, the
practice is the outcome of a principle (viz. that power
comes with exercise) wrongly applied, bringing it thereby

---

[1] Cp. *Swansong* (G., pp. 299-302).
[2] *How Gertrude Teaches her Children*, Letter I., § 42.
[3] *Vide* Stanz Letter, § 195.

into strong opposition with the principle that exercise must have meaning for the child, that is to say, must be related to life.

Pestalozzi's verbalism was further accentuated by his view of the function of words. We have seen how, in the step prior to the teaching of language, the child is to learn long lists of names of objects with which he is not yet acquainted. By this means "the representation of the object is preceded by the fluency of the sound which describes the object, and from the moment when by observation the child can combine the object with the sound which denotes it he cannot possibly forget it." Pestalozzi is here thinking of the nursery, where the young child acquires many words whose content is at first exceedingly thin, but additional experience deepens their meaning and narrows their application.

The Function of Words.

This natural method of acquiring a vocabulary in early childhood is extended by Pestalozzi to the school. Amongst the points that Krusi notes in the method at Burgdorf is " that through a well-arranged nomenclature indelibly impressed, a general foundation for all kinds of knowledge was laid." [1] In this way the child was to enjoy the advantages of one whose home is in a great house of business, and who therefore acquires every day from his cradle upwards the names of countless objects. The words are thus " ready like nets to catch meanings, as experience gives the opportunity." [2]

This practice of Pestalozzi's struck Herbart very forcibly, as he tells us in his review of *How Gertrude Teaches her Children*.[3] He admitted that the little children seemed to

[1] *How Gertrude Teaches her Children*, i. 43.
[2] Wiget, *op. cit.*
[3] Herbart's *Sämmtliche Werke*, Vol. I., p. 142.

enjoy the exercise, and in talking over the matter with
Pestalozzi it occurred to him that possibly an *inner sense of
the meaning* of what is being taught them is even more
important than its instantaneous apprehension. " Most of
that which they learned by heart had to do with objects
immediately about them. The child left the school with
his words in his head, saw the object, and now for the
first time perhaps realised what the words meant, and
that in a much more perfect way than he would have
done, had the teacher tried to explain them through other
words.

" The lesson gives the word and puts together what
should go together in thought, time and opportunity
attach ideas to the words and fuse into an intimate whole
what were until then only laid side by side. At the same
time we must not forget that Pestalozzi was dealing
with little children. To them a word is not as it
is to us, merely the sign of a thing, but a thing in
itself. They stop over the sound, and only when that
is quite familiar to them, do they learn to forget it in
the thing."

If further support were wanted for what developed into
an empty teaching of words, Pestalozzi's view of the nature
and function of language provided it. The point is, as
usual, excellently put by Wiget: " Since language is
originally ' the giving back of all the impressions which
Nature in her whole course has made upon the race,' and
since, according to Herder—Pestalozzi's authority for the
origin of language—' the impression of a thing must be
similar upon all the members of one species,' so Pestalozzi
(perhaps under the influence of older traditions which
ascribed a certain reality to words) held it for possible
' by means of her spoken sounds, to awaken in the child
the very impressions which these tones have always

produced on the race.' [1]   And this idea took such hold of
him that the principle of observation was overshadowed.
Things were pushed aside by words, and into the place
of nature teaching the dictionary stepped.[2] The contradiction between theory and practice is thus again ' a
contradiction between two principles, justified in themselves, but with regard to the range of their applicability
not sufficiently delimited.' "

[1] Cp. *How Gertrude Teaches her Children*, Letter VII., § 46 (G.,
p. 116).   [2] Cp. *ibid.*, § 3 (G., p. 112).

CHAPTER XII.

PRACTICAL EDUCATION.

Intellectual and Physical Foundations. "To have knowledge without practical power, to have insight and yet to be incapable of applying it in everyday life—could an unfriendly spirit devise a more fearful lot for a human being than this?" The feeling of practical power and its exercise are as essential to man as knowledge and thought, and indeed knowing and doing, impression and expression, are so closely connected that when one ceases, the other ceases with it. It is therefore as important to cultivate practical capacity—without which our wants and wishes cannot be satisfied—and to carry it through to the same degree of perfection, as it is to train thought-power and intellectual insight. Both alike are fundamental necessities of the human organism.[1]

In this chapter we are concerned with the cultivation of practical capacity (*Kunstkraft*), with the "psychological unfolding of the many-sided physical powers which dwell in the child's nature."

The letters which constitute *How Gertrude Teaches her Children* only treat this part of the problem of education very slightly. Pestalozzi's more detailed ideas upon the subject must be looked for in other of his writings. Thus it is in the *Swansong*[2] that he tells us what he means by "practical capacity." The term includes the power of

[1] *How Gertrude Teaches her Children*, xii. 5 (G., p. 136).
[2] Vide *Swansong*, § 28 (G., p. 279).

giving external expression to the products of the intellect, of giving external effectiveness to the impulses of the heart, and of performing the practical duties which belong to home and civic life. Without dwelling upon the obvious defects of this statement as a logical classification, it is useful as showing how widely the term is to be understood; it implies effectiveness in action of any and every kind.

The impulse to action lies, of course, in human nature itself. The teacher's business is to understand the conditions, psychological and physiological, under which action may be effectively controlled and purposefully directed. In attacking this problem, Pestalozzi, as always, endeavours to go to the root of the matter. He finds that the foundations of practical power are partly intellectual and partly physical. Definite action implies an idea of what is to be done, as well as the power of doing it. The importance of this preliminary intellectual condition, as we may call it, is well brought out in Pestalozzi's treatment of drawing—the typical school dexterity—to which he has paid a good deal of attention in the seventh of the Gessner Letters. As we shall see, the initial stage must provide for (1) the clear apprehension of form, (2) the desire to imitate form, and (3) the necessary power of muscular direction.

Before drawing of any kind is attempted, he tells us, the child should be able to apprehend form.
Ideational Elements in Drawing. A child cannot draw an object properly "until he has ideas about the proportion of the form, and is able to express himself concerning them." To this end he devised what he called an "A B C of Spatial Perception." "This 'alphahet,'" says Dean Ith in his report,[1] "is a square, decimally divided by horizontal, perpendicular, and slanting lines," which was to be applied

[1] *Vide* p. 97.

to the analysis of forms as the alphabet is used for the analysis of sounds. It was at first used in actual measurement, the divided square being traced on transparent horn which could be superposed upon other forms. In the course of this exercise, a feeling for proportion insensibly arises, by means of which "measurements" may be made without mechanical aid.

The "power to observe form" has now been acquired. Obviously only the geometrical aspects of objects repre-

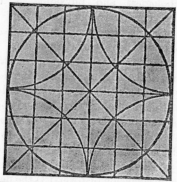

Fig. IV.   (See note at the end of the chapter.)

sented or seen "in the flat" is referred to. So far, however, "the eye has been trained," not in the sense of having been made optically more delicate, but in the only way which "sense training" can have a meaning. It is the *mind* that has been trained by exercise to deal effectively with certain sense material. The "idea of measurement" has been acquired, which of course involves ideas of proportion and the power to express proportion numerically—as twice this or that, the half of something else etc. Thus "the idea of drawing is not only founded upon the power of the hand, but upon the inward processes of the human mind." So far there has been no thought of manual dexterity, but the preliminary geometrical and arithmetical ideas have been in process of formation.

What is true of drawing is true of all dexterities. It is essential for the efficiency of practical power of any kind, artistic or technical, that the "powers of thought and judgment should undergo a preliminary training, which always begins with the exercise of the perceptual powers"[1] —not, of course, generally, but in the particular direction demanded by the sphere of practical activity with which we are concerned.

Practical Training in Drawing. Having secured the necessary intellectual foundations, the physical side of the training begins. The aim now is to establish practical skill (*Fertigkeit*), which rests on the highest possible degree of what Pestalozzi calls "nerve-tact," that is to say, upon the ready and certain action of delicate nerve coordinations which ensure certainty of movement in the hundred different directions demanded by a complicated physical action. Here again, however, is a parallel mental condition. Muscular control from the side of mind rests ultimately upon "sensations of motion" which are only obtained by moving; hence, Pestalozzi points out that while in order "to know" we may often remain passive, in order to acquire practical skill and power we must *do*. Sensations of motion frequently repeated and attended to acquire a certain fixity as "motor habits," and as such are instantly at the service of conceived action involving them. The perfect coordination of the various "motor habits" is the mental parallel to the nerve-tact of which Pestalozzi speaks.[2]

---

[1] Vide *Swansong*, § 28 (G., p. 279).

[2] The student should compare this with the chapter on Habit in any modern psychology, *e.g.* James's *Text-Book of Psychology*, Chap. X. James says that "Habit depends on sensations not

These then are the preliminary physical (physiological) and mental conditions of practical power. Advance in physical dexterity is, however, in no way parallel to the intellectual advance described in the last chapter. The latter depends upon the purely mental power of abstraction, the former upon mere repetition. Pestalozzi puts it in this way. "The laws which govern the development of the physical powers are physical, because the mechanism which gives power to the human limbs is itself physical." As James puts it: "The principle of habit is at bottom a physical principle." "The phenomena of habit in living beings are due to the plasticity of the organic materials of which their bodies are composed."

At the same time, in endeavouring to provide practice, the intellectual background is not to be overlooked. Mind is always behind effective action, and merely mechanical exercise of the limbs is deficient as an educational instrument, because it makes no demands upon intellectual activity. Who does not know the musician who reads perfectly at sight but, in spite of his admirable technical skill, never succeeds in interpreting the music he renders. It conveys no meaning to him and he cannot therefore convey one to us. The habit is there. It works with unfailing accuracy, but there is no mind controlling it. Exercises which give results of that kind are bad in themselves and bad in their general influence. *The practice of purely mechanical exercises which are not the result of an intellectual stimulus has no part in human education;*

"**Mind**" **must always enter into Training.**

attended to." This sentence aptly expresses the "mental" side of practical skill to which Pestalozzi refers. At first of course these sensations are attended to, but with repetition the nervous impulses are linked up into a series which functions automatically.

such exercises tend to blunt intellectual and moral power.[1]

This is a vital principle of Pestalozzianism. It means simply that the child is to put himself into what he is doing, and that can only be achieved when his activity is prompted by some purpose or need. We shall understand what Pestalozzi means if we look again at his ideas on the teaching of drawing. " Let the child use his chalk or pencil freely, assisted and occasionally stimulated by his teacher, but do not force him into directions which do not appeal to him. He will finally become sensible of the need for greater accuracy. At that moment methodical training may properly begin." " Not until the thought arises in the child that his mother might help him in what he wishes to do, but cannot do properly, has the time come for the guidance of the teacher's art to find ready access to the child's mind." [2] The teacher is to guard against being regarded as an interfering person, and also to avoid the danger of crushing the child's spontaneity by drilling him into a machine.

In the face of the infinite complexities of movement involved in the many specialised forms of practical skill, and in face of Pestalozzi's constant endeavour to elementarise all forms of instruction, it is not surprising to find him considering the possibility of discovering an " A B C of practical capacity " which " should be a series of exercises advancing gradually from the simplest to the most complicated dexterities." This third " alphabet " should include the elements of all physical activity; it should be a " general gymnastic of power."

An A B C of Movements, i.e. of Practical Capacity.

---

[1] Lenzburg-Address (M., iii. 470).   [2] *Swansong*, § 77 (G., p. 313).

" Unhappily," he says, " this A B C of practical capacity
is not yet found, and one rarely hears of anybody trying to
work it out." Yet he thinks that, if somebody would
take it seriously in hand, the problem would not be
found to present great inherent difficulties. His idea is
that such an alphabet would " begin with the simplest
natural expressions of physical power in which lie the
foundations of the most complex human dexterities : striking and carrying, thrusting and throwing, pulling and
twisting, wrestling and swinging." [1]

Although he has not himself worked out such a system
as he suggests, his occasional references suggest important
principles.[2] It is clear that in Pestalozzi's view, general
physical training is to precede such specialised physical
training as would be given by learning one particular
dexterity—as for example that involved in a highly
specialised manual occupation.

Such a training would be very partial and one-sided.
It would be bad for two reasons. On the purely physical
side, it would fix certain movements prematurely, and
make it difficult either to acquire skill in a new direction
or to rearrange, even in a slight degree, the composite
system of movements which has become a habit. On
mind itself the consequences would be even worse. It
is acquiring a fixed series of motor ideas, and " while
the hand loses versatility, imagination withers away." [3]

---

[1] *How Gertrude Teaches her Children*, XII., 8 (G., p. 139).

[2] It is interesting to find that Fichte in his *Addresses to the
German Nation* emphasises the importance of Pestalozzi's suggestion
and laments the fact that he had not worked out the idea. This
was in 1808, when as a matter of fact the idea had been elaborated
by one of Pestalozzi's colleagues (Niederer) in the *Wochenschrift*.
(See below, p. 215.)

[3] Wiget, *op. cit.*

"The spirit of power dies and with it the spirit of discovery and the elevating sense of self-respect."

What Pestalozzi means will be perhaps best understood from an illustration. Suppose the *only* training in hand-movements a child received was concerned with knitting stockings. He would become very skilful as a stocking knitter, but quite useless for anything else because not only would those movements be the only series that practice had made automatic, but they would be the only notions of movement his mind could deal with. The case is of course absurd. We could never get such complete specialisation of movement, but the more nearly physical training approaches this impossible extreme the more uneducative it is. Pestalozzi means that a gradual sharpening of the sense of motion, richness of possible motor representations, is the general task which an elementary gymnastic of dexterity has to fulfil.[1] To substitute for such a general preliminary training a manual training limited to the acquisition of dexterities which will be of direct service to him in his future life is mere "routine education," leading to a "fractional humanity" —an expression of the *Researches*.

Pestalozzi's views on the teaching of writing before drawing are an interesting illustration of these **Writing.** principles, which he means of course to be of general application. "Nature herself has subordinated this art to the art of drawing. Writing is a special kind of linear drawing, and suffers no arbitrary deviation from the fixed direction of its form. If the child has been made an expert in writing before he can draw, his hand must necessarily have been spoiled, because it has been set into particular forms before the suppleness

---

[1] Wiget, *op. cit.*

required for skill in drawing has been sufficiently and certainly established. Further, when drawing precedes writing, the right formation of the letters becomes immeasurably easier, and the child is spared the great waste of time involved in the process of again overcoming his tendency to crooked and inaccurate forms."[1]

Here, of course, he is thinking of writing as a purely mechanical art, without taking into consideration fundamental differences between writing and drawing which make vast differences in our mode of treating them. The motor control I have gained in practising drawing does help me to copy letters, but as everybody knows it is possible to copy letters and indeed to make them freely and to group them into pseudo-verbal (if I may be forgiven the hybrid) forms without in the least being able to write in the meaningful sense of the word. Most schoolmasters of experience will have come across cases of the kind and schools for mentally deficient children commonly have them. Whether such children might not be taught to write in the proper sense of the word by adopting special methods based on their psychical peculiarities is not a question that concerns us at the moment.

It is characteristic of Niederer that he should have attempted to fill up the gap noted by Pesta-

Drill.

lozzi in respect of an A B C of practical power, and that in so doing he should have applied a single general principle to the point of absurdity. In an essay in the *Wochenschrift* he approached the problem of a "general elementary gymnastic" from the point of view of the "elementary method," a leading feature of which, it will be remembered, is "unbroken continuity of

---

[1] *How Gertrude Teaches her Children*, VII., § 68.

advance in scarcely perceptible steps." His physical exercises rival *The Mother's Book* in the pedantry with which the principle is applied. To find out the correct order for such a series of movements one has only to ask : "What movements can I make with every single member of my body and with every single joint of the same ? In what direction can these movements take place, and in what positions ? How can the movements of several members and several joints be combined with one another ? " "The range of all possible exercises must be exhausted at each stage." This is a marked change from the running and jumping which are regarded in *How Gertrude Teaches her Children* as the fitting starting-points of physical training, and a curious departure from the principle on which Pestalozzi set great store—" that no physical activity is educative which does not spring from an intellectual stimulus."

Although Niederer's elaborate " drill" was published with Pestalozzi's approval, and although, in a letter to Stapfer in 1811, he talks of a "perfected and general training of the joints of the boy's arms and the girl's fingers which shall make the learning of every sort of manual occupation the easiest of games," as a matter of fact, a very small place is assigned to this sort of thing in the *Report to Parents*, which describes the scheme of physical education practised at Yverdun.[1] " We ascribe the good health of our children partly to their careful nourishment but more particularly to the free active lives they lead." Among the daily exercises which occupy the recreation hours, the first place is given to walking, swimming, sledging, skating, etc. When these are not possible, the boys are led to an open place, where they are

---

[1] *Vide* p. 336.

divided into groups determined by their physical strength or their inclinations, and there they choose for themselves the exercise or game they prefer. When bad weather makes outdoor freedom impossible, the boys are drilled inside the building, on the lines set forth in the *Wochenschrift*. On free afternoons they take long walks or are put through military exercises. Formal "elementary" drill is at best, therefore, a stop-gap, and is no real substitute for the free movements involved in games. The interest that comes from spontaneous activity is as essential to the physical as to the intellectual side of education.

Practical Training and Actual Life. We have learned already that physical education, as we understand it, does not include all that Pestalozzi meant by the term. He had in mind the general training in "those dexterities upon whose possession depends both the power to do and the habit of doing everything demanded by a cultivated mind and a noble heart." His aim, in this regard, was to fit the child for the physical conditions of his existence. Clearly the individual requirements in such a matter will vary enormously, and to this fact Pestalozzi was keenly alive.

He pours scorn upon a physical education based upon "dancing, fencing, swimming, climbing, vaulting," and the like, the result of which is to make one want to ride when one has no horse, or to dance when one has no shoes, to lead one to spend money and time at the social evenings of the small towns, in which young women waste the hard-earned wages of their fathers, and young men learn to despise the very manual labour which has put it in their power to enjoy all these fine things."[1]

---

[1] Pestalozzi's *Brief Account of his Method*, 1802, Morf, ii., p. 152.

Or, as the same point is put in the Lenzburg Address, "it would be an ill service to humanity if gymnastics brought the children of the farmer and the artisan to such a pass that, while they could climb and leap like wild things, they were unwilling to help the mother in the house, and were strangers to the quiet workshop of the father or to the toilsome labour of the plough."[1]

It was, of course, a general principle of Pestalozzi's that every influence which leads us to apply our powers and activities in a way that turns us from the actual calls of practical life, or puts us out of accord with them, must be regarded as a deviation from the laws of nature, as destructive of the harmony between self and surroundings, and as a hindrance to self-culture.[2]

Illustrations of these principles occur throughout Pestalozzi's writings, especially in those concerning concrete problems, such as that of the education of the poor. In his letters " On the education of the poor children of the country," whilst he emphasises the importance of games and physical exercises, he lays still greater stress upon work in field and kitchen garden, where interesting instruction in useful knowledge concerning sowing and planting, protecting and grafting, and other garden dexterities is combined with muscular exertion.

In the *Picture of a Poor-house*[3] which appeared in the *Wochenschrift*, he tells us " the children learn how to run by being set to take care of geese, sheep, and goats, seeking lost ones till they are found, and running quickly on errands. They do not learn to climb on poles set up for the purpose, but on the trees in order to gather the

---

[1] Lenzburg Address, M., iii. 473.
[2] *How Gertrude Teaches her Children*, XII. 11.
[3] Seyffarth, x., p. 366.

fruit. They work in the most varied positions, they weed, rake, and gather stones ; they are given tools early, they carry burdens on their backs and on their heads, they stamp clay on the threshing floor."

These tasks are not set indiscriminately, but in an order determined by their relative complexity. It is an attempt to find a useful and interesting employment for those physical movements which Niederer's drill also provided, but without exciting the intellectual accompaniment which makes physical exercise educative; it is an attempt to subordinate physical training to the demands of the future, without, however, sacrificing any of that general bodily training, which is as much the absolute right of the poor man's child as it is of the child of the rich. As partially determining the order of such occupations, Pestalozzi suggests that the exercising of several parts of the body should precede that of single parts ; the exercise of the larger limbs should precede that of the smaller, and work which necessitates bodily motion should precede sedentary occupation.

In the case of the more fortunate children who enjoy a home life, the household duties themselves are the best of all instruments for physical education. "The careful and wise use of the means of education afforded by home life is just as important in regard to physical as to moral and intellectual education."[1] Here, as nowhere else, the practical duties which the wise mother assigns to her children have a meaning and a motive which appeals to both the head and the heart. It is real life, and the nearer the school can approach to it the more valuable its practical training will be.

Similar considerations led him to draw a sharp dis-

[1] *Swansong*, § 30 (G., p. 280).

tinction between the practical education of the countryman and the townsman. "The countryman who has been
sufficiently educated for his position will not need a
carpenter to mend every broken board, nor a smith to
drive a hook into his wall or to straighten a bent nail."
He will understand field work of course, and besides this
he will know the use of the hammer, the tongs, and the
plane, and be able to do his own repairs. The townsman's
practical education must rest on a broader foundation. He
must not only obtain an insight into the essential features
of local industries, but he should receive such a mathematical and aesthetical training as will cultivate in him
any latent capacity for invention.

Pestalozzi is always at his best when he is writing in the
concrete, when he is discussing a practical issue and facing
actual fact. In such places one feels that it is the real
Pestalozzi who is speaking, and that his practical intuitions
are often better guides to the truth than his abstract
generalisations, coloured as they so frequently are by his
mouthpiece Niederer, who had more feeling for philosophical principle than for the concrete child, limited as he
is on every side by the facts of life. Pestalozzi in practice
never loses sight of the actual boy. The "average child"
has no place in his philosophy. "Life educates," and
artificial devices which are not based upon that principle
are unnatural, and therefore harmful. But "life" is a
concrete, limited fact, differing for each individual within
other broad differences which mark off the rich from the
poor, the artisan from the peasant, the cotton-spinner from
the iron-worker, the ship-builder from the mason.

In so far as all are men, having bodily organs whose
movements are governed by mechanical laws, a general
scheme of physical exercises may be thought out which will
ennoble the specialised education for a calling, and assume

for it " the pure foundation of humanity," if this general scheme is accompanied by that intellectual preparation typified in the lessons prior to the teaching of drawing. But the " learning time " is short, and much may be done —particularly in country schools—to give an all-round physical training in combination with instruction in the occupations which in all probability will be the children's life-work. Such instruction will have the incalculable advantage of close connection with life. It must not, however, be mechanical. The intellectual preparation is essential, that freedom and inventiveness may be assured. The exercises must be varied, graded, and purposeful, that the " hand may not lose its suppleness," and that interest may be kept up.

Having secured the intellectual foundations and accuracy in the elementary movements, so that their representation for the purposes of development of real power is possible, progress in the acquisition of any dexterity is marked by these stages : (1) correctness of form, (2) power in repro- ducing it, (3) delicacy in its representation, (4) freedom and independence in its application.[1] When he wrote this Pestalozzi had been convinced by his critics that his A B C of Spatial Perception—based on the geometrically divided square—leading as it did to the geometrical apprehension of form, was mistaken.

Progress in Practical Skill.

At Burgdorf practical work in drawing " began with the horizontal line, and its application to the various objects which lay around. Next came the vertical line, then the right angle, and soon, as the child by easy application of these forms became stronger, the figures were gradually varied." " Every drawing, even the first beginning, was

---

[1] *Swansong*, § 81 (G., p. 314).

brought to perfection before the children proceeded further, developing in them a consciousness of perfected power, even in the first steps of the art." [1]

At Yverdun the purely geometrical teaching of drawing was abandoned. The prospectus of 1804,[2] drawn up for the joint Fellenberg-Pestalozzi Institute, does not mention the A B C of Spatial Perception, and the aim is rather to establish a sense of the beautiful than to develope a sense of mathematical proportions. In 1809 a book of Schmid's was adopted, *The Elements of Drawing in accordance with Pestalozzian Principles*, the chief feature of which was the " unbroken continuity and scarcely perceptible advance " of its graduated exercises—straight lines and curved lines combined in a great variety of ways. The children mastered the elements, copied the combinations, and invented new ones for themselves. Natural objects and drawings of ornament were rigidly excluded. The obvious one-sidedness of such a training should have prevented Pestalozzi from accepting it, but it was another application of a much-loved principle, and Pestalozzi was too little of an artist himself to have a keen sense of artistic error.[3]

In respect of the remaining school dexterities, we have already noted that the teaching of writing is to follow that of drawing. It will be easy for the child who has gained command of his pencil in the drawing lessons to learn to form the letters. " At four or five he should do this, first with a pencil on a slate, because it is easier to manage than a pen, and because mistakes are easily erased, instead of having to remain before the child, thereby becoming the source of further errors." " When he is familiar with the forms of the letters and their combinations, he is given a

---

[1] *How Gertrude Teaches her Children*, VIII. 67, 68.
[2] See Chapter XVIII. [3] Cp. Froebel's Drawing Exercises. No doubt he owed much to Schmid.

pen and a copy-book with graduated exercises." "His first writing with the pen is merely his pencil progress over again, and he should at first make the letters the same size as he drew them on the slate, and only gradually be exercised in copying the ordinary small writing."

He has now passed through stages (1) and (2) of his progress in the art. Learning to write is, however, a kind of learning to talk. When he knows the forms of the letters and is skilled in their reproduction, he needs no more special copies. He has in his head their essence.[1] He writes from his own experience and uses his power of memory and imagination. Delicacy, freedom, independence, are qualities in this art, as in every other, intimately bound up with intellectual power, a further indication of the ultimate unity of the whole problem of education.

Another characteristic school dexterity is music, progress in which follows the same course as in drawing.

Music.

At its base are sensory observations involving ideas of "more or less," that is to say of comparative, length, loudness, pitch, and tone. "He who has been introduced on 'elementary' principles into the art of measuring and reckoning has already got a start towards a clear knowledge of the intellectual foundations of music."

The method was worked out in detail by W. T. Pfeiffer and H. G. Nägeli, the former of whom had spent two years with Pestalozzi at Burgdorf, and published in a book, *The Teaching of Music on Pestalozzian Principles* (1810). Both men were doing much for the popularisation of music in Switzerland, and Pestalozzi invited them to apply his

---

[1] *How Gertrude Teaches her Children*, Letter VII. (G., p. 121).

general educational principles to the teaching of music, and help in that way to introduce it into the life of the people.[1] This book was the result. It is divided into two parts; in the first there are three steps, in which Pestalozzian principles are clearly to be observed. (1) Exercises in the observation of tones in respect of (*a*) their (time) length, (*b*) their pitch, (*c*) their loudness and softness. (2) The methodical connection of these three elements—time, melody, and force. (3) Musical notation.

After this general preliminary training—an "elementary" musical gymnastic—there followed more specialised courses, as follows: (1) The singing of words. (2) The relative time and word emphasis. (3) The connection of music and poetry. (4) The introduction to musical works. It was only in this last stage that actual songs were sung. The "elementary" principle has once again been allowed to overshadow every other.

The educational value of "manual training" is so frequently urged in the present day that Pesta-
Manual Training. lozzi's views upon the subject have a particular interest. We have already seen on what a high educational level he places manual work, and the point is repeatedly urged throughout his writings. The school at Bonnal, described in *Leonard and Gertrude*, Part III., Chapters LXVI.-LXVIII., is a school of industry; in *Christopher and Elizabeth* he writes: "If I had time and patience and could be a village schoolmaster, I would take spinning-wheels and weaving-stools into my school, and the children should learn to speak, to read, and to reckon, whilst their hands were busily employed." "Every day the schoolmaster realised more fully how work cultivates the intelligence, gives force to the feelings of the heart, and keeps

alive the sense of duty." In 1807 he wrote, "I now regard it as a clear and incontrovertible principle, that man is much more truly educated through that which he does than through that which he learns."

We also know how differently he would apply this principle in respect of the town and country child, and the question naturally suggests itself as to whether the principle of work would overcome the principle that is equally characteristic of Pestalozzi—that school education should be a chapter of real life, that its arrangements should always take into consideration the probable future of the children. With the child of the artisan and the peasant, work is the starting-point of the whole Pestalozzian system; instruction is fastened upon or developed out of it.

In the case of the higher classes, he says, " their children must not and cannot be led through the activity of their hands to the activity of the intellect and the raising of their affections; on the contrary, they must be stimulated and guided by the activity of their minds to the activity of their hands."[1] But the " practical capacity " required by the upper classes is something different from the practical capacity of the artisan. " The power they need depends upon the extent and the solidity of their knowledge, *i.e.* their knowledge of objects and the manner of dealing with them, though for the actual handling they frequently have other people's hands at their call, which they must and ought to make use of."[1] Doing is not essential, but they should know how to do. " Instead of technique they require technology."[2]

At the same time, Pestalozzi does not suggest abandoning the " practice of mechanical dexterities " in the case of

---

[1] *Swansong*, §§ 119-123 (G., pp. 320-1).   [2] Wiget, *op. cit.*

children of the well-to-do, indeed he laments its neglect as one of the signs of educational degeneracy, but in their case the manual work occupies quite a different place in the system. It is not the centre around which all other teaching is grouped. It is an occasional—though, of course, regular and systematic—putting of the hand to occupations interesting in themselves, or having a close connection with the surroundings of home or school. At Yverdun, for example, the boys learned to dig and to saw, they practised turning and bookbinding, though letters of visitors tell us that this side of the school work was irregular and spasmodic.

In concluding this account of Pestalozzi's theory and practice in respect of the education of practical power, it may be useful to point again to the intimate interaction of intellectual and physical activity, and to the fundamental unity of the whole problem of education.

He sought a gymnastic through which the training we give to the body shall itself be a means of intellectual and moral training. He sought to make the body a perfect instrument for carrying out the mind's behests. Intellectual training and physical training are not two separate things —the one for the mind and the other for the body—both are introduced "mainly for the sake of the soul." [1] It is in fact exactly the Platonic view which animated Pestalozzi.

His analysis of the process of acquiring practical skill shows that from the beginning mental factors are involved. Observation is fundamental as furnishing materials from which the mind builds up standards wherewith to measure

---

[1] Plato, *Republic*, Bk. III. (Davies and Vaughan's Translation, p. 107).

the results produced by the physical activities which it, in due course, initiates and directs to definite ends.

Schemes of physical training which do not take into account this intellectual factor fall short of Pestalozzi's idea of the educative; on the other hand, properly treated, the mere "whittling of a stick with a knife" may in the fullest sense answer to that idea. When, however, we regard practical efficiency more closely, it is obvious that the combination of intellectual insight and practical skill is still only a preliminary condition. Without the will to do, skill and insight are lame incompetents. This side of education, the keystone to the arch, is the subject of our next chapter.

NOTE TO FIG. IV.

This Figure is given by Biber (*Henry Pestalozzi and his Plan of Education*, p. 205) as the A B C of Form. It is, however, clearly not the one referred to by Ith, who speaks of it as decimally divided. In any case, it does not seem to have been long used, being superseded by riper methods. Seyffarth does not print it.

CHAPTER XIII.

Moral Education.

In Pestalozzi's best known work, *How Gertrude Teaches her Children,* he is in the main occupied with intellectual education. This was due to the circumstances of the time, and it is significant that, in a scheme for the revision of that work, he takes up the subject of moral education first. Indeed we saw in an earlier chapter (Principle of Spontaneity) that he looked on the possibility of moral development as constituting the ultimate difference between man and the lower animals.

Moral Progress of Mankind.

For Pestalozzi moral education is the key to his whole system. " The final aim of education—humanity— is only to be reached by subordinating the demands of our intellectual and practical capacities to the higher demands of morality and religion." He points out that this subordination characterises nature's own proceeding. The child trusts and loves long before he thinks and works. His belief in his mother and his love for her are already lively, strong, and imperishable at a time when he is intellectually and physically powerless. Thus we may say that nature postpones intellectual and practical education in favour of the education of the heart, an order which must never be departed from. Man must be intellectually and practically cultivated, but only by putting these sides of his culture at the service of faith and love can he be ennobled and inwardly satisfied by his education. "That is God's order in respect of head, heart, and hand."

Pestalozzi tells us what he means by morality in the book he wrote at Fichte's suggestion—*Researches into the Course of Nature in the Development of the Human Race.*[1] He there recognises three grades of mankind—the natural man, the social man, and the moral man.[2]

The Natural Man. The *natural man* is, after Rousseau's pattern, a harmless, good-natured being whose wants are in perfect equilibrium with his power.

" Man in this condition is a pure child of his instincts which lead him directly and harmlessly to the satisfaction of his sensory desires."

" In an entirely benevolent way he loves his wife, his child, his dog, and his horse ; he does not know what God is, nor is he acquainted with sin. He has small fear of evil spirits. The daylight, the forest, and the meadow are to him holy in the state which God created them ; ploughed lands are a curse ; he spends his time in sleeping and sensory enjoyment. . . . He will give away his only cow for a string of corals."

" So long as this continues we call him an unspoiled natural man, but so soon as he finds difficulty in satisfying his desires he loses his harmlessness and his natural good nature ; he is now *a natural man spoiled*. Just as the whole human race began its development as an innocent child of nature, so the development of each child has this state of innocence as its point of departure."

The natural man has neither religion nor morality, and the child at the moment of his birth is precisely in the same position. Like the natural man, " he knows nothing of evil, of pain, of hunger, of care, of mistrust, of feelings of independence or insecurity." " This, however, does not last, for so soon as the moment of birth is over the purity

---

[1] This is translated in G. (p. 53 ff.).

[2] Compare also *How Gertrude Teaches her Children*, VII. 33,

of the natural man in the child passes away." His first cry is the sign of unsatisfied desire, of coming struggles and pain which will carry him further and further away from the condition in which God first placed him. The natural man as such is lost from the moment when his instincts are insufficient to maintain him securely.

The *natural man spoiled* is in a sad position. Selfishness has taken the place of natural kindliness, and his life is a battle from beginning to end. It is a struggle of all against each, and each against all. He is religious now, but his religion is a superstition. In this condition he remains a long time, escaping from it by means of what political philosophers of the eighteenth century called a *social contract*, under which each individual gives up certain of his natural rights to the whole community in return for the protection which in its turn the community undertakes to give him. This, according to eighteenth century social theory, is the origin of society and of law.

Social man is, however, not moral. He has no need of morality. His actions are regulated by his contract, that is, by law; and social life is quite possible without any further guiding principle of conduct. But man may easily deceive himself and mistake the actions of organised masses of men for moral action. Such action is, at best, only a modification of natural action due to the obligation entered into under the social contract. Societies may have religion, but it is essentially external—a legal contrivance which has nothing to do with the religion of true morality.

Social Man.

Social man may realise the difference between the innocent independence of his God-given natural condition and his present condition, which is based upon selfishness only limited in its extent by the control of the law. In the midst of it all he feels a need in his innermost self, and the feeling arises that it is within his power to make himself a nobler being than nature and society can possibly make him.

Most men are satisfied to live their lives under law. They give what the law demands and take what the law allows. Their citizenship is unquestionable, they live socially well-ordered lives, and socially they are approved. But morality is for Pestalozzi an absolutely individual matter. "No man can feel for me that I am moral." Legality and morality are different in their essence. It is the difference between necessity and freedom. Morality has its seat in the good-will, it consists in the pure will to do right "according to the measure of my knowledge." "Of good works Pestalozzi is sceptical, because he is not sure that they may not be merely legal acts." [1]

The perfectly *moral man* is the unattainable ideal. **Moral Man.** Mankind as a whole is as incapable of living upon earth "a life of pure morality as of remaining in the innocence of his original nature." Few men strive after this ideal; social life makes too many claims upon them, and native selfishness is too strong. But the germ of morality is in every man, as is shown by that sense of inward dissatisfaction which most men feel at some time or other. The feeling is an expression of man's true self, the higher nature which he lost when his desires and his powers ceased to be in equilibrium, the divine element in him which is everlastingly opposed to the selfishness of the spoiled animal nature. Between these two sides of man there is a livelong struggle; one or the other must be in the ascendant, equilibrium is not possible. How are we to ensure the predominance of the higher nature? This is the problem of moral and religious education.

[1] Wiget, *op. cit.*

As in his treatment of intellectual and physical education, Pestalozzi subjects the " moral powers" of man to a psychological analysis. He endeavours, that is to say, to find the elements which lie at the base of moral development, and which are therefore the starting-points of moral training. For these elements he uses the same word, *Anschauung*, as he employs for the sensory observations and practical experiences which are the point of departure for, and the bed rock of, intellectual education ; but in this latter case attention is outwardly directed, we are concerned with external objects (*äussere Anschauung*), whereas in the former he speaks of an inner sense (*innere Anschauung*) by which the feelings which are native and inseparable from man's soul are perceived. The stimulus in both cases comes from experience. Upon the one his knowledge, in so far as it relates to the external world, rests. From the other, that is from the feelings of love, gratitude, trust, and sympathy, which are native and inseparable from his soul, his religion and morality develop.[1]

The process is the same in principle as the process which governs intellectual education. In both cases the materials provided by experience are " by analogy " made to do duty for new and even for imaginary situations. In both cases the actual experience must precede the word. " Just as, in the ' elementary ' training of the intellect, the sensory impression of an object must be in the child's mind before the word which denotes the object may be put into his mouth, so must the feelings which lie at the root of moral ideas in the mind of the child be already there before the words which denote them are known to him." [2]

(Marginal note:) Psychological Foundations of Morality: Law of " Natural " Nearness.

---

[1] Cp. p. 119 f.   [2] Morf, ii. 159.

As already said, it is experience which provides the stimulus which calls into existence the "inner feelings," but all experiences do not excite them in the same degree, and as in relation to intellectual education Pestalozzi enunciates a law of physical nearness which states the ground of variation in the sensory clearness of impressions, so in relation to these "inner feelings" he finds that their intensity varies in accordance with the *law of natural (tierischen) nearness and remoteness.*

The word *tierischen* means of course *animal*, but if we remember what the natural man is like, and that the word "natural" in this connection refers to that state, we shall arrive at Pestalozzi's meaning. We might indeed describe the principle as the *law of nearness and remoteness to the feelings of the natural man.* We are in fact reminded of the fundamental innocence of man's nature, and even in his social state the objects which would have made the strongest appeal to his innocent animal nature are more effective in rousing moral feelings than those which appeal simply to his sense of duty.

A parent, for example, stands to his child in such a relation. The child is "naturally near" to

Parent and Child.

him, and is in consequence a fertile source of those feelings which are fundamental to morality. In effect, therefore, the law amounts to the statement that the sympathetic feelings are the root of morality. At the same time it must be remembered that this only relates to psychological foundations. To do good out of sympathy is not in itself moral, but sympathy, operating as defined by the law of natural nearness, provides the bridge which enables the merely social man to pass over into the moral man.[1]

[1] Cp. *Enquiries* . . . (G., p. 79 f.).

Of course, when moral objects are "physically" as well as "naturally" near, their effectiveness as agents in the development of sympathetic feelings is greatly enhanced. The "physical" distance of a father separated from his child dulls the action of the law of "natural" nearness. "The mere idea of a father's duty is less favourable to the development of morality in him, than the smiles and tears of his child lying in the cradle before his eyes."

Here, then, we have the psychological ground for Pestalozzi's insistence upon family life as the true source of religion and morality. All the objects that surround the child are "physically" as well as "naturally" near to him, and the child's earliest experiences in his relations with his mother are the main sources of "inner feelings," the strength and character of which largely determine his moral and religious future. Pestalozzi never dissociates religion and morality : whilst the one represents man in his attitude towards God, the other in his attitude towards himself and his fellow men, they both have their origin in family life.

In his intercourse with his mother, the germs of love, of trust, and of gratitude are developed in the **Mother the** child. "The development of the human race **source of** begins in a strong passionate desire for the **Morality and** satisfaction of physical wants. The mother's **Religion.** breast satisfies the physical cravings, and generates *love* ; soon after, *fear* is developed, but the mother's protecting arm drives it away and the child *trusts*. Love and trust united produce the first germs of gratitude." He learns to be *patient* and *obedient* ; he discovers that his brothers and sisters have claims upon his mother's attention, that she is not there entirely for him, and that he himself is not in the world just for his own sake. Here are the germs of the *social feelings* and of

sympathy. In his relations with his father and mother
he discovers what *duty* means, not through any verbal
teaching on their part, but through the education of life
itself. The first conditions of moral self-development are
thus satisfied, and at the same time there is produced the
whole essence of that state of mind which is characteristic
of human dependence on God.

The child's dependence upon his mother is the prototype
of such dependence. He is not conscious of the extent to
which he trusts in her, and as he develops physically he
becomes more and more independent. " He becomes conscious of his own personality and secretly begins to feel
that he no longer needs his mother. She reads the growing thought in his eyes, she presses her darling to her heart,
and says in a voice he has not heard before, ' Child, there
is a God whom you need, who will take you in His arms
when I can no longer shelter you.'

" Then an inexpressible something arises in his heart, a
holy feeling, a mysterious sense of things unseen, that calls
for faith and raises him above himself. He rejoices in the
name of God as soon as he hears his mother pronounce it.
The feelings of love, gratitude, and trust, that were developed at her bosom, extend to God and embrace Him as
father and mother. Obedience has now a wider field."
The child does right now for God's sake as he formerly did
for his mother's sake.[1] This, however, cannot come about
unless the mother herself is actuated by other motives than
those which would stir the simple natural man. She herself must be moral; the germ of the divine in her must
have developed and brought about the transition from the
social to the moral stage. Morality cannot issue from man's
nature without God's help, and the mother, divinely actuated, is God's first instrument to that end.

[1] *How Gertrude Teaches her Children*, XIII.

As the child grows the physical relations between him and his mother become less intimate, and with increasing independence he comes more into contact with the outer world. Egoistic feelings and bad examples may now choke the germs of good just stimulated into promising life. " Man's feeling for the right and for duty, for virtue and wisdom, dies out completely when he is surrounded by examples of wickedness, cruelty, forgetfulness of duty, unfaithfulness, selfishness, and tyranny." [1] The transition period is a critical point in the child's life, and it cannot be left to chance to settle his fate. The whole art of education must be applied " to keep the feelings of love, gratitude, trust, and obedience pure in the child." " Now for the first time Nature cannot be trusted ; we must do everything in our power to take the reins out of her *blind* hands and put them into the hands of principles." [2]

There are some admirable passages dealing with this period in the child's life in Pestalozzi's diary (*v.* pp. 37-44). He discusses with great clearness and insight the relations between freedom and obedience. Rousseau, he says, was wrong in separating the period of freedom from that of obedience. The transition must be gradual. It demands the greatest care and forethought on the side of the parents.

But it is in the home pictures of *Leonard and Gertrude* that Pestalozzi has best described the matter and the manner of early moral training—the home in which the mother's coming and going is like that of the sun in its daily traverse of the sky. The sun does its work so silently and unobtrusively that we do not notice it, only when it sets we remember that it will come again to warm the earth and ripen the fruits thereof. So in Gertrude, you notice nothing particular about her ; you think that any other

[1] Seyff., viii. 30, 31. [2] *How Gertrude Teaches her Children*, XIII.

woman could do all she does just as well. But "you need
not say more than that to make her great in my eyes," said
Glüphi. "The Sublime is so simple that children and
babes believe they could accomplish still more." [1]

In respect of family life the poor have the advantage of
the rich; their homes offer them so many more opportunities for mutual helpfulness, self-sacrifice, and loving
sympathy. No school can take the place of an ideally constituted family, where the intellectual, moral, and physical
relations are the most natural and therefore the most intimate and the most educative.

In the exigences of modern life schools are essential—
establishments, that is to say, which are designed to carry on the process of education from
the point at which the family can no longer
undertake it. The transition from the family to the school
should not be violent. The school is to aim at continuing
the family life, and it *may measure its success by its nearness
to or remoteness from the family ideal*. This was his guiding
principle both at Stanz and Yverdun. "School instruction which is not founded on the family model (*i.e.* is not
conducted in a social atmosphere of mutual helpfulness and
love) is like an artificial blight upon the people." [2] The
environment of the home is continuous. The child's experiences are repeated, not as so many mechanical contrivances—such, for example, as those which Rousseau

School and
Home.

[1] Cp. Tolstoi's "A healthy child when he comes into the world
realises completely the absolute harmony with the true, the beautiful, and the good which we carry in us . . . he is much nearer
than I am, or any grown man, to the true, beautiful, and good to
which I undertake to raise him. The consciousness of this ideal
lives in him much more intensely than in me, and all that he requires
of me is the material with which to perfect himself harmoniously in
all directions."—Quoted by Crosby in *Tolstoi as Schoolmaster*, p. 30.

[2] Cp. Stanz Letter, p. 72.

suggests for the "natural" education of Emile—but as the outcome of living intercourse. "The Elementary Method," he says in his Address of 1818, "is in its essentia form, nothing else than a return to the simplicity of home education."

The relation between parents and children is the model towards which the teacher should work in dealing with his boys. "My first efforts at Stanz were to make these seventy children feel like brothers and sisters of a large family, and to make them affectionate and considerate one towards another." Such a relationship makes both example and teaching more telling, and only as the school atmosphere approximates to that of the living room can corporal punishment be effective. "Parental punishment rarely makes a bad impression on the child. Far otherwise is the case with the punishments of school teachers who do not live night and day with their children in the purity of family relationship."[1]

Punishments.

"Blows are in general an unworthy instrument of education. . . . I am profoundly opposed to corporal punishment inflicted by a stranger teacher upon a stranger child; but not to such punishment at the hands of parents. There are cases in which corporal punishment is the best, but only those teachers who feel towards their pupils as a father towards his children should inflict it." He reserved that right to himself in Yverdun, but only in such cases as he felt he enjoyed the unconditional confidence of the parents. But whole years passed by without any punishment of the kind being necessary.

Notably at Stanz[2] he tried to broaden the children's sympathies and bring love and kindness into such unceasing contact with their daily activities that these sentiments

[1] Cp. Stanz Letter, p. 77. [2] Vide Stanz Letter, Ch. IV.

might be engrafted in their hearts; he made the daily
events of the house serviceable for the awakening of these
feelings, and utilised for the same purpose things that
happened outside whenever they touched the household.
He taught them " neither morality nor religion," and gave
them few explanations.   The important thing was to
establish firmly that inner sense of right and wrong
which rests upon the feelings of love, confidence, and
sympathy; these come from actions, not from words:
they are insensibly acquired, breathed in as it were
from the atmosphere created by the thousand tender
and considerate acts which are hourly observable in the
intimacy of family life.

At Yverdun as at Stanz, although the circumstances
were poles asunder, Pestalozzi strove to make
Supervision environment, not formal religious instruction,
at
Yverdun.   the chief factor in the moral education of his
pupils.

In the *Report to Parents* of 1808 he says : " Our educa-
cational machinery has only a value in so far as it approaches
in character to that of a well ordered house in all its details.
Our teachers wake the children; they are present when
they get up and when they dress; they observe their bodily
condition and the state of their clothes; they see to their
personal cleanliness; they place them in rows twice a day
and examine their apparel; they accompany them to morning and evening prayers, take their meals with them, go
with them into the playground, join in their games, take
walks with them; in short they never leave them out of
school hours except when they are in bed and asleep.   All
the unmarried teachers live in the house and sleep in the
dormitories."   We may not now approve of such unceasing
supervision, but we must keep in mind the spirit of it all.
Home life was the model, and everything which helped to

secure intimate personal intercourse between pupils and teachers was good in Pestalozzi's eyes.

To lighten the burden upon the younger teachers, they were divided into three sets, so that "house duties" only fell upon them every third day. Over them were the older members of the staff, each of whom had from twelve to sixteen children under his immediate care. He was their school-father and was, as such, held responsible for them. Once a week each of these groups was taken by its guardian to Pestalozzi himself, who in earnest and loving conversation with them endeavoured especially to touch their innermost natures, and to lead them to view their relations one to another in the spirit of loving consideration. At morning and evening prayers he talked to the whole school as a father to his family.[1]

In large establishments, with many teachers there is great danger of lack of unity of purpose. Boys may be differently viewed and differently treated by various masters, each of whom has only partial knowledge. This stumbling-block must be got out of the way. At Yverdun weekly staff meetings were held, in which the teachers discussed every pupil, his progress, his character, his inclinations and weaknesses, and the measures that should be taken to suit the particular case. The possibility of one-sided, unconfirmed, and inaccurate opinions was in that way excluded.[2]

Pestalozzi regarded the study of the individuality of children as one of the most important duties of the teacher. One may lay down general principles, but in the concrete one has not to deal with a generalised being. The individual is limited and one-sided in his natural inclinations.

---

[1] *Vide* p. 325 f. Cp. also Gertrude's talks with her children in *Leonard and Gertrude* (G., p. 33).

[2] *Vide* p. 326.

He is a problem in himself, and the teacher's first object
should be to find what forces in him are likely to be a help,
and what forces to be a hindrance, to moral development.
This is the meaning of his Yverdun practice, and the whole
tenor of the *Report to Parents* shows the importance he
attached to this principle alike in the intellectual and the
moral sphere.[1]

Although there is no talk of an A B C of the moral
feelings (*innere Anschauungen*), yet one finds
in the thirteenth letter of *How Gertrude Teaches
her Children* the idea of a " feeling-series "
advancing by " elementary " steps. He wonders
why mankind does not set about the task of opening out
a perfect gradation of means for developing the intellect
and the feelings.   On his own lines he endeavoured to
solve the problem for the intellect, but in the matter of the
feelings we only have indirect evidence of the direction of
Pestalozzi's thoughts.

A B C of
Moral
Feelings.

Thus one of his students, Grüner, wrote : " I learned
from several talks with Pestalozzi that in his evening and
morning conversations with the small groups of boys, he
looked to the following points : what feelings awake first
in the child's heart, and may therefore be looked on as the
simplest and most natural ; which feelings come from the
lowest depths and influence them most strongly ; how
the feelings which awake early and those which are easily
made permanent, connect themselves with others which
awake later and are more difficult to fix and make perfect ;
and how, in accordance with these observations, moral
feelings or experiences might be reduced to a natural progressive order through reciprocity in the child's life."[2]

In any case, however, the environment cannot be ordered

---

[1] Cp. Chapter V., p. 111.   [2] Quoted by Wiget, *op. cit.*

so perfectly as to offer a graded series of stimuli corresponding to a gradation of feelings such as was in Pestalozzi's mind. But in this respect there is no difference between the merely sensory environment and what may perhaps be called the "moral" environment. As in the former case, so in the latter, it rests largely with the educator to decide to which of the multitude of impressions the child's attention shall be directed. Clearly there is room here for gradation, and the teacher's art consists in determining whether the "moral" circumstances of the moment are or are not fitted, by the simplicity or the complexity of the motive underlying them, to be brought more prominently into the child's consciousness at his particular stage of development. Mere chance, mere "subjective selection," "blind Nature's way" cannot be left supreme in moral, any more than in physical or intellectual, education.

We may now examine in detail how the psychological elements which Pestalozzi held to be the bases of morality are to be worked out. The family and the school constitute the environment which calls the feelings into life, but morality means something more than feelings. In the thirteenth letter of *How Gertrude Teaches her Children* we are told that through the gradual development of the child's numerous feelings he may ultimately pass to the *recognition and veneration of the moral law*.

Moral
Progress :
Purity of
Feeling and
Discipline
of Will.

As he tells us in the Prospectus, the idea of law comes when the boy is able to distinguish it from the person in whom it is represented, when he accepts it as the guide of his higher nature.[1] It is a general notion of a highly abstract character, and the school may only be able to

---

[1] *Vide* pp. 315, 316.

carry its pupils one step towards it. In any case, the method is the same as that followed in the development of the general notion on the purely intellectual side. Here, however, it is feelings—(*innere Anschauungen*)—which are preliminary. "The first instruction of the child should appeal to the heart, and not to the head." [1] "It remains for a long time the business of the heart, it is for a long time the business of the woman before it begins to be the business of the man." [2]

In the *Anschauung* stage the essential thing is to see that the *right* feeling is roused. Pestalozzi's practice at Stanz is suggestive of the care he took at this point. In conversation with his boys he led them to express their feelings with freedom and confidence. These confidences offered opportunity for kindly criticism, for correction, or for approval. "Activity and purity of feeling must come first in elementary moral education."

But if feelings, however pure and refined they may be, do not find an issue in action they are useless **Training of the Will.** as moral agencies. Morality involves will; and will involves action with definite purpose and confidence in one's power to carry it through. The sense of power can only be won in action. When Pestalozzi felt sure that the children felt rightly upon the subject of his talk with them, he followed it up by exercises to teach them self-control and to bring the good in them to practical expression. [3] In a sense, therefore, moral education is a special sort of practical education, and in this way Wiget accounts for the fact that Pestalozzi treats of Intellectual and Practical Education before Moral Education in *How Gertrude Teaches her Children*. "The

---

[1] *How Gertrude Teaches her Children*, XIII. 23.
[2] *Ibid.*, XIII. 24. [3] *Vide* Stanz Letter, Ch. IV., p. 76.

discipline provided by intellectual and practical training ensures a willing servant in mind and body," ready for the guidance of law when the conception of law is reached. This preparatory discipline of mind and body is, for Pestalozzi, the second step in moral education. It is, of course to be found in the concrete experiences of school and home.

The immediate aims of such a discipline will be: (1) to increase the power of withstanding the unpleasant, *e.g.* to accustom a child to submit with good grace to the limitations of actual life, to exercise him in the manful acceptance of deserved punishment, and in cheerful submission to legitimate authority; (2) to increase the energy of the active will. The life of the child in the home and in the school offers two chief means of exercise; these are (*a*) manual work and physical exercises, (*b*) instruction.

With regard to (*a*), what has been said in the previous chapter indicates Pestalozzi's preference. The interest and the immediate usefulness of manual and particularly of household work appeal to children. It is an admirable agent for the cultivation of continuous attention. "Work in general is the surest of all exercises for the attention, because it is impossible to do it well without attending continuously to it." [1] With regard to the more characteristic exercises of school life—those connected with (*b*)—Pestalozzi has a deep sense of their value as effective instruments for the preliminary discipline of the will.

Again, however, it is a question of stimulus only. "The teacher must transplant himself completely to the child's point of view—step with him from one discovery to another. This is, I admit, much harder than to follow a good handbook, introducing the young people to its contents by instruction, dictation and demonstration." But energy of

----

[1] *Schweizerblatt*, M., iii., p. 43.

will only grows by its own activity; keen observations, instructive comparisons and abstractions, free thought-activity in fact, leading to independent extension of knowledge, is what is wanted. Only when instruction induces this sort of spirit in the child is it morally effective. The same point is touched on in the seventh letter of *How Gertrude Teaches her Children*; he writes: "That which I gain through the spontaneous exercise of my will in endeavouring to extend my knowledge, my insight, and my practical capacities, has a special value in relation to my moral development.

"But if the energies are directed to any end other than that of doing the work itself in the best possible way, the moral value of the effort is greatly diminished, for it is motive which determines the relation of work to moral development." For this reason Pestalozzi will have nothing to do with any external motive such as love of praise or fear of shame. A sense of duty he will admit. The only reward for work done is to come from the ennobling feeling that it has been well done.

In a remarkable interview with Dr. Bell in 1816 at Yverdun, Pestalozzi, speaking of stimulating the child to effort, said that " he never appealed to all-too-easily excited motives like that of love of praise. The children were expected to respond to purer ones, such, for example, as love of duty, of parents, of teachers, and above all love for the subject itself, to which the child must be won by such a treatment of the subject as corresponded to his intellectual standpoint."[1]

---

[1] Bell was too much in love with his own ideas to see anything in Pestalozzi's, and left Yverdun confidently assuring his companion that in twelve years nobody would hear a word of Pestalozzian method, and by that time his own ideas (*i.e.* his monitorial system) would have spread over the whole earth ! (Morf, vol. iv., 330.)

Motives like fear or inordinate ambition may stimulate to exertion, intellectual or physical, but they cannot warm the heart. There is not in them that life which makes the heart of youth burn with the delight of knowledge—with the honest consciousness of talent—with the honourable wish for distinction—with the kindly glow of genuine feeling. Such motives are inadequate in their source, and inefficient in their application, for they are nothing to the heart, and " out of the heart come the issues of life." [1]

"Love for the subject itself," "spontaneous effort to increase knowledge," which the teacher is to

Interest and Whole-heartedness. inspire, we are accustomed to call *interest*—*intellectual interest*, that is to say, as opposed to interest which is only excited by novelty. Pestalozzi attached the greatest importance to it, on grounds closely related to moral development.

"The interest in study is the first thing which a teacher should endeavour to excite and keep alive. There are scarcely any circumstances, in which a want of application in children does not proceed from a want of interest; and there are perhaps none, under which a want of interest does not originate in the mode of treatment adopted by a teacher. I would go as far as to lay it down for a rule, that whenever children are inattentive, and apparently take no interest in a lesson, the teacher should always first look to himself for the reason." Too often " children are punished when the master is to blame." "There is a remarkable reciprocal action between the interest which the teacher takes and that which he communicates to his pupils. If he is not present with his whole mind in the subject; if he does not care whether it is understood or not, whether his manner is liked or not, he will never fail

[1] *Letters to Greaves*, 1827 (G., p. 253 f.).

of alienating the affections of his pupils, and of rendering them indifferent to what he says. But real interest taken in the task of instruction—kind words and kinder feelings —the very expression of the features and the glance of the eye—are never lost upon children."

As we have seen, he is concerned to give to the will the highest possible degree of energy, and instruction properly conceived is a powerful instrument in the teacher's hands. It should stimulate cheerful response and lay the founda- tion of a *habit of wholeheartedness* before which difficulties are bravely met and successfully surmounted.

In providing work for his children, the teacher must make them feel that they need to use their whole powers. " When I recommend a mother to avoid wearying her child by her instructions, I do not wish to encourage the notion that instruction should always take the character of amusement, or even of play. I am convinced that such a notion, where it is entertained and acted upon by a teacher, will ever preclude solidity of knowledge, and from a want of sufficient exertions on the part of the pupils will lead to that very result which I wish to avoid by my principle of a constant employment of the thinking powers. A child must, very early in life, be taught a lesson which frequently comes too late, and is then a most painful one—that exertion is indispensable for the attainment of knowledge. A child should not be taught to look upon exertion as an avoidable evil." [1]

So far as mere experience is concerned, nothing more can be done for the child in the direction of moral education. Experience rightly managed is the source of purity of feeling, and experience again affords a field for action in response to feeling.

School-boy Morals.

[1] *Letters to Greaves* (G., p. 252).

By its means, in the ways indicated, home and school should combine to establish firmly in the child what may be called the elements of a strong moral sense. Unselfish love and sympathy for others, warmhearted confidence in his fellows, and a humble trust in God, combined with intellectual and physical keenness, should be the aim of his training to this point. "The boy should have an inner feeling for what ought to be, and he should be conscious of serviceable power." When he has attained to the moral frame of mind, when he has been trained in the habit of right action, it remains to produce in him the idea of moral purpose, through reflection upon the concrete circumstances in the midst of which he lives.

But the difficulty is much greater than in the corresponding stage of intellectual training. Feelings are elusive, and words are dangerous, for they come very often when the feeling is not there, and in any case verbal expression weakens them. A treatment which would satisfy a logician is therefore absolutely impossible at the school age. Pestalozzi finds *silence* the essential factor.

Writing of his experiences at Burgdorf and München-büchsee in the *Views and Experiences* he says : " What we do in respect of moral education cannot of course be so striking (to the observer) as that which we have accomplished in respect of the intellect. The true moral ' elementary ' education, on account of its nature, leads first to feeling, then to silence, and finally to action. Every distracting and superfluous word tends to falsify the inner feeling, or to weaken its vitalising effect."[1] On the same grounds he objects to the children memorising catechisms of religion. He regarded true religion as a matter of deep feeling, and he believed that in

[1] *Vide* M., vol. iii., p. 319.

reducing religion to set forms of words, the effect was rather to blunt feeling than to deepen it. "It is enough if, out of the child's home and school life, certain principles, certain views hardly yet formulated, have attained to predominance."

In his actions, however, the child has a more concrete material to work upon. What he has done and is doing every day forms, as it were, a generalised picture of himself in action, that is to say, of the general tendencies of his will. In this general picture he recognises himself, and if he were asked to describe it, it would take the form of a person who in such-and-such circumstances always acts in such-and-such a way, of a person whose conduct has come to be guided by certain rules. In other words, maxims of conduct have been developed. This is what Pestalozzi means, in the twelfth letter of *How Gertrude Teaches her Children*, when he speaks of our activities as being "the sense-foundation of our virtue," and of a general kind of education, suitable to the life-duties of the human race, which "goes from complete efficiency in action to the *recognition of rules*."

From the school point of view this is the end of the matter. School training in morals must not pass beyond "the limitations of actual life, where the transition from feeling to action is easy." Abstract ethical systems must be left to maturer minds.

We may understand now what Pestalozzi means by regarding moral education as the key to his whole system. In a later chapter we shall see that intellectual and practical education cannot be considered separately. The one involves the other from bottom to top. So, in the course of moral education, we find that he sees in intellectual and practical training the chief means of discipline for the will, and in the acquisition of knowledge the source of its enlightenment. " My morality is nothing else than the way in which I apply my pure will to do right, to the measure of my knowledge and to the concrete circumstances of my life."[1] Purity of will rests upon purity of feeling, which comes from living in an atmosphere of love and faith, like that tenderly pictured by Pestalozzi in the household of Gertrude, and conspicuously created by him in his own institutions. Effectiveness involves insight and discipline, which come from reflection and action.

[1] *Enquiries concerning the Course of Nature*, etc. (G., p. 77).

CHAPTER XIV.

THE SCIENCE OF EDUCATION AND THE TRAINING OF TEACHERS.

What Pestalozzi Means by a Science of Education. Pestalozzi's investigations, as described in *How Gertrude Teaches her Children*, are clearly those of a man who was inspired by the true scientific spirit, that is to say, by the spirit of men who place fact above theory, and never allow their anxiety to establish a hypothesis to affect their judgment in regard to the significance of everything which comes under their observation. The spirit of research could hardly have been better expressed than in the opening paragraph of the sixth letter : " I lived at the highest nerve-tension at every point within the sphere in which I was working. I knew what I was looking for. I took no thought for the morrow, and at each moment I was keenly conscious of just what was essential for the object I was pursuing, but if my imagination carried me to-day a hundred steps beyond the firm ground which I had found, the next day I retraced those hundred steps. This happened thousands of times. Thousands and thousands of times I believed I was approaching my goal, and suddenly found that what I had imagined to be my end was only a new difficulty to be surmounted."

But Pestalozzi saw that science means more than the mere accumulation of facts. He aimed at determining their causal connections, at the formulation of the facts into

a logical system resting ultimately upon general principles
which would give unity to the whole. He realised that
neither an aggregation of facts nor an aggregation of rules
constitutes a science. There must be a theory which
explains the facts and gives coherence to the rules.

At Stanz "the whole scheme of a general method of instruction revealed itself to him." At Burgdorf, as he carried
his investigations into the teaching of reading, arithmetic,
writing and drawing further and further back, he felt that
isolated aids to this and that subject of instruction were
not enough; they only made him realise that " he did not
yet know the true scope and inner depth of his subject."
He was seeking a common psychological origin for all those
means of instruction, because he was convinced "that only
through this could he discover the form in which the
education of mankind is determined, through the very laws
of Nature herself." The same idea is expressed in the
Report to Parents, in which he describes himself as trying to drag education as far as possible out of the confusion of its empirical contradictions and raise it to a
science resting on indisputable principles.[1]

He objected strongly to the practice of selecting
particular practical points, technical " tips," from his
doctrines. " I do not doubt," he says in a letter to
Tobler in 1802, " that the tendency to recognise in my
doctrines certain ideas as helpful practical contributions
to the art of teaching will be a danger to the doctrines as
a whole, but we must strive unconditionally for the
recognition of them in their entirety as an indivisible
whole. Only in that way can we maintain their spirit and
prevent, as it were, my building from being set on fire
with torches borrowed from myself."[2]

[1] Seyffarth, xvii. 152.   [2] Morf, ii. 67.

His belief in the ultimate unity of the whole problem is still more directly expressed in the New Year's Address of 1818. There he thanks God that his long experience in educating the children of the people has led him to the conviction that " Education in all its parts must necessarily be raised to the dignity of a science which must find its foundations in the deepest knowledge of human nature." He adds, "I am myself, of course, far from being acquainted with this science. The idea of it is scarcely yet complete in my own mind, yet my mind accepts it as an absolute truth, and the circumstances of the time have made it a necessity for the world." As he says elsewhere, " such a science is the most important of all branches of nature knowledge, the centre of all the investigations of nature which humanity as such is concerned in." [1]

When Pestalozzi speaks of a " Science of Education," he means a body of principles arrived at by the investigation of human nature viewed as a developing organism, and serving to give authoritative guidance to the practical teacher. The unity of the investigation is determined by its aim, and the possibility of arriving at useful results rests upon the assumption common to all the sciences that the course of Nature is uniform. Over and over again, in *How Gertrude Teaches her Children*, it is assumed that psychical process is as subject to law as physical process. The various expressions, "psychological necessity," "physical necessity," " mechanical law," " physico-mechanical law," " a mechanism of human nature," " the mechanical form of all instruction," all have reference, as Wiget points out, " to the natural necessity of intellectual happenings," to the law of cause and effect as applicable to mental process.

---

[1] *A Word concerning the Present Condition*, etc., 1820 (S., vol. xii.).

But although the teacher cannot override natural laws, he may make them serve his purpose. That is just the difference between his educative activities and those which Nature herself might exert. Nature is "blind," says Pestalozzi,—that is to say, the operations of nature are not purposeful; the teacher, on the other hand, has a definite aim, and deliberately makes use of natural forces in order to attain it. He orders his means to his end, and since the means are in the main the laws that govern mental process, his science is largely built upon psychology. At the same time, Pestalozzi did not distinguish very sharply the physical from the psychical, as the "principles of uninterrupted continuity of progress in scarcely perceptible steps" and the "law of physical nearness" show.

The Relation of the Teacher to the Science.

We have discussed already (in Chapter IV.) what Pestalozzi regarded as the final aim of education—the harmonious unfolding of the human powers, the maturity of which he describes in his picture of the man who is all that his neighbours think a man ought to be, a description which, while it lacks philosophical form, really includes all that we are accustomed to include under the word "character." The aim of education is, then, to establish character.

To attain this end the teacher has to make such use of the means provided by Nature as seems to him best, but as the laws governing the development of human nature are fixed, the question may be asked as to whether there can be more than one right way of using them. Pestalozzi says, in *How Gertrude Teaches her Children*, "that he has come to the conclusion that while there are many bad methods, there is only one good one." But he is here really thinking of the principles underlying method of the psychological foundations which are fixed and unchangeable. He is clearer in the *Swansong* : " We must understand this point carefully—a method of education and instruction which will satisfy completely the principles of the elementary method is inconceivable. However clearly these principles are laid down, however perfectly we simplify the means to be employed, every teacher will adapt both principles and means to his purpose differently in accordance with his own individuality."

One man is distinguished by the warmth of his sympathies, another is of the colder intellectual type, and a third tends to view all things from the point of view of their practical application. Inevitably the " frame of his mind " will affect the teacher's procedure.

Equally varying is the individuality of the children, and both in theory and practice Pestalozzi emphasised the importance of doing nothing to crush what is the child's source of strength. The idiosyncrasies of individuals are amongst the greatest blessings of human nature, and should be respected in the highest degree.[1]

" No institution can, therefore, furnish models of all recognisable methods suitable for all conditions of children, no matter how richly it may be endowed." Even the same teacher may often find it necessary to let principle give way partly to the exigences of circumstance. Time-tables, curricula, unintelligent demands of parents are all facts which have to be taken into account, but so long as he is *on the whole* satisfied that his practice is based on sound scientific principles (*i.e.* is according to the " laws of human nature ") he need not be troubled by external deviations in the form, always provided that these deviations are

---

[1] See also p. 346 f. for an account of this principle in application, and compare his doctrines relating to social position and education, p. 224.

consciously made.   He might otherwise lose sight entirely
of his principles.[1]

    We may now notice more in detail how Pestalozzi
endeavoured to build up this science.   He was
Method of quite conscious of the incompleteness of his
Building-up work, and, indeed, of his incompetence to com-
the Science :
Experiment. plete it.   " Whilst I have done very little in
my life to reach ideas that can be defined with
philosophic certainty, yet in my own way I have found a
few means to my end.   These I should never have found
by such philosophical endeavours to reach clear ideas of
my subjects as I was myself capable of making."   His
view that education might and ought to be raised to
the dignity of a science did not come from any *a priori*
principles as to the nature of mind and the universe.
Although Niederer frequently attributed to his master
current philosophical ideas, Herbart's view is truer, that it
was quite contrary to Pestalozzi's intentions to introduce
into his teachings the ideas of critical or idealistic philosophers.[2]

  [1] *Lenzburg Address*, pars. 223-5 (M., iii., p. 357).

  [2] Yet Pestalozzi is mistaken when he attributes such results as he
had reached entirely to experience.   Although he belongs to no
particular school of philosophy, he assumes all through his investigations that there is a special power of the soul at the basis of every
sort of intellectual activity.   He was trained in the faculty-psycho-
logy of Wolff which held sway until Beneke and Herbart destroyed
it.   Again, in the sixth letter of *How Gertrude Teaches her Children*,
he speaks of the possibility of discovering the *form* in which the
cultivation of mankind is determined by the laws of Nature itself.
"It is evident that this form is found in the general organisation
of the mind itself, by means of which our intelligence binds the
impressions received through the senses into a system."   We have
here the presumption of an *a priori* activity of the mind in
accordance with the nature of which the manifold of experience is
synthesised, a doctrine which one identifies with Kant, whose

Pestalozzi deliberately disavows an *a priori* method; in spite of certain tacit assumptions, one may fairly regard his position as that of the investigator in natural science, who looks upon the facts of experience as the final source of knowledge, and the ultimate test of theoretical validity. "The way of my life is the way of experiments." He took a great risk at Burgdorf in order to have free play for his experiments, and he never let himself be troubled by complaints and criticisms which charged him with sacrificing the welfare of the children to his investigation. His experiments were usually unsystematic, but he never ceased to make them, even after his staff at Yverdun begged him to adhere to arrangements, and not, by "his everlasting experiments, to throw all the classes in confusion, thereby utterly destroying the possibility of connected instruction." [1]

He was quite frank with the public in the matter. In an open letter relating to the difficulties at München-buchsee he writes, "To run a successful boarding-school was not my reason for beginning my independent work at Burgdorf. I have always wished to be in a position to examine, by means of continuous and sufficient experiences, certain ideas relating to the education of mankind. . . . Although my energies were divided between my new discoveries and the fulfilment of my duties in respect of the children entrusted to me, . . . my method proved its influence upon man's inner nature. At the same time, under the circumstances we could not satisfy completely all the general and individual requirements of the children. We did all we could in really essential matters, and here

categorical imperative stands side by side with Fichte's transcendental Ego, vaguely and implicitly, in the ethical doctrines which Pestalozzi endeavoured to expound in his *Enquiries.*

[1] 1813. Morf, iv. 416.

and there were decidedly successful." He goes on to suggest that the division in their work could not, however, continue, and that the study of method would have had to be separated from the conduct of the boarding-school they had founded, that " they were just ready for the change in organisation when the necessity of leaving Burgdorf was forced upon them, and the burden of starting a new institution was placed upon his shoulders." The suggestion that experiment was to be abandoned must have been a momentary concession to criticism at a time of serious anxiety. The teachers' memorial already referred to is proof of his actual practice at a later date.

But although he saw that some positive results had been reached by his own experimental work, he was aware that more remained to be done than one institution under one direction could hope to accomplish. " We require on the one side the freest and widest room for experiments in schools organised for the purpose which would fill up the existing gaps in educational knowledge by the results of their work; and on the other hand, we require that these results should be tested by daily experience." " For a work of this embracing character one institution could not suffice. We have, for example, the needs of the children of better-class artisans, which, in addition to the more general aspects of the problem of education, call for their particular application to the scientific side of culture; and equally essential is the working out of a natural education suited to the home life and calling of the unskilled labourers, and finally, there are the claims of the children of the poor and unfortunate who are not in a position to fulfil their duties as parents." [1]

Experimental Schools.

[1] *Views and Experiences*, 1805 (M., iii. 326).

Whilst calling for experimental schools, Pestalozzi depre-
cated the hasty adoption of results on a large scale. The
spirit of his whole work might easily be lost in the hands of
a man who, having acquired the mechanism of Pestalozzianism, is set over a large province to reorganise the
schools. In this sense he wrote to Nicolovius, who had
called Zeller, a student of Pestalozzi's method, to preside
over the educational activities of one of the provinces of
Prussia. "The business is not yet ripe enough to be made
applicable to a whole state. . . . I have the greatest respect
for Zeller: he is keen about national education, and he
has a wonderful acquaintance with the mechanism of our
teaching of reading, writing, singing, and to some extent
of language also. . . . But he has not gone beyond a
formalism in which he is fixed and satisfied. . . . The
greater the results he effects in six months, the more
important it is that you should know exactly the point
beyond which he cannot go. . . . Great as he is, he
falls short of the very highest, both in his head and
heart." [1]

Even Froebel has not suffered more than Pestalozzi in
reputation and in effectiveness from the ten-
Pestalozzi's Imitators. dency to mere imitation. History is eloquent
of the fact that there have been few good edu-
cational ideas which teachers themselves have not spoiled.
Earnest men and women, impatient to obtain practical

---

[1] Results proved how completely Pestalozzi's doubts were justified
in this case. There is an interesting account of Zeller's work at the
"Orphanotrophy" of Königsberg in No. XX. of the *Quarterly
Journal of Education* (U.S.A.). It is reprinted in the first of two
volumes entitled *The Schoolmaster*, published by Knight in 1836.
The writer says of Zeller "his efforts not being directed by sufficient
knowledge of human nature, his zeal and activity were rather
detrimental to the cause which he had undertaken."

skill, take hold of a mechanism which is not meant to be universal, which is in its very concreteness limited to the circumstances of a moment, a first approximation, perhaps, in an endeavour to give a principle practical shape. They mistake the mechanism for the truth that lies behind it, become expert in its use, and carry it away to be applied with absolute faithfulness of detail, but without " the spirit that giveth life."

To some extent Pestalozzi and his assistants were to blame for this in their case, and the less gifted visitors were either disappointed because they could not see through the mechanism of the Pestalozzian formulae, or they saw in them the key to the practical success of the Yverdun Institution and enthusiastically practised "the method" until they could be pronounced expert. Although the master himself saw the danger, as the letter quoted above shows, his example " in never reading a book for forty years" was calculated to make inferior men working with him attach too much importance to their own particular proceedings, and, therefore, to be more concerned to train the visitors in their characteristic dexterities (*e.g.* in the use of the Alphabets of Observation and of Number Relation) than to inspire them with Pestalozzi's fundamental ideas and fact-regarding temperament.

A conspicuous and not solitary example of failure was doubtless often present to Pestalozzi's mind. Certain Danish students had founded a school in their native country, which in six months accomplished wonderful results in the teaching of the three elementary subjects, but another year saw the end. The teachers were unable to move outside " the elementary books," and the children proved utterly helpless in all matters not covered by them. The public lost interest in the school, and the critics condemned Pestalozzi and his mechanical methods, which were, of course, no substitute for soundness of principle and insight.[1]

It was, in Pestalozzi's view, the business of the experimental school to establish principles, to investigate the nature of education in its absolute purity, under circumstances which free the school from the prejudices and private requirements of individuals. By its side should stand the "testing" school (*Probeschule*), and in connection with both should be a Training College in which men might learn, not the mechanism of a method, but the spirit of research. Men who are going to teach cannot be treated like mechanics who are apprenticed to a trade. Each one will have in his professional career a special set of problems to solve, in its details different from that of any other teacher. The best training, therefore, will be given by associating the students with experimental enquiry, with the actual working out of principles and methods, in the course of which they will arrive at the point of view which will enable them to attack successfully the special problems to which in the future each may be assigned. By such a training he may acquire less technique, but he will have gained insight.

(Margin note: The Aim of the Experimental School.)

Ideas of this kind give the tone to all that Pestalozzi wrote in the last years at Yverdun, and, with Pestalozzi, to have an idea meant to strive for its realisation. He felt the need keenly. Hence his appeal for funds in the Address of 1818, and his defence of Yverdun in 1820. In the latter document he writes :—

"It is obvious that there is probably no calling which requires trained, psychological tact, and the many-sided

[1] Similar failures in Würtemberg led to a royal edict banishing Pestalozzianism in every shape and form from the schools. (Schmid, vol. iv., p. 600.)

insight which comes from repeated experiments and varied practice so much as that of the teacher. The material upon which he is engaged and which he must be in a position to handle effectively is the masterpiece of creation— it is Man himself. He must be able to watch over his charge as a good gardener watches over the most delicate plant from the moment of its first germination to the time of its fruit-bearing maturity. He must know all the child's possibilities exactly, and guide his development effectively in all its directions and in all its intricate relations. There is no profession on earth which pre-supposes a deeper knowledge of human nature and greater skill and adroitness in its management." Man takes the utmost possible pains to understand his dogs and his horses, but there is no institution in which the lofty calling of the schoolmaster can be completely and satis-factorily learned; not merely is there nowhere a professor-ship of the science of education, but there is nowhere an institution exclusively devoted to the training of teachers in the exercise of their profession in the spirit of the best type of family life.

"The experimental school is, for Pestalozzi, the fructify-ing centre of pedagogical experience"; it is at once the source and the testing-place of theory, the centre from which a higher idea of the aims of education and the function of the teacher may radiate, the means whereby the most fruitful pedagogical ideas may be spread over the widest area.

As Wiget points out, the idea of "experimental schools" was in Pestalozzi's mind some years before he wrote his *Views and Experiences*. Both Fischer and Tobler remarked upon it in the Burgdorf days, and Niederer's defence of Yverdun, after the report of the Commission of Enquiry of 1810, is based upon this idea. Kant, in his *Lectures upon Pedagogy* (published in 1803), has also insisted upon the necessity of institutions of the kind. " Men should first set up experimental schools and then normal schools."

People imagine, he adds, " that experiments in education are unnecessary, and that we can judge from our reason whether anything is good or not. This is a great mistake, and experience teaches us that the results of an experiment are often entirely different from what we expected. And since we must be guided by experiments, no one generation can set forth a complete scheme of education," applicable, that is to say, to all future times. Kant had in his mind the "model" schools which the Jesuit Felbiger had set up under Maria Theresa in Austria.[1] The idea of a fixed method, which still survives in our phrase " Normal Schools " and " Normal Colleges," and which these Austrian " normal" schools carried to excess, was as un-Pestalozzian as it was repugnant to the judgment of Kant. Basedow's idea, as carried out in Dessau, was better, in spite of its many mistakes.

In addition to the results derived from his own experiments, he sought to widen the basis of his facts by inviting old students to send him the results of their own observations and enquiries. Thus he writes to Ström in Copenhagen : "All our teachers meet several times a week and compare the notes each has made in the course of his particular work ; the experience of most of them is thereby ripened and much useful material for our journal[2] comes from their discussions. We are, however, collecting notes from outside, and we beg that you will lend us a helping hand, for you live in a circle which might furnish us with important material for publication. Send us, therefore,

Accumulation of Materials from Wider Sources.

---

[1] *Vide* p. 13.   [2] *I.e.* the *Wochenschrift*.

as much as you can; in particular historical and psychological notes relating to your work. It is very important that we should be able to give the reading public information about the progress of our work from all possible sides."

But important as the accumulation of facts is, a science must endeavour to formulate its facts into generalisations which shall throw light upon their connections, and contribute to their explanation. Pestalozzi knew the truth of this. "I naturally at every moment struck upon facts which seemed to throw light upon the existence of physico-mechanical laws in accordance with which our minds pick up and retain outer impressions." His experimental work gave rise to a "feeling for psychological rules," which he was anxious to convert into knowledge. But he never really reached this third step. He collected materials, and *felt* the existence of law, but he was not equal to the task of its formulation. His generalisations, such for example as his "law of physical nearness" and the abstract reasoning by which he attempted to establish his three elementary means, were not happy. As Niederer put it in his estimate of Pestalozzi: "His feelings gave rise to an inner conviction of the existence of law, but he succumbed in the struggle to derive and express it exactly."

His services in a certain sense may not have been more than to have confirmed the Philanthropinist idea of a Science of Education, but his method of confirmation was important enough to establish his claims as the founder. His adherence to the facts of experience may not have been absolute, but in spirit at least that was his method. He set himself consciously against a speculative method, which lost sight of the concrete child, and emphasised the necessity of an empirical foundation if there was to be any prospect of a " Science of Education." He left the problem unsolved, but at least he pointed to one essential factor in its solution.

To his credit it should also be added that he never dreamed of attaining finality in his or any other time. In 1800, when he drew up the first statement of his method, he asked those for whom it was written to accept it as a provisional contribution only—the mite he would wish to give in a great cause. "I beg you carefully to distinguish those ideas upon which doubt may rest from those about which there can be no doubt. I would have my final results rest upon irrefragable proofs, or to be deduced from absolutely established premises." In a like spirit he wrote the opening words of the *Swansong*. "Examine everything; adhere to what is sound, and if you can improve upon anything let it be done in the spirit in which these pages themselves are written." Human progress is always piecemeal and halting,[1] no less in the theory and practice of education than in other aspects of culture. Pestalozzi would not in 1827 have quarrelled with what he wrote in 1800. "We have not yet fathomed either Education or the Child."[2]

[1] How much nearer are we in 1912 ?
[2] *Vide* Monograph of 1800, p. 300.

CHAPTER XV.

The Influence of Pestalozzi.

The Humanitarian Motive in Education. A comparison of the organisation, of the aims and spirit of the methods of instruction in respect of popular education at the beginning of the nineteenth and the beginning of the twentieth century would give a good general indication of the influence which the Pestalozzian spirit has exerted. Although it is true that Pestalozzi was in many respects a child of his age, and that had he lived in the time of Comenius his work would have had even less historical results, we must also give him the credit which is properly due to men who give form and life to the vague aspirations of their age—aspirations which also serve their purpose in affording the environment necessary for the full historical fruitfulness of the master's ideas.

No single feature of popular education has failed to receive stimulus and profit from the work of Pestalozzi. Alike in its general conception and in its detailed practice, there is so much that we now take for granted that we often seem to be dealing with the obvious when we are reading Pestalozzian principles. We are so accustomed now, even in England, to think of the elementary school as the great nursery of the nation, by means of which the State endeavours to prepare its children for responsible citizenship, that it is difficult to realise how comparatively recently this view has prevailed among the nations of Western Europe. It was precisely this social aspect of education which was Pestalozzi's inspiring motive, and of all purely Pestalozzian doctrines this is at once the greatest and least vulnerable. The nineteenth century humanitarian motive in education takes its definite beginning from him, not from the superficial inconsistencies of Rousseau, nor the abstract theoretical legislation of the French revolutionaries, nor the benevolent intentions of the Philanthropinists.

Heralded by *Leonard and Gertrude*, Pestalozzianism as a social factor of the highest importance at

Prussian Interest and Activity. once attracted the attention of thoughtful Governments. Its concreteness was its strength and its charm. It was no dangerous social doctrine which Pestalozzi preached, and Frederick the Great had abandoned the idea that peoples were easy to govern in proportion to their ignorance. The difficulty had been to educate men without at the same time unfitting them for actual life. In *Leonard and Gertrude*, education is from the beginning intimately connected with the home, directly adapted to the duties the child will probably have to fulfil in the future. At the same time, it affords escape for the talented whose capacities would find their best employment in higher social spheres. Upon the Prussian Queen Louisa the book made a profound impression. In her diary she wrote, "I am now reading *Leonard and Gertrude*, by Pestalozzi. How refreshing this story of the Swiss village is! Were I my own master, I would go straightway to Switzerland to shake hands with the noble man, and to thank him with all my heart. How deep is his love for his fellow men. Yes, in the name of Humanity, I thank him."

Not only in Prussia, but in Spain, in Denmark, in

France, in Italy, in Austria, and even in Russia, this book prepared the way for the time when Pestalozzi himself should become a schoolmaster, and after the appearance of *How Gertrude Teaches her Children* a steady stream of visitors, official and unofficial, poured first into Burgdorf and then into Yverdun from all these countries; it was Prussia, however, that took to the new doctrines most seriously.

Even before the great defeat of the German armies at Jena (1806), a Pestalozzian school was opened in Berlin —the Plamannsche Institut—under royal auspices, partly as experiment, but chiefly with the idea of training teachers in the method. In Frankfort in the same year, Grüner, who, as a Philanthropinist, had gone to Burgdorf as a critic of Pestalozzi's claims and had come back an ardent convert, opened the school in which Froebel first found his vocation, and still earlier in Bremen Herbart had excited a good deal of interest in the work which he himself had seen in Burgdorf. Then came the crushing events of 1806, followed, in the winter of 1807, by Fichte's stirring *Addresses to the German Nation* in which the Prussian people were exhorted to seek national regeneration in the education of their children. Although Fichte criticised sharply certain details in Pestalozzi's theory and practice, speaking generally, he urged the Pestalozzian school as the true type.

Prussia was at that time fortunate in its ministers. Von Stein and von Humboldt, who successively guided her educational policy, were full of understanding for the ideas of Nicolovius and Süvern, their chief subordinates, who were keen disciples of Pestalozzi. At their instance a regular succession of teachers were sent to Switzerland not merely to learn the "school machinery," but to catch the spirit of the master. On their return, these men were placed in positions of responsibility over the country, with the deliberate intention of giving new life to the whole organisation. Of course there were some failures. Zeller, for example, was placed over the province of Königsberg, but through his woodenness and vanity the result was a fiasco. In Prussia, however, such cases did not stop reform, as they did in Denmark, Würtemberg, Spain, and elsewhere. Too many officials, teachers, and clergymen had penetrated beyond the formalism which encrusted the truths for which Pestalozzi stood to let an occasional failure stop the current of reform which was producing a great spiritual change in the schools.

In 1809 the Prussian State made itself definitely responsible for the primary school system, and laid it down that the first business of the schools was to train the judgment and to develop the moral and religious sense, and that teachers were to be specially trained for their work. Although a great school system had been organised by Frederick the Great, it had remained a machine which stood outside the lives of the people. " Now for the first time the German school was a fact in Prussia, for the first time it had a genuine content, and took its inspiration from teachers filled with genuine pedagogical spirit—the country had become one great Pestalozzi school."

The example which Prussia had set in the storm and stress of national feeling, was more or less speedily followed by the other German states. Still more slowly the Prussian example spread over Europe. It was not until 1870 that our own country persuaded itself that primary education was of sufficient social importance to demand comprehensive treatment, on the principle of the compulsory attendance of all children not otherwise adequately provided for.

The emphasis which Pestalozzi placed upon home training, and the fact that Comenius, in his scheme for the national organisation of education, had suggested six to fourteen as age limits for the primary schools, led Prussia to fix the lower limit of compulsory school attendance at six, and the ages suggested by Comenius became the standard for all the German States.

It was not only in respect of the State organisation of education that Pestalozzi's influence was felt. **Influence upon Educational thinkers: Herbart, Froebel, Niemeyer.** In respect also of the theory and practice of education, he is the founder of a new epoch. The educational literature directly or indirectly inspired by his work is so abundant that it is only possible in the limits of a short chapter to indicate its character in very general terms. His own writings and the books issued under his superintendence were subject to the keenest criticism, particularly *How Gertrude Teaches her Children*, and the three elementary books published in 1803. His most distinguished critic was Herbart, whose public work for education really began with expositions of Pestalozzian doctrine.

To estimate exactly Herbart's indebtedness to Pestalozzi is hardly possible. He was of course a man of different intellectual calibre, a distinguished philosopher and mathematician. We know, however, that he was never ashamed to acknowledge himself a Pestalozzian, even when in a period of reaction educational opinion in Prussia tended to despise the term. He saw of course that Pestalozzi had not a rounded-off theory at his command, but he recognised the value of the work he had done and was still endeavouring to accomplish.

In his comments upon the Gessner Letters, written in December 1801, he says that in 1799 he had found Pestalozzi working at problems which he himself had been engaged upon as a private tutor. "I had long felt that to give our children the feeling which comes from clear comprehension was the true object of instruction, and that the only means of attaining this lay in a perfect graduation of the subjects of instruction, a graduation which should satisfy every point of view. This was precisely the problem upon which Pestalozzi was working—the problem of the organisation of the material of instruction, the determination of the order in which subjects should be taught both within themselves and with respect to one another." [1]

In the Bremen address, "On the point of view from which Pestalozzi's method of instruction should be judged," he says : " Pestalozzi is especially wanting in respect of sound scientific background, and still more in respect of the cool-headedness necessary to the use of a scientific method, or even for the successful mixture and adaptation of learned generalisations out of which orderly prescriptions might have resulted, such as would have been of immediate service to us who would learn from him his art. He cannot, therefore, object to others attempting to set forth some parts of his method in a more orderly fashion, if he has any hope of its becoming widespread."

One may therefore conclude that Pestalozzi at least gave Herbart his starting-points, that in expounding and criticising Pestalozzi his own educational ideas were to some extent cleared up. The fact that one of his most important educational publications, "Concerning the Aesthetic Revelation of the World as the chief concern of Education," appeared as a supplementary chapter to the second edition of his book, *Pestalozzi's Idea of an A B C of Sense-Perception examined and scientifically worked out* (1804), sufficiently demonstrates the intimate relation of the one man to the other.

---

[1] Herbart, *Sämmtliche Werke*, Vol. I., pp. 141, 142.

It was probably Herbart's active support of the Pestalozzian principle that secured his nomination to the chair of philosophy at Königsberg in 1808, in the hope that he would be helpful in correcting the all-too-ready tendency to see nothing in the new ideas but the pedantry which had amused itself in filling a thick book with dull exercises upon the multiplication table. For the rest Herbart, with a new psychology and a definite ethical system, was able to give to the vague intuitions of Pestalozzi a more definite form, to organise them into a system capable of practical interpretation, free from the one-sidedness and mechanism into which Pestalozzi himself was often led, through the absence of fixed guiding principles.

The whole literature which has followed upon Herbart's educational writings may thus be said to spring, in the first instance, from Pestalozzi, whose fundamental doctrines, so imperfectly expressed but so deeply felt, have been developed into an elaborate system such as Pestalozzi certainly would recognise with difficulty.[1]

Amongst the many visitors to Yverdun during its most brilliant period, not the least interesting was Froebel, who, first in 1805, on the advice of Grüner of Frankfort, and again in 1808, was studying the practice of his recently adopted profession under Pestalozzi. That he learned very much from Pestalozzi's work is clear. The *Education of Man* is throughout reminiscent of Pestalozzi. As an illustration one may compare Froebel's early number lessons with the suggestions made by Pestalozzi in the introduction to the A B C of number relations.[2] Froebel's "Come, let us live with

Froebel.

---

[1] *Vide* Ziller, *Allgemeine Pädagogik*; De Garmo, *Herbart and the Herbartians*; Rein, *Outlines of Pedagogics*.

[2] *Education of Man,* International Education Series (Arnold), p. 81 ff. *Vide* also p. 193 of this book.

our children," [1] precisely reflects what he had seen in practice at Yverdun.

In addition to the philosophic turn that was given to Pestalozzianism by Herbart, the literature of educational theory and practice of a less general and scientific character which had already begun to appear in Germany increased enormously. Men who had seen the work at Burgdorf were keen to describe what they had seen, or to apply what they had learned to the special problems of their own country, and they in turn inspired others to work at some one or other of the many points at issue in relation to natural education.

Even the men who had written educational treatises before Pestalozzi took definitely to the profession were affected by the new wave of enthusiasm. Niemeyer, for example, whose *Principles of Education and Instruction* (*Grundsätze der Erziehung und des Unterrichts*, 1796) Herbart, in 1802, described as containing the very best that modern pedagogy had said upon the subject,[2] discussed his own attitude to Pestalozzi's doctrines in a special booklet, *Contributions to the criticism of Pestalozzian Principles and Methods of Instruction*. While the claims of his more ardent followers to the originality of their master are discounted, and the formalism of some of his methods of instruction are sharply criticised, Niemeyer closes with a warm appreciation. "Anything which awakens such a widespread interest as Pestalozzi's educational ideas have done, must necessarily contain, if we can only view it as a whole, much that is both true and useful." "The influence in this case can only be for good, and that in the highest degree, if men will look to the spirit rather than to the letter."

Niemeyer.

---

[1] *Education of Man*, p. 89.   [2] *Werke*, Vol. I., p. 283.

We have seen already how the whole educational machinery of the German states was being overhauled ; both public and professional opinion was in course of formation upon all points of detail and many questions of principle. The way was therefore open for a more or less ephemeral literature in relation to the many points at issue.

The question of the training of teachers, of the relation of the church to the school, of the organisation of continuation schools, of modern types of secondary schools, the discussion of methods of teaching, the preparation of school books based on Pestalozzian principles, etc., kept and still keep the educational press in Germany busy. This volume of educational literature is a purely nineteenth century product and is a standing monument to the influence of Pestalozzi upon educational history.

Even amongst Pestalozzians it would be impossible to expect unanimity in a matter which involved so many traditional points of view. Gradually

Harnisch.

two wings, so to speak, formed themselves in the ranks of the reformers. The right wing led by Harnisch[1] (1787-1864) emphasised the need for definite religious instruction in the primary schools. Harnisch had learned the Pestalozzi method as a teacher in Plamann's school in Berlin. As rector of the teachers' seminary at Breslau he did much to work out the application of the method of sense-perception to the subjects of the elementary school.[2] But

---

[1] Vide *Bibliothek Pädagogischer Classiker* (Langensalza), which includes the chief educational writings of Niemeyer and Harnisch.

[2] An interesting letter from Harnisch to Pestalozzi in 1814 is quoted by Morf, vol. iv., p. 363. It is valuable testimony to the way in which the latter affected educational opinion in Prussia. Amongst other things he suggests that an educational newspaper should be published in Yverdun, that all Germany might be kept in touch with the parent institution.

his churchmanship always affected his view of the function of the school. He emphasised more and more the importance of dogmatic religion, and became the acknowledged leader of an apparently reactionary party, which often appeared to its opponents to be aiming at the restriction of the work of the primary school to the teaching of reading, writing and the catechism.

The leader of the left wing was Diesterweg, without whom Prussian education is hardly to be understood. A stimulating writer, he did much to work out and popularise the methodology of the various school subjects on Pestalozzian lines. In 1827 he founded *Die Rheinischen Blätter*, a journal devoted to the professional interests of teachers, in which for many years he fought for the better education, the better training, and the better remuneration of teachers. In 1832 he became principal of the Berlin Training College, which he soon converted into a pattern professional school. " As the artist is best trained in the studio, so is the teacher best trained in the pattern school. His profession is a practical one. The sharp division of professional knowledge into theory and practice has no significance for him. Pure theory cannot make a teacher. It only leads him astray. The one thing necessary for a teacher's seminary is therefore a well-equipped model school."

In accordance with his ideals, a school was provided in which Diesterweg tried to give practical shape to Pestalozzian doctrine. " The development of the child is to be stimulated according to his own inner needs. Instruction is to begin with observation and to advance step by step to the general notion. The children are to be trained by encouraging the spontaneous exercise of their own activity. The teachers are not to regard themselves as the centre of interest, still less the subject-matter of instruction. The children themselves are to occupy this place; the teacher and the subject-matter form as it were their environment; they are the tools skilfully placed at the service of the children in their instinctive efforts towards development.[1]

Penetrated with Pestalozzian views as to the great social significance of the school, he fought strenuously against the reactionary tendency which in Prussia reached its climax under Frederick William IV. (1840-1861). Unable to adapt himself to the "policy of regulations" which stifled the freedom of the teachers and destroyed all possibility of educational growth, he gave up the direction of the Berlin seminary only to fight for his cause with still greater zeal in the press, and as an elected representative of the people in the government of the city of Berlin. The high place which the school in Germany takes, the clear views held by both the governed and the governing classes as to its importance in relation to the future of the fatherland, are in no small degree due to the Pestalozzian spirit, as kept alive at a critical time by Diesterweg,[2] who died three days after Sadowa, July 7th, 1866.

In respect of the training of teachers generally, it may be said that the fame of the Pestalozzian institutions at Burgdorf and Yverdun, and the large number of enthusiastic practical teachers and organisers who took their inspiration thence, gave a stamp of reality to the idea which has resulted in the general acceptance of the principle in nearly all civilised countries. Of course the idea was not new. In our own country Mulcaster, in the sixteenth century, had urged its importance, and in various German states

The Training of Teachers.

---

[1] Schmidt, *Geschichte der Pädagogik*, Bd. iv., p. 227 ff.

[2] A selection of Diesterweg's pedagogical writings is published in the *Bibliothek Pädagogischer Classiker*.

teachers' training classes had been actually called into being in the seventeenth and eighteenth centuries, like those of Ratke at Koethen and Francke at Halle. The Philanthropinists also took up the cause, and in Switzerland under their influence Stapfer made an attempt to create a national system of training colleges. Almost at the same time the training idea was finding favour in England through the successful application of the monitorial system by Lancaster and Bell.

It was Pestalozzi, however, who convinced the Prussian authorities both of its necessity and of its practicability. The reorganisation of schools there included the provision of teachers' seminaries, but the necessity of securing a good general education for the future teachers in the elementary schools gradually led to the abandonment of the idea that such institutions should be devoted primarily to professional studies. A mixture of the academic and professional elements, in which the academic tends more and more to displace the professional, is leading reformers in Prussia back to the Pestalozzian ideal, which demands first a good liberal education free from all professional bias, and lastly a period of purely professional training. Neither at Yverdun nor at Burgdorf was there any suggestion of such a conflict of aims as a concurrent academic and professional training necessarily entails, to the inevitable cost of both. It scarcely needs to be pointed out how completely the usual English practice has gone in the opposite direction, though recent reforms show signs of a closer approach to the Pestalozzian ideal. Amongst other changes a new type of training college has been created in which students whose general education has reached a certain minimum standard will devote their time wholly to the study of the theory and practice of their profession.

In the elementary schools themselves Pestalozzi's influence has been enormous. The curriculum has been reformed to answer at least in part to his fundamental doctrine that the schools should prepare for life; new methods of teaching have been worked out, based upon the fact that interested observation is the child's natural way of collecting material which the mind spontaneously, though imperfectly, systematises. Lastly, what is commonly called " School Method," that is to say, all that large body of literature which deals with specific prescriptions for teaching this and that subject of instruction, is to a large extent the result of Pestalozzi's attempt to " elementarise " the curriculum at Burgdorf.

School Aims.

The whole spirit of the elementary school has changed. Discipline is gentler because the aims are higher, and because a specially trained staff has replaced the cobbler-schoolmaster of Pestalozzi's own experience. Finally, the subjects of instruction themselves have been systematised, graduated, illustrated, and variously prepared for school purposes by competent authorities who have grasped the true teacher's point of view. In all these directions there can, of course, be no finality in practice, but to Pestalozzi we must give the credit of having put us upon the never-ending path of progress.

In respect of the curriculum of the schools, we may note the growing tendency to base it upon the principle of the spontaneous and harmonious reaction of the child upon his environment. The difficulty which was felt at Bonnal—viz. that the school is cut off from the rest of the everyday life of the child—is still a pressing one. The child at play and the child at his lessons are not, in the full sense, one and the same person. Professor Dewey's school in Chicago was, perhaps, the best known attempt to realise Pestalozzi's ideal, and the questions which guide his teachers in arranging the school work are precisely the same in character as those which Glüphi, with Gertrude's assistance, set himself to solve. "What can be done, and how can it be done, to bring the school into closer relations with the home and neighbourhood life? What can be done in the way of introducing subject-matter in history and science and art that shall have a real significance in the child's own life? How can instruction in reading, writing, and the use of figures be carried on with everyday experience and occupation as their background and in definite relation to other studies" which shall give them a meaning? How shall we adapt ourselves to the individual needs of the children? [1]

Although few schools have been organised so completely upon this ideal, the dangers involved in completely severing the school from the home life of the children are being recognised, and a system of education which is alleged by its critics to produce "the clerk at the top and the hooligan at the bottom" is being very properly subjected to scrutiny.

The modern insistence upon manual activities in the primary schools is a step towards the Pestalozzian ideal, and Herr Salomon's system of educational handwork in wood (*Slojd*) is an interesting and valuable attempt to apply Pestalozzianism to the conditions of national life.

As to methods of teaching and the organisation of instruction, one sees on every hand the influence of Pestalozzi's cardinal doctrines. The modern treatment of geography as a school subject takes its standard of excellence from the practice at Burgdorf and Yverdun. In the practical study of the home neighbourhood the child lays the foundations of all future intelligent geographical

Methods of Teaching Particular Subjects. — Geography.

---

[1] Dewey, *The School and Society*, p. 116 ff.

work. Karl Ritter, an old pupil of Salzmann's in Schnep-
fenthal, who, with his friend Alexander von Humboldt,
shares the honour of having founded the science of
geography, spoke in enthusiastic terms of Tobler's
geographical lessons. For the first time he saw his own
ideas as to the possibilities of the subject carried out in
the school.

When he visited Yverdun for the second time Tobler
had gone, but his successor, Henning, was elaborating his
ideas, and at Ritter's suggestion the first book upon
method in geographical teaching was published. Henning's *Leitfaden beim methodischen Unterricht in der Geo-
graphie* is the forerunner of an ever-increasing number
of books upon what the Germans call *Heimatskunde*, in
the course of which the child not only acquires direct
acquaintance with the methods of the geographer, but
also, through his directed observation of natural phenomena—wind, rain, frost, heat, and cold—as well as of
the animals and plants of his neighbourhood, is provided with a stock of experiences which constitute a
broad foundation for any future specialised work in
science. " Look at all things from the point of view
of their interaction " is one of Henning's fundamental principles, but his book is chiefly devoted to
the geographical side. It was reserved for Harnisch
to apply Pestalozzi's idea to natural history for the first
time.

Geography is, however, only one example of the way the
ideas expressed in *How Gertrude Teaches her
Children* have been applied to instruction in
special subjects. The teaching of arithmetic
has been revolutionised by Pestalozzi's insistence upon
a sensory foundation for the subject, and although
the *Lessons in the Apprehension of Number Relations*,

Arithmetic.

as worked out by Krusi with thousands of abstract
exercises, offends by its mechanical formalism against
more fundamental principles, the book was epoch-making
in respect of this department of school work, and a new type
of arithmetic text-book was not slow to appear, in which the
idea of the acquisition of formal dexterity was subordinated
to that of training for actual life by means of concrete
examples—the truer Pestalozzian view which Krusi, and
therefore Pestalozzi himself, lost sight of in their keenness
to produce that marvellous dexterity which excited the
astonished admiration of visitors to Burgdorf.[1]

In this way a school of Pestalozzians was formed which
insisted on the value of mental arithmetic as " strengthening the thought-powers." Joseph Schmid, von Türk, and
Kamerau, all at one time or other members of Pestalozzi's
staff, each published books upon the subject which
emphasised its formal value, that is to say, the logical
training which is given by abstract arithmetical exercises.
But even for them all early work with numbers is concrete, and it has remained so whatever the views of
teachers about the ultimate value of the subject in the
higher branches may be.

In regard to drawing Pestalozzi made the first attempt
to bring it within the range of the elementary
Drawing.   school. His practical success cannot be questioned, and his psychological analysis of the
problem was sound, but his desire to begin at the beginning
and to go forward on the principles of the " elementary
method " led to the drawing of lines, angles, and geometrical
figures, which for long remained the standard procedure
in the lower classes of the elementary schools.[2] Pestalozzi
had said " Nature gives the child no lines ; she only

[1] *Vide* p. 205.

[2] With this paragraph cp. *Letters to Greaves* (G., p. 232 f.).

offers objects, and lines must only be given to him that he may see objects correctly"—but the mechanism of the "elementary method" survived the spirit which gave it birth. The books of Schmid, von Türk, Ramsauer, and Tobler only served still further to stiffen the formal and, to the child, meaningless nature of the drawing lesson. We are now revising our ideas and practice, but the problem of drawing in the elementary school cannot yet be said to be solved.

Pestalozzi's method of teaching children to use their native tongue has become, in its broad outlines, the standard practice of the elementary schools.

Mother Tongue.

The child is first taught to speak properly. Through direct observation he learns the right word for the right thing, and when he has got a stock of words which are real to him, he is exercised in their use. All lessons are, at least indirectly, lessons in the mother tongue. Within his range the child is required to express himself exactly about that which he knows. When he can do this satisfactorily in speech and in writing, the language as such is studied. The grammatical generalisations under these circumstances are as real to him as his own thoughts which insensibly involve them. The passage from the vague to the definite idea in this relatively abstract sphere is now possible. As we have seen, Pestalozzi's own lessons often pursued the formal end to an unjustifiable extreme, but here, as in so many other cases, the formalism of his practice must not blind us to the soundness of the principles which he lays down.

His attempt in this regard, to reduce to order the language teaching of the nursery [1] in particular, gave rise to much misunderstanding of the true Pestalozzian point of

---

[1] *I.e.* in *The Mother's Book, vide* p. 177.

view.   Even when abandoning the idea that such instruction should begin with the human body, von Türk, in his
*Sensory Perception as the Foundation of Instruction in the
Mother Tongue* (1811), applies the "elementary method"
to the child's environment with equal thoroughness. He
finds, for example, twenty-two different shades of red for
the child to attend to and speak in set terms about. The
Pestalozzians were first brought into the right path by
Denzel, who had worked with the master at Burgdorf,
but always took a wide and independent view in matters
of practice.

His *Introduction to the Principles of Education and
Instruction* (1835) accepts the fact that the impressions
with which the child is already equipped when he comes
to school must be disorderly, and lays it down that the
problem of the school is first of all gradually to reduce
these ideas to some sort of form, and to train the child's
flighty attention to regard one thing at a time. The whole
range of the child's thoughts is in this way disciplined.
Then the objects of his immediate environment are brought
to his notice in a systematic way ; he is taught to notice
in them whatever is noteworthy, and he is allowed to
speak freely about them. Instruction goes from the indefinite to the definite, from the impression of the object
as a whole to the consideration of its parts.[1]

Pestalozzi's attempt to solve the problem of the teaching
of reading was never quite satisfactory to himself, but he
did not succeed in improving upon it.[2]

Lastly we may note that the systematisation of instruction in music began under Pestalozzi's auspices.
Music.   The work of Pfeiffer and Nageli aimed at
enabling the children in the elementary school to sing from

---

[1] *Vide* Scherer, *Pestalozzische Pädagogik*, p. 186.

[2] It was a purely syllabic method, *vide* p. 188 f.

notes, and they applied the elementary method somewhat rigidly to the solution of this problem.[1] Natorp, an enthusiastic colleague of Nicolovius and Süvern, improved thereon in his *Guide to Instruction in Music for Elementary School Teachers* (1813) by introducing songs at a certain stage, since which time the importance of the subject has led to many devices for making it easily applicable to the conditions of the elementary school, not the least important of which is the Tonic-Solfa system, which has, however, so far found little favour in any country but our own.

It is of course in Germany, and particularly in Prussia, that Pestalozzi's influence made itself chiefly felt, partly because he was a German-speaking Swiss, but chiefly on account of the historical situation.

In our own country education was much in the air during the first quarter of the nineteenth century, and Pestalozzian doctrine was enthusiastically taken up by a small band of admirers who had themselves been in Yverdun.[2] Chief amongst these perhaps was Biber, who had been on Pestalozzi's staff. He published a life of his master and a critical account of his doctrines in 1831. Admirable as the book is in some respects, it is tinged with personal unfriendliness and not therefore authoritative, though it has played a considerable part in English accounts of Yverdun. Biber had given courses of lectures in London in 1828 and in 1829 on the principles and methods of Pestalozzi, which appeared in book form as *The Christian Monitor* and *Christian Education* respectively.

Influence in England.

But Pestalozzi himself had sent a message to this

---

[1] *Vide* also p. 222.

[2] Amongst other English visitors were Andrew Bell and Lord Brougham. Brougham, however, thought most highly of Fellenberg, and Bell was enamoured of his own system.

country in a series of letters to J. P. Greaves. These were translated at Greaves' request, possibly by Biber himself, and published as *Letters on Early Education* in 1827, just after their writer's death. So far as I know these important letters never reached a second edition.[1]

Several years before that, however, P. H. Pullen had published *The Mother's Book*, " exemplifying Pestalozzi's Plan of awakening the Understanding of Children in Language, Drawing, Geometry, Geography and Nature," and in 1821 the same author published *Pestalozzi's Intellectual or Intuitive Arithmetic*. In the same period a series of six pamphlets entitled *Hints to Parents* were published, each one being devoted to a special aspect of Pestalozzian method (Language, Form, Number, etc.). They were in truth *Mother's Books* which seem to have had a considerable vogue. One in my possession is the fifth edition and was published in 1827.

The work of the Mayos has probably had the greatest direct influence in introducing Pestalozzian practice into our schools. Mayo, who was in Yverdun in 1819, opened a Pestalozzian school first at Epsom and afterwards in larger premises at Cheam. He was intimately connected with the Home and Colonial Infant School Society, and with his sister he published for the benefit of the students of the Society's Training College *Practical Remarks on Infant Education*, which breathe the spirit of their master. It was, however, Miss Mayo's *Lessons on Objects* which brought Pestalozzi into the schools of the country, a book which was the forerunner of the crowds of object-lesson manuals which are now perhaps passing away. As exemplifying the earliest English interpretations of Pestalozzian doctrine,

[1] A selection containing the chief letters will be found in G., p. 211 f.

two lessons are given in Part III., one from the work of Biber already mentioned and one from Miss Mayo.[1] They are interesting as showing a distinct step forward in the development of teaching methods. Crude as we should now regard the Mayo lessons, they are an improvement upon Biber, whose rigid formalism is worthy of the author of *The Mother's Book*.

It was, however, the political questions involved in the educational question that chiefly interested the British people. We were too much occupied with the struggle between the "National" schools and the Lancasterian schools to be much affected by fundamental doctrines. In 1863, however, Herbert Spencer's essays upon education once again brought Pestalozzian doctrine before the English public.

But it is not in the wealth of literature that has gathered round Pestalozzi's name in England that we may see his influence. We must look rather to the practice of the schools, and especially to the present tendency to allow the schools greater freedom, in the hope that they may adapt themselves more closely to the home life of the children in the districts which they serve. "Normal schools" such as Felbiger created in Austria—code-bound schools and code-bound teachers—could never carry out the Pestalozzian ideal.

[1] *Vide* Chapter XXI.

PART III.

ADDITIONAL TRANSLATIONS, ETC.

CHAPTER XVI.

A Letter on the Education of Poor Country Children.[1]

(1776)

The poor man is usually poor because he has not learned how to support himself. We must deal with his poverty at its source. Whilst giving him a general education, we must pay particular attention to his special circumstances. The poor must be trained for poverty. This is the test that we should apply to institutions that profess to educate them.

The education of the poor demands a deep and accurate knowledge of poverty, its needs, difficulties, and circumstances. It demands a detailed acquaintance with the life the children will probably lead in the future. For, generally speaking, it is true that men in all ranks should prepare their children especially for the difficulties and limitations of later days, and I think that a characteristic feature of the apprenticeship to any calling should consist in practising its difficulties, in patiently overcoming all desires which might prove a hindrance to the continuous

---

[1] *Vide* Chapter III., p. 48 f.

execution of future duties. This seems to me especially true of the education of the poor to the most difficult calling in life.

The would-be philanthropist should find out how the suffering poor live. He must see the poor man in his badly lighted room, his wife in the smoke-ridden kitchen, and his child at a task that is almost too much for him. That is the sort of place in which a lad brought up in a publicly supported school must live in the future ; his wife will probably have to conduct her household in a similar kitchen with few contrivances, and with very little change of food ; to engage in one or other branch of heavy labour will be his only means of livelihood. Children who live in this way with poor parents are so accustomed to all these restrictions that they do not find them grievous. They may live happily and quietly in spite of them.

An educational institute should not rob children of the possibility of living quiet, contented lives, yet that will happen if the philanthropist who wishes to educate poor children is not sufficiently acquainted with poverty and the means of helping it ; and unless, in the conduct of such an institution, he always remembers that the children will be poor people in the future, that they will have to support themselves and to make themselves comfortable on such resources as local circumstances afford.

A wise founder will regard it as the best feature of his institution, that it trains those capacities which will to all appearances afford the surest means of livelihood in that place where the lot of the children is likely to be cast ; he will so organise their education that the hardships which belong to lowlier callings will not be strange or loathsome or burdensome to them ; he will feel keenly that the success of the training depends on the careful emphasis which is laid on industry, and on estimating as modestly as possible the real necessities of life; adaptive resourcefulness, obedient and yielding modesty, practice in quietly facing the various modes of livelihood open to the poor are the most important things to teach—these lessons, or rather these capacities, must be the compensation for his poverty; his adaptive resourcefulness, the readiness of his hand and his head for any work that comes to hand, must give him his advantage in usefulness over the people of means.

Whenever men think of plans for an orphanage, they should keep their minds on the future needs and circumstances of the children, and remember that the institution must be a school for training the capacities suited to the case, and guard against the consequences of error in this respect.

Rest, pleasure, abundance, do not stimulate activity; ample provision does not rouse active search; to preach gratitude does not of itself make for diligence, sensitive dreams about what is good do not give strength, and carefully explained catechisms furnish no compensation when the children leave the comforts which beneficence has provided for them, to take their place amidst the hardships of humble life which will be their lot.

We must not think that work which even in our eyes is not difficult, and which presents no persistent hardships to be overcome, can be a satisfactory training for poverty. The boys will have to face without flinching such work as there is for them. They will not be able to choose. In one place they must not fight shy of the damp of the weaver's cellar, in another they must accustom themselves to the dust of the cotton mill, and elsewhere it is the nasty fat of the wool they will have to endure, or even the unpleasantness of the scavenger service—but I will avoid further detail, though it is certain that neither open air, nor draught, nor steam-laden atmosphere must affect their health. The schoolroom must resemble as far as may be the future home of the boys ; they must learn to submit their will to that of another in the workshop ; whether the bed is a poor one, whether it is soft or hard, whether it is shared with another or not should alike be indifferent, but that will never be if school beds are always soft and warm and single.

My noble friend ! I know your gentle heart will think this very severe, but I tremble for the suffering of those unfortunates who have been ruined by the unwisdom of philanthropists, when I see them struggling with tears in their eyes under the burden of unfamiliar poverty, eating their bread with tears, when I see them like sickly children . . . their lives through. My heart, too, burns within me on behalf of these lost ones. But I can only see one way to their well-being—accustoming them strictly to severe restrictions, training them suitably to be diligent and industrious, and to endure such hardships of all kinds as are common to the various callings open to the poor in our land. You yourself, however, have in your letter accepted the ideas of restrictions and of industry as the underlying principles of your own institution, but you are in an elevated district, where agriculture will always offer a sure means of livelihood to poor boys.

Are there in existence public institutions where these principles are actually put into practice, where the future of the children is specially considered ? On the contrary, I think the arrangements of most of our richly-endowed institutions are of a dangerously opposite character. Too liberal for their purpose, by satisfying all the children's needs without calling for effort on their part they commonly hinder the germ of industry and of bread-seeking resourcefulness from developing. The capacities which the actual needs of the poor call into existence in a

natural way are undeveloped. The state is no gainer from
such wealthy institutions, which are nothing but nurseries
of unskilled men who are made utterly unfit to cope with
the chances and restrictions of humble life ; having no
capacity to lift themselves out of that station, they pass
over from the orphanage into the poor-house. The education of the poor is nowhere so bad as it is in such institutions. Their founders knew nothing of the poor; the
external magnificence of their foundations appeals to their
ambitions, and the real objects of the foundation are lost
sight of.

What is then to be done? Can these public institutions be improved? Is it possible to introduce the spirit
of hard work, of anxious economy, of brave effort in face
of overwhelming difficulties, into places whose founders
were wealthy and ignorant of the lives of the poor, whose
salaried chiefs command a well-organised service, where
abundance removes all motive for effort, economy, and
resourcefulness, and actually encourages carelessness, waste,
and dishonesty? Is it possible, in spite of all difficulties,
to achieve in such circumstances the real objects of a
school for poor children? I should not wish to utter a too
decided *No*. Men's powers can accomplish much when
they set their minds to it, and I wish all success to him
who essayed such a task. But the men who would undertake it are *rari nantes in gurgite vasto*—I would not count
too surely on finding one. My own ideas run in another
direction. I think the object would be best attained if
special schools of this kind were definitely associated with
some branch of industry. Of this, however, I will speak
in later letters.

CHAPTER XVII.

THE PAMPHLET OF 1800.

Introductory. This pamphlet (*Denkschrift*) was written by Pestalozzi in 1800, in response to an invitation from one of the members of the "Society of Friends of Education," which Stapfer had founded with the special object of supporting Pestalozzi's work. As Morf remarks, "it is particularly interesting because it is a product of his workshop that comes from the very time when his ideas were beginning to clear up." It was published in 1828, a year after Pestalozzi's death, by Niederer in a monthly journal (Rossel's *Allgemeine Monatschrift*). In the introduction Niederer wrote, "This valuable original document comes directly from the Pestalozzi circle at the moment when the Method was created. It contains the germ of the whole system as it was developed in his later writings."

The student is strongly advised to compare it with (i) *The Evening Hours of a Hermit*, (ii) *How Gertrude Teaches her Children*, (iii) *Views and Experiences*, and (iv) *The Swansong*.[1] He should, of course, read it in the light of the exposition of Pestalozzian doctrine given in this book.

The Pamphlet. I am trying to psychologise education; I am trying to bring it into harmonious relations with mind as it is, and with actual life. Setting aside all presuppositions, I put this question to myself: What course would you follow if you undertook to give a child such knowledge and such practical skill as would

---

[1] Translations of these documents or selected portions of them will be found in G.

enable him with reasonable use of his opportunities to lead a happy and contented life ? For whatever procedure would be suited to a single child would be equally applicable to others. It seems to me, too, that we should pay more attention to the education of the children of the poor than to that of the children of the rich.

It is true that Nature herself does much for man, but we no longer follow in her steps; the poor man has little share in her blessings, and the rich man is surfeited with them to his consequent destruction.

Severe as is this judgment, it rests on experience. Hence the force of my desire, not merely to hide the blunders of the schools which are destroying the manhood of Europe, but to heal them at their sources.

This, however, can only be done by bringing instruction of all kinds into line with the laws which govern the progress of mind from sensory experience to definite ideas.

I have tried to simplify the elements of human knowledge. I have tried to bring the elements of knowledge themselves into line with these laws, and to arrange them in series the psychological sequence of which will bring within the reach of everybody a knowledge of the world of nature, general clearness in all essential ideas and fruitful practice in the most necessary dexterities.

I quite realise the gravity of the claims I am advancing, but neither the difficulties of the undertaking nor my own limitations shall prevent me from contributing my mite towards an object of such importance to the whole world. And when I put before you, gentlemen, the results of my long and arduous labours, I hope that you will carefully distinguish those ideas upon which doubt may be cast from those which cannot be questioned. I want my final results to rest upon irrefragable proofs, or to be themselves derived from absolutely established premises.

I start with the idea that sensory contact with the out-side world is the only true foundation of human instruc-tion, because it is the only foundation of human know-ledge.   All that we know is a consequence of, or an abstraction from, sensory experience.   Thus, whenever this is imperfect, partial, or immature, the superstructure is at fault—deception and error creep in.

I then enquire what Nature herself does to make the world (or that part of it with which I actually come into contact) appear to me in its true light.   Or, to put it in another way, what measures does she take to ensure that my sensory acquaintance with the chief things about me shall mature satisfactorily in my mind?   This must surely be dependent on my particular locality, my specific needs, and my actual dependence on other things.

My specific locality determines my (sensory) outlook upon the world, my needs direct my efforts, and my relations to other things necessitate attention and give the occasion for foresight and care.   Thus, by means of the first Nature fixes the sensory foundations of my knowledge, by the second she does the same thing for my vocation, and by the third a similar service is rendered to propriety of conduct.

I next ask what instruments the long experience of the race has found for strengthening these natural influences, and I find them to be Speech, Drawing, Writing, Count-ing, and Measurement.

If I now seek after the common source of these elemen-tary human instruments, I find it in the common constitu-tion of our minds, by means of which our intelligence works up the sensory impressions from the outside world into unities, that is to say, into conceptions.

From this description it is clear that whenever instruc-tion does not move forward step by step with sensory experience, but hurries on ahead, it dulls the senses themselves and thus leads inevitably to one-sidedness, crookedness, superficiality, and all the presumptions of ignorance. Every word, every number, every measurement, is the intellectual result of ripe sensory experience.

But the stages through which sensory impressions are gradually raised to definite ideas proceed in perfect harmony with the laws of the nervous system, up to the point at which they come within the range of the understanding which is quite independent of external stimuli.

Gesture precedes hieroglyphs, hieroglyphs precede cultivated speech, just as the specific names precede the generic.

Further, it is only when Education follows a course in harmony with the processes of the nervous system as it brings before me the confused mass of sense-impressions that I am conscious of definite sensory experiences, and from these I am enabled to reach clear and definite ideas.

Teaching devices are thus based upon certain physico-mechanical [1] laws. The chief of these are:—

1. See that things are related to each other in your mind, as they are related to each other in actuality.

2. Carefully distinguish between essentials and unessentials, subordinating the one to the other. Take especial care to distinguish between the

---

[1] This is the literal translation of the German words, but by *physisch* Pestalozzi means not merely the bodily machinery—it is the whole nature of man (physical, intellectual, and moral) that the word refers to. Similarly *mechanisch* means *organisch*. The phrase might therefore be translated : Teaching devices are based upon the laws that govern the working of the human organism.

    pedagogic view of things and things as they really are.

3. Let the emphasis you put upon particular things correspond with their actual importance.

4. Classify objects in accordance with their likenesses.

5. In cases of importance, let the impression be strengthened by an appeal to various senses.

6. In every subject aim at perfect graduation. Every step forward should be a scarcely noticeable addition to that which has already been perfectly and unforgettably acquired.

7. Be quite sure that the simple has been perfectly mastered before you proceed to the complicated.

8. Watch the ripening fruit, how perfect are its parts! So every sound judgment should be the fruit of complete sensory acquaintance with the object concerned. Beware of appearances in this respect, as you are careful of the apparent perfection of fruit that may be worm-eaten.

9. Nature's effects in the physical world are inevitable— this inevitableness is, as it were, a result of Nature's methods, her steadiness in uniting apparently differing elements to the achievement of her ends. In imitation of her, education must seek to make the results at which she aims a physical necessity, bringing her various devices harmoniously and steadily to bear.

10. Richness and variety of stimulus and application give natural processes and natural effects the appearance of freedom and spontaneity in spite of their being inevitable.

11. Above all, the great law of our physical constitution— that which states the relation between impressions and the physical nearness or distance of the objects

that produce them—must be recognised. Never
forget that this physical nearness or distance of
the objects in your environment determines the
positive character of your sensory experience, your
vocational development and even that of your conduct. But this law has not independent value,
It operates as it were around another, namely,
the law of your own being—your innermost self.
Do not forget that all that you are, your purposes and all that you ought to be, have their
origin in yourself. Even your sensory experience must have a common centre, and that centre
is yourself. The educator's contribution to the
work of Nature is simply this : he gathers together things Nature has scattered over wide areas
and brings them, in due relation, nearer to our
five senses, thereby lightening the burden on
memory capacity. In this way he improves
enormously the apprehensive powers of the senses,
and through practice makes it every day easier
accurately to recall the objects with which they
have come into touch.

The procedure of Nature is always lofty and simple.
She produces the greatest tree from the tiny seed—unfolding each day and each hour in scarcely noticeable
additions first the beginnings of the stem, then the
boughs, then the branches, and finally the extreme twigs
on which hangs the perishable foliage. She is our model.
Think carefully of this great natural process—how each
part is separately formed and perfected and how when this
achievement is permanent new elements are added.

Watch the bright blossom unfolding from its hiding-
place in the bud. See how it rapidly loses its pristine
beauty as the weak but nevertheless perfect fruit develops.

The fruit grows quietly for months as it hangs on the nourishing twig—finally, when it is ripe and perfect in all its parts it falls to the ground.

Consider too how Nature cherishes the root as well as the rising shoot. She buries the noblest part of the tree deep down in the earth. Think how that sturdy tree trunk gets its nourishment from the very heart of the root, and how the boughs are nourished from the trunk and the branches from the boughs. Every part of the tree, even to the frailest twig, receives strength in perfect proportion to its needs.

Man's sensory mechanism is subject to the same laws as govern organic life generally. Accordingly instruction should bury, as it were, the essentials of knowledge deep down in the human mind; then connect the less essential in unbroken gradation to these well-established essentials, always keeping a strict eye on the living harmony of the whole.

Such are the fundamental principles. But what has been done in Europe along these lines? What use has been made of them in the schools, in the teaching of language, drawing, writing, reading, arithmetic and measurement?

I see no trace of their influence, at any rate in the schools for the poorer classes.[1] As a rule indeed all that is *done is directly contrary to my principles, to the consequent* undoing of the people.

My problem is thus that of bringing the elementary procedure for each subject into line with the inner constitution of the mind—that is to say into line with the laws which govern development from sensory impressions to definite ideas.

---

[1] Pestalozzi could not forget what Basedow and his followers were doing for the well-to-do.

In the course of our work we should not, however, fail to make full use of two means of attracting our pupils which Nature has given us in their Love for Song and their general Aesthetic Sensibility. The mother sings her child to sleep; but here as always we ignore the moral. Before the child is a year old, his mother stops singing. She is no longer his mother. The child is weaned, and for him as for others she is only a distracted overburdened woman. Alas, that it should be so! How is it that we have not discovered how to connect the nursery lullaby to a graduated series of national songs from the lullabies of infancy to the sublime hymn of praise, such as should be heard in the cottages of the people? I cannot fill this gap, though I must at any rate point it out.

So is it in respect of our aesthetic sensibilities. Nature is full of impressive and magnificent forms, but Europe has done nothing to awaken a sense of these things in the minds of her people or to arrange them in series the sensory acquaintance with which would develop this feeling on right lines. Sunrises and sunsets are vain. The indefinable charm of flower and field, mountain and valley, makes no appeal to us.

In this respect also my work has little to offer, but the gaps must be filled if popular education is ever to rise above the meaninglessness of the present barbarities to agreement with the natural constitution of our minds.

I must now leave these general methods of attraction, and apply myself to the special devices for teaching language, etc.

Before the child himself voluntarily utters a sound, he is already aware of all the sensory facts which his special circumstances have brought within his experience. In practice he knows the differences between pebbles and wood, and between wood and glass. This misty awareness is cleared up by speech. He must have names for the different things that he knows and for their qualities.

Thus I attach language to knowledge and I extend his knowledge that I may enlarge his vocabulary; at the same time his sensory impressions of things are cleared up. This clearing up of consciousness is the general form which instruction should take. It may follow one of two directions :—

We must lead children either through a knowledge of words to a knowledge of things, or through acquaintance with things to acquaintance with words. This latter is my course. I insist that actual sensory acquaintance should always precede the name, and that distinct knowledge should precede the judgment. I wish to make mere words and talk valueless in men's minds and to give all the weight to actual sensory experience—the best protection against noisy assertion. From the outset I want to put the child into the heart of Nature in the midst of which he lives; I want to organise his learning to talk by means of a collection of common natural products; I want to teach him to distinguish the particular from the general quite early, and to give him corresponding words; in general, I hope to substitute physical generalisations for the metaphysical with which we nowadays begin our instruction, and only when the general foundations of knowledge—sensory experience—have been soundly laid shall I begin the difficult abstract studies from books.

But my A B C book is simply a collection of easy stories by means of which any mother who makes use of the sound of each letter may put her children in effective command of the essential features of its own body.. . . .

There follows a summarised description of his methods of teaching language, etc., with illustrative appendices. As these have already been given in the text of this book, they are not repeated here. (*Vide* p. 185 ff.)

In this way, gentlemen, I try to apply the laws which govern our progress from sensory impressions to definite ideas to the problems of elementary education. . . . I follow in Nature's path. If the child is already familiar with elementary bodies—air, earth, fire, water—I show him their effects on other things that he knows, and as he learns the properties of the elements I show him the effects of bringing one element to bear upon another, and through simple sensory experience I lead him to the boundaries of the exact sciences.

We must put all our procedure into such a form that mothers can use it. It is also important that children should not be misled by the arrogant ignorance of their teachers, and my method will, I think, lead a child of seven to seek out the teacher who really knows his subject and will lead him to take an independent view of their own.

But we have fathomed neither education nor the child.

Sensory impressions, the sources of knowledge, are in their detail unnoticeable, and in Nature's order there is nothing but confusion. But the important parts of all this chaos do not amount to very much; and when order is attained they are easily surveyed. On the other side, the child's own grasp of things—if power in this regard is used with psychological insight—is of infinite importance. At the same time we must make full use of what our ancestors have done for us linguistically. By means of language, distinctness and individuality is given to our sense impressions—in language we have the infinite details of sense already reduced to order and purposeful sequence. It would be egregious folly to make no use of this. My procedure is here determined by the child's ultimate destiny, though I am only thinking of that within the limits of his present physical constitution, into the nature and bounds of which I am concerned to enquire. I am thus brought back again to the *Law of Physical Nearness* as it bears on my sensory experience and my purposeful endeavour.

Surely a child who runs about for an hour to find a tree that grows at his own door will never know a tree. The child who finds no stimulus to effort at home will not find it easily in the outside world, nor will he who is not moved to love by his mother's eye, feel moved to kindness by the tears of men in his journey through the world. The reflecting man becomes an angel if he makes use of the incentives to virtuous behaviour which lie about him; he becomes a devil if these are neglected and other distant stimuli are sought. The things of the world that lie far off cannot help being sources of illusion and error—and therefore of vice. But I must say again that this law operates around a higher law—the law of man's own being, that is, of himself. Self-knowledge is the central point from which instruction must start.[1]

This self-knowledge is, however, of two kinds:—

1. It is the knowledge of my physical constitution (*i.e.* my body). (Vide *Mother's Book*.) This I strive to make the starting-point of instruction.
2. It is the knowledge of my spiritual existence—my individuality; myself as a responsible person, as consciously striving to be true to principles. Mere sensory experience of the environment is not enough to awaken this knowledge. For this reason Nature has implanted within the child confidence in his mother, and the consequent

---

[1] This is of course the guiding principle of *The Mother's Book* (*vide* p. 177 f.), though in this case it is very superficially interpreted.

readiness to obey her; this kind of experience sets up dispositions which make a life devoted to duty easier for him later on.

Nourished at his mother's breast, seeing love in her every glance, dependent upon her for the gratification of his every wish, obedience is for him a physical necessity. It is an easy duty the performance of which gives him great pleasure.

So it is with man. The whirl of his existence and his sensory experiences do not furnish enough motives to induce him to subject himself to a life of duty. To fill up this gap Nature has endowed him with faith in God and the consequent readiness to yield Him obedience; this sort of experience establishes within him the dispositions necessary to steady effort towards self-improvement. In like manner he is nourished in the bosom of Nature, and finds there all his joys. So it comes about that obedience to truth and right, and to his Maker who needs him, is in origin a natural result of his position, in its fulfilment an easy duty, and in its consequences the source of all his pleasures.

For this reason I find the keystone of my plan of instruction in the early development of the sensory stimuli to the fear of God; for though I am sure that religion as a subject of intellectual exercise and instruction is put to bad use, I am equally certain that as an affair of the emotions it is a necessity of my sensory nature in its tenderest years, that as such its pure and ennobling influences can never be called into activity too early. All the prophets from Moses to Christ Himself have connected religious feeling with childlike innocence; they have sought to develop and nourish it through actual experience of Nature as a whole.

I follow in their steps. My instruction is simply a

series of demonstrations of the wisdom and greatness of the Creator, and of the wisdom and greatness of man's nature in so far as he has not degraded it. The carefully worked out methods which I use open the child's eyes to the world; he no longer *suspects* the existence of God, he sees Him and worships Him.

I do not think you can find any surer means of raising unreflecting man to a devout feeling towards God, and to a sense of his own worth. It is my profoundest wish to establish my method of instruction on the foundation of human contentedness. I know that a child brought up without trust in God is like a motherless waif or like an unhappy daughter who has lost her mother's love.

But it is now time to stop. Gentlemen, this is the preliminary sketch of my principles and my methods, which I offer for your careful examination and criticism.

CHAPTER XVIII.

THE PROSPECTUS OF MÜNCHENBUCHSEE (1804).

The circumstances of this prospectus have been described in Chapter VI. It was largely owing to the additions which Fellenberg inserted without the consent of Pestalozzi and his staff that the rupture took place. The text used for the translation is given in Morf, vol. iii., pp. 187-201. It represents what was drawn up and agreed upon before Fellenberg's unauthorised additions.

It should be carefully compared with the *Report to Parents* in the next chapter. Such a comparison will bring out both Pestalozzi's strength and his weakness. Here we have an orderly, almost scientific document, a cold statement of ideals and plans; there Pestalozzi is writing from his heart. He gives us a concrete picture of school realities, not an abstract disquisition.

PROSPECTUS.

In our work we propose to include everything that is really essential to the happiness and well-being of all worthy men. To that end we shall make full use of the natural inclinations and dispositions of the boys.

The happiness and well-being of men depends absolutely upon three conditions :—

(1) Their mental and bodily health and purity, that is to say upon their knowing and doing none of those things which are injurious to either.

(2) Their being strong and capable of looking after themselves in all matters which concern their individual

honour and welfare, or their capacity to maintain their self-respect.

(3) Their serviceableness in the home and in the State; their capacity and willingness to lend the helping hand of fellowship to others.

When these conditions are fulfilled, men are in a position to do their duty to God, to society, and even to the animals, within human limitations. They may expect to satisfy all the needs which properly belong to human nature. They are then what men should be—mature in mind, independent and well disposed, a source of happiness alike to themselves and to others, just as wise parents would wish to see their sons.

Just how independent, how worthy and how useful each individual is depends upon the degree of bodily, intellectual and moral strength which he brings with him into the world. Providence has reserved to himself the power of defining the amount. The educator cannot alter this. He can give nothing that is not there already in germ. Nor can he change the natural order in which each of man's capacities unfolds and develops into power. It is in fact the teacher's most sacred duty to honour and make use of that which God has put into the child, for that is greater and nobler than anything that man can give, or any pedagogic method man may devise. He should build absolutely upon these foundations. He must give free play to the natural course of development and make full and honest use of the means which Nature and man's primitive circumstances provide. By just those means he should plan to stimulate each faculty, put it to active and varied use, give it the necessary direction and thus give it organic form. But besides this separate attention to each faculty, he must bring them into coordinate lines of work and maintain this coordination. He must not produce one-sided men—whether they are practical, intellectual or emotional—but men who are many-sided, cheerful, happy, frank, and sensitive to all that is good, beautiful and true; men who are at peace with themselves and in harmony with all that is purposeful and right about them.

Such is the ideal of the Institutions at Hofwyl and Münchenbuchsee. Their methods, their courses, and indeed all their arrangements are concentrated on its attainment, making allowance for personal limitations of the staff and the means at their disposal. The specific methods adopted are designed, singly and in combination, to stimulate, exercise and train the physical, intellectual and moral sides of our pupils harmoniously. On these foundations they endeavour to instruct the boys with reference to their lives as citizens and as members of particular professions. Above all things we hope the boys will leave us far-seeing, strong and well disposed—capable, that is to say, of leading really human lives; we hope too that parents will be satisfied with what we can do for the welfare of their boys on the side of domestic and vocational training. Such a programme will do much also to meet the urgent needs of our land and of our times, indeed of posterity also. So much harm has been done by the accumulation of useless knowledge and by showy and superficial education on the one hand and by the complete neglect of education on the other, that a speedy remedy is essential.

We hope in all sincerity to accomplish our aim so far as human failings will permit. The more detailed account of our work in each subject is given below.

This should aim to develop, exercise and strengthen the **Physical Education.** bodily powers in order that they may be in a position to carry out the behests of a cultivated mind moved by high ideals. The training begins in movements ; it ends in free open-air life and in social intercourse. At this last stage it is a valuable stimulus to the imagination and indeed to the whole inner life. To come to details.

(i) *Of Bodily Health.* This we hope to ensure by means of suitable dietary and clothing, cleanliness, open-air exercise, and the many-sided activities which *the actual class-room instruction inspires* ; by preventing the boys from adopting bodily attitudes which hinder free physiological activities and check growth ; by means of games, recreation and rest ; by good nursing in sickness, and above all by protecting the boys from impurity and its consequences.

(ii) *Of Exercise and Hardening.* A sequence of exercises beginning with simple and easy and proceeding to complex and difficult movements for individuals and for groups has been arranged, with the object of teaching the boys to use their limbs in harmonious combination ; taking care however not to over-emphasise skill in these exercises for its own sake, but rather to subordinate it to the call of wisdom and love. The pupil will learn to use his body in the service of his mind and of his affections. The work will always have reference to the boys' actual efficiency as members of a community dependent on mutual service.

(iii) *Of deportment and grace in movement.* The special dexterities of movement are not excluded—dancing, boxing, riding. We are, however, anxious to avoid placing a deceptive veneer of politeness and polish upon the boys.

(iv) *Of instruction in Hygiene.* This is connected with the daily life of the boys—thoroughly direct and practical. We tell the boys the rules of health as experience teaches them, but habit is the main thing. Prescriptions and rules are only useful when they express what the child has learned in his own experience. They must be orderly, active, clean, etc., from habit, before we speak to them about such things. This is the only way to keep the boys clear of the dangers to health which are so prevalent in these days.

We aim in this regard to develop and exercise the capacities which make up and give expression **Intellectual Education.** to the understanding and the intelligence. It includes, therefore, everything which is necessary to enable a man to acquire, maintain, and put to use intelligent and clear insight into the problems which press upon him. It begins with simple sensory experience of the things which the child's spontaneous activity brings forward, as soon as he begins to look at, to notice and to describe objects about him.

From the intellectual point of view his original impressions are concerned with Form, Number, Language or Drawing. Either through these things being emphasised by other people or through his own attention to them, he becomes conscious of his own intellectual existence, and at the same time he becomes aware of the external use of the eye, the hand, and his vocal organs. As his powers of observant attention increase, or as his knowledge of the relations which develop out of form, number and speech, and his power to describe these relations grow, he advances to understanding ; when he has grasped these relationships in their entirety he has attained to intelligence. His concrete work with these elements carries with it the exercise and development of all his other intellectual powers—memory, discrimination, imagination, judgment, etc. His work at the various subjects of the curriculum continues the same processes in unbroken connection. The subjects include all those which an educated man must know, as well as those which are conventionally required and useful and those which are necessary for particular professions.

The first instrument for intellectual development on these lines concerns the observation of form.   This includes—

(1) *The capacity to apprehend and to describe visible objects.*   For this purpose we have a collection of mathematical models of different shapes and construction.   The pupils take them to pieces and put them together, they name the lines, figures, angles, surfaces, etc.   Thus they learn to name, describe and compare accurately the shapes of objects which they happen to come across.

(2) *The capacity to apprehend Form in and for itself, with corresponding exercises, making use of the eye and of the hand and of the power to define the proportions of each form considered.*

For this purpose we have our own A B C of observation.   It begins with the straight line.   The pupils learn for themselves the various positions which one, two, three or four lines may occupy one towards another, and to describe them.   In this exercise head, eye, hand and speech are employed.   They must find out everything without exception.   It is really very easy, because each step forward involves only a very slight addition to what has gone before.   At the same time they learn to measure by means of the square each of these forms and to express it in numbers.   Similarly they compare the forms in respect of size, shape, the number and division of their parts, etc., using algebraic symbols to that end.

(3) *They are thus led directly to Geometry.*

Their previous work has prepared them admirably, but only those go on who like the subject or who need it vocationally.   A specialist teacher has the subject in hand.   Those who do not proceed, have already had a sufficient training in recognising, estimating and measuring forms, proportions and sizes for all the necessities of ordinary life.

The second instrument for intellectual development which we use concerns number—equally original with form in human activity.

(1) As to consciousness of number.

This takes place with sensory objects; in very young children with the parts of the body, the fingers especially. We also make use of a series of squares. We put these together, divide them, compare sum with sum—in general we make the changes and numerical comparisons in a continuously and gradually ascending order of difficulty without noticeable breaks.

(2) The actual apprehension of Number relations.

The series and the devices employed are described in the Pestalozzi Elementary Books. This activity carries the pupil into the realms of pure thought—he thinks himself and steadily acquires power. He learns what absolute unity is as opposed to divisible wholes, and to divide, compare and build up wholes by means of parts of steadily increasing complexity—thus he gains the capacity to define the relationships in such complexes. He does everything that intelligence can suggest in this direct dealing with number. He learns perfectly the real value of each number or of the wholes and of their parts. He solves exceedingly complex problems with extraordinary ease and accuracy, once he has gained the mastery of number relations. The objection that this is a mere mechanical task is too foolish to reply to.

(3) Of written Arithmetic.

The rules, etc., have all been unconsciously used in the oral work. Progress will therefore be easy when the figures, etc., are familiar. He not only knows the rules, he sees their necessity, *i.e.* how they follow from the actual nature of number. Any other kind of arithmetic is mechanical; it has no claim to offer an intellectual training.

(4) Algebra stands in the same relation to arithmetic as geometry to the A B C of observation.

(5) The applications of arithmetic include bookkeeping and such other work as is necessary to the higher branches of industry.

The third instrument for intellectual training of which we make especial use here is Language. This demands

(1) Exercises in the perception of sensory details. This is necessary to description and actually gives it occasion.

In these exercises we teach our boys to attend carefully to and to name the various sensory qualities of the objects about them—colour, form, etc. We begin with the body itself. Work in this direction gives them as it were a type of the complexity and many-sidedness of other objects which will be brought to their notice. They will learn from it how to look at other things in every possible way. The little wonder-world which they discover in themselves is extraordinarily stimulating. Learning appropriate names gives them a rich vocabulary for the description of other things. They learn to know themselves thoroughly, the foundation of all other knowledge. They rise to the idea of what they can and ought to be amongst other things, and to understand what is everywhere available for their activity, their insight, their needs and their duty. They cannot but think about these things under such circumstances. They learn to know the tools which they must use when they undertake to examine an object. They know what an exhaustive examination means. From the body itself they go to objects around them—selecting those which they ought to know well. It should be noted further that, after the first exercises, even the body itself cannot be described without reference to a crowd of other objects.

(2) Exercises in speech are inseparable from the above.
We give the boys practice calculated to teach them to
express themselves easily on any occasion. They must, to
that end, learn to articulate clearly and to use words in
their right sense. This comes partly from always requiring
them to repeat after their teachers. This they do in
rhythm; the impression on their minds is so much clearer,
the pleasure and stimulus from the volume of sound is so
much greater, and their vocal organs are proportionately
strengthened. The work consists of a series of exercises
in utterance, beginning with the speech elements, and
leading up to the complete mastery of their combinations.
The *first* exercises consist of elementary sounds and their
combinations into every variety of syllable—the aim being
to stimulate independent power in making new changes
and combinations, and to make the boys fluent and unhesi-
tating in the clear use of the right pronunciation.

The *second* step is to teach them words. We begin with
nouns to which other words are added until small sentences
are formed, by means of which the pupils are made
familiar with all kinds of words. No word is used unless
it has a meaning in the child's own experience, and unless
the pupils themselves have provided it, that they may
acquire the habit in later life of always looking for the meanings which lie behind the words that pour into their ears.
To that end they need lessons in the observation of word
relations—training, that is to say, in detailed verbal
description of visible objects in order to learn to use and
to understand accurately words which have reference to
objects or their logical relations.

(3) Along with these exercises, the pupils learn to read
both printed and written texts.

(4) We teach writing from the point of view of clearness, primness, beauty and rapidity.

(5) Grammar and spelling are connected with all this work.

(6) The syntactical side of grammar is also taught in connection with the above. It is, of course, nothing but a practical exercise of the intelligence.

(7) The last stage in the teaching of language from the point of view of intelligence as well as the starting-point for history and for the study of present realities is the Dictionary (?).

All that is said above is carried through in French and German. Latin and Greek will also be taught to those who ask for it.

In addition the following subjects are taught:—

1. Geography.

2. Natural History.

3. Physics and Chemistry (*Naturlehre*).

4. History.

5. Incidentally we may mention the Biographies of Great Men with which we make our pupils acquainted, in the hope of putting in their minds a picture of man's higher life and thus of showing them concretely what they have to strive for and what to avoid. Here intellectual and moral education meet.

In the education of the heart we hope to succeed through **Moral Education.** methods designed to awaken, exercise and further the development of those powers and points of view which make up and express the good will. Nothing is neglected which has a bearing on this problem. We take our start in the feelings and affections which the mother has already implanted in her child through the loving care he has enjoyed at her hands. The essential feelings looked for are love, gratitude and confidence. He becomes conscious of these feelings through the continuance of maternal care.

Experience of her kindly and unselfish behaviour, or of that of his parents and guardians in general, gives the boy a sense of morality; experience of their piety awakens religious feelings in his heart.

This development can only take place when all the capacities and all the activities that belong to morality are duly developed. This advance proceeds in line with his advancing intelligence—in this union the child grows in wisdom.

To make morality and religion play their part in the life of the boys is the most sacred part of our work. Success depends primarily upon—

1. Stimulating those feelings of love, gratitude and confidence which are fundamental to morality and religion.

2. Finding connected means of putting to practical service the principles and points of view to which those feelings give rise.

3. Moral and religious instruction.

(a) The feelings of love, gratitude and confidence— the holy ground on which alone virtue and reverence germinate and flourish—are aroused and fixed in the child through the sense of being kindly treated and of being taken care of. Our first care is therefore to work on those lines.

(b) Next we endeavour to put these feelings to practical expression—to raise them, that is to say, to the moral level. Love must become obedience and power to conquer the self; gratitude must become devotion, confidence must become reverence. At this point the boy does not yet know the law of duty; indeed, he has no idea of the word, nor can words supply the idea. He must first see this law in personified form—in the person of his tutor. We try therefore to lead him, through example, to the moral attitude of mind, in order that we may call upon him unconditionally to do his whole duty to himself and to others whatever effort and sacrifice it may cost. All our work on the intellectual side is the greatest help. It is so completely in accordance with his own nature that the pupil falls into it without question or difficulty.

The calls of duty are widened by his intercourse with companions of all ages, not forgetting the animals entrusted to his care.

(c) Our third object is to see that he makes use of his opportunities. Love must be transformed into sympathy in joy and in sorrow, gratitude into effort to return the "kindness" he has received, confidence into willing recognition of mutual rights. Through actual experience our boys must learn to do to others as they would be done by. The sense of right and of duty which awakes in the boy through his intercourse with parent and teacher begins to take clear form in his mind as a law of his nature, as an unmistakable demand of his inner life. His conscience has been stimulated into effective life.

As we endeavour to develop the true spirit of morality in the boys, so we try through words to make their ideas on the subject explicit and clear. Moral instruction is based absolutely upon their inner experience. They are made clear about what they ought to do and to be in respect of themselves, and what they should do and be to others. We try to put them into the position in which the moral ideal burns within them and leads them to exert their whole strength to its attainment. In this way they are brought quite naturally to revere and obey the behests of duty and conscience. The ideal is separated from its personal embodiment, and the boys realise that they are rendering obedience to their own higher nature. There remains only one step more to take in order that their goodness of heart shall open out to all men, that they may conceive the idea of the moral worth of human nature, that their love may become entirely self-forgetful and self-sacrificing in its warmth, that their gratitude may lead to the recognition of the sacred rights of others and to a struggle against irregular and unworthy conduct, that their confidence may develop into indestructible faith in truth, right, virtue, and holiness.

But religion alone can do this. In religion man sees his race in its perfection and does it reverence. Only in religion does man realise himself and his fellows as cast in the image of God, then only does he feel that duty, truth, and right are divine institutions to which he must devote his whole life.

Religion is only possible when the foundations of love, gratitude and confidence are safely laid in the heart. These feelings give the desire for things not of this world. We therefore strive to establish these feelings in their simple sincerity. Then we try to win them Godwards. The Father-word of God, the simplest and loftiest idea of Christianity, is the first thing to be implanted in boys in whom you wish religion to develop.

Then we try to make this child-like attitude to God habitual in the boys. We teach them to see God around them and to feel Him in their hearts. The good mother is our model. It is in an atmosphere like this that, morning and evening, an address and prayers are held.

To raise the religious attitude of mind to its loftiest and worthiest, we lead the boys to contemplate our Lord Himself. Instruction in Christian doctrine is given by special teachers. The children of Catholic parents are taught by a priest in the neighbourhood.

Aesthetic Development. Aesthetic development and the education of taste in our judgment follow from the harmonious education of body and mind. The joys of complete freedom in his corporate outdoor games stimulate and embolden his imagination. Gradually developing intelligence reveals to the mind the harmony of the outer relationships of the beautiful and constitutes the necessary foundation for the skilful use of the eye, the hand and the voice in recognising, understanding and creating those relationships. The education of the heart means teaching it to recognise and to give form to everything in itself beautiful, noble and divine; it is based on enthusiastic and devoted love.

Those who object to our methods, on the ground that they weaken the sense for the beautiful, seem to have neither a real grasp of its spirit nor a knowledge of its connection with man's essential needs and with the foundations of the beautiful.

We have seen that physical education must be based on the development of mind and heart; so it is with the education of the taste. Only in that way does it bring harmony into life, such as we desire; only then is beauty of outward form the fitting dwelling-place of a noble soul.

To make our procedure in this respect clear, we give details concerning the special points and special dexterities which enter into our programme.

The elements of the various practical dexterities—the only ones which can be clearly apprehended and demonstrated—spring from the same source and the same period of time as the elements of intellectual power. In form it is the curved line, in number it is rhythm, in language it is song. Here are the simple starting-points, provided by Nature, of man's capacity for giving expression to the beautiful.

To attain to power we must give practice in observing these elements accompanied by practical exercise in form, number and speech.

(1) The first (form) comes through drawing, by which we mean linear drawing and drawing from objects, which our pupils soon excel in. They draw straight and curved lines of all kinds on slates. From these lines they build up their own designs, so that the hand gets practice in every kind of movement, and their imaginative powers find stimulus and free play. Then they proceed to the imitation of mathematical forms with the special object of making eye measurements; sometimes their drawings are of equal size, sometimes they show proportional changes; the models are drawn from every possible point of view. They do the outlines first, and later on shading and perspective.

(2) From this type of exercise the children pass to the sketching of landscape, to making rough sketches and models of anything; in short we wish to impress so deeply upon them the things they see that they can make use of the impressions at any time.

(3) How the development of artistic drawing takes place from these beginnings is clear.

Its progressive steps are light and easy to define. We have a special teacher for those boys whose talent warrants further development. He aims at introducing the boys to independent work. But do we not need an A B C of forms of beauty, starting from the curved line? We leave the point for artists to deal with.

(4) We do not neglect the aesthetic training given by song. We think it as important for the contentedness, cheerfulness and higher life of the soul as it is for forms of worship. The rhythmic movements, the choice of songs and poems, the common effort, everything tends to mould

the plastic minds of the boys in wise and virtuous directions. Choral music strengthens the social bond. Dancing
is related to this work. We treat it as the poetry of
gesture.

(5) Rhythm is necessarily bound up with movement,
song and poetry. The union leads to the full enjoyment
of the beautiful. The poetic sense is awakened through
free and happy life in nature and in warmth of heart;
poetic power comes through language which enables us to
communicate our feelings to others.

This is the threefold foundation of the higher life; to
it we add the reading aloud of carefully chosen poetry,
the simpler the better, as affording a clear union of nature
and of mind.

CHAPTER XIX.

Report to Parents.[1]

I have for a long time felt the necessity of writing a
general report to the parents of my pupils in
order to give them a short, but, as far as possible, a definite and clear statement of my
educational principles, of the point of view from which my
present methods are directed, and of my opinions, needs,
hopes, and expectations in general. They ought, I feel, to
know the present position of the institute which embodies
my principles, the condition of the children and of everything which could directly concern them. I should like
at the same time to tell them the feelings which move my
heart towards them, and to call upon them for intimate
co-operation in all our work. I hope in this way to put
them in a position to form a right judgment concerning
matters which touch them so nearly, and, at the same
time, to reassure them where there might be misunderstanding or doubt in regard to the children entrusted to
my care. Moreover, the constant increase in the number
of enquiries which reach us from so many sources compels
me to provide for the general public a summary account of
the school and what it stands for.

Owing to want of leisure, I have tried to meet both
needs at once. I hope, nevertheless, that parents may

Object of the Report.

[1] The translation is from the text of Seyffarth (vol. x., pp. 331-61).
Vide p. 107.

accept the document as a token of affection and confidence, and that interested enquirers may accept it as a partial fulfilment of my intention to make what I have done and hope still to do as helpful to others as possible, until I am in a position to publish a more complete and connected account of the school.

From the outset we have had many difficulties to over-come—want of money in the first instance, and **Early Diffi-** adverse public opinion in the second. People **culties and** **Criticisms.** thought neither I nor my colleagues were equal to the undertaking. Many asserted that the reputation of my early experiments was based on a flimsy illusion. I was a charlatan whom profounder men would very soon expose. Men who, by common consent, were hard-headed took it for granted that I should accomplish nothing. Men discussed among themselves why this should be so.

Some said there was nothing in it beyond a simple little mechanism for teaching children to reel off alphabets and multiplication tables. Others thought that the children did nothing but memorise. Even the difficult mathe-matical problems which they seemed to solve spontaneously were nothing but memorised results, and, of course, this stupefied their other intellectual powers. The under-standing in particular was sacrificed to the memory. Others would have it that the children's imagination suffered most in the attainment of such wonderful skill in dealing with figures. In like fashion, it was urged by others that our methods would make the handwriting of the boys altogether wooden. They said it would end in everybody's writing being precisely alike, to the utter con-fusion of our social relations.

Another type of critic seriously believed that we stimu-lated the intellect too much, thereby running the risk of confusing the child; that we did not appeal sufficiently to memory, for children learned nothing by heart; they could repeat no stories, historical or mythological, no grammatical rules, no catechism, and for that reason difficulties arose when it was necessary to transfer a child to another school. Even the emotions were sacrificed to the intellect. Some said that we neither had nor taught any religion; others that we were revolutionary in our politics; some thought indeed I was a tool of the Jesuits, and some . . . but I have given enough of these judgments to show how the most essential and obvious matters can be misinterpreted and misrepresented with superficial perversity by men who do not wish to understand.

For the most part, however, these errors have now been given up. Men began later on to look into our work more closely, and they admitted that there was good in it. Still, a large number of our critics thought the "natural education" which we stood for was only fit for little children, that it would be best if the pupils were removed at ten and taught on other lines the subjects of a conventional education. In their view the Institute was merely a preparatory school. The instruction that was given was so easy and attractive that there was reason to fear the boys would quail before the more difficult work.

Others thought, however, that such an education as we gave was fit only for the children of the poor. The children of the wealthier people should not be taught in the "natural way," but in accordance with accepted traditions, for they were destined at some time or other to live in a world which took such and such for granted. On the other hand, many held the opposite view and thought that such a slowly progressing education, which aimed at the harmonious development and training of all the children's powers, belonged exclusively to the higher classes; it would be a national calamity if the children of the common people were educated in this way.

The harm which this conflict of opinion might have caused was, thank God, avoided. The mere fact of the existence of the Institute has appealed to so many distinguished men that people nowadays speak respectfully of it and of the ideas which it represents. Men of deserved reputation have examined our principles from all sides, and what they have yet to say rests on enquiries concerning which irresponsible gossip is now usually silent. The struggle therefore grows both keener and more honourable every day.

And as to the Institute itself, we are surely in a position to say that, after passing safely through the fire of eight years' criticism, it has not been found wanting. We may quietly rest our case on the testimony of all those who have taken the trouble to enquire into our work carefully and without prejudice. We can say to the world with a good conscience : Our children are thoroughly happy; their native innocence is unimpaired, their religion is strengthened, their minds have been developed, their knowledge has increased, and their feelings have been ennobled. Our arrangements to these various ends have the quiet force which comes from the devotion and love of the teachers, supported as it is by their inspiring energy. The spirit of a great household rules the place ; it is everywhere illumined by paternal and filial feelings. The children feel free; their occupations are such as stimulate the love of doing; their loyalty and confidence are unbounded.

I should like, first of all, in a word or two to touch on the steps we take to ensure the welfare of individual children as well as of the general body and to describe our arrangements for the moral and religious education of the pupils.

The life of the house is, in the fullest sense of the words,
stimulating and instructive ; this does not
The School refer to the transitory quickening of interest
Household. in particular directions, nor do I mean instructive merely in the school sense of that word.   Beyond all
such limitations, the life of the place quickens the whole
disposition of the children ; their instruction is natural,
arising as it does from the freedom and independence enjoyed by all ; the school is a picture of home-like loyalty
and unity on a very large scale.   The majority of the
teachers live all day with the children as though they were
of them, in full community of mind and heart, of interest,
and of effort.   They live, eat and sleep in the same rooms.
All the details which directly concern the well-being of the
children are, for the most part, in the teachers' own hands.
They look after the rooms, the apparatus for teaching, the
children's clothes, their cleanliness, health, etc.   In this
way they are brought into intimate and varied relations
with the children, and their influence is wider than the
walls of the class-room.

One and all, we do for every one of our many children what
the careful mother does for her small family.   Our educational machinery has only a value in so far as it approaches
the character of a well-ordered house in all its details.
Our teachers wake the children ; they are present when they
get up and when they dress ; they observe their bodily condition and the state of their clothes ; they see to their personal cleanliness ; they place them in rows twice a day and
examine their apparel ; they accompany them to morning and
evening prayers, take their meals with them, go with them
into the playground, join in their games, take walks with
them—in short, they never leave them out of school hours
except when they are in bed and asleep.   All the unmarried
teachers live in the house and sleep in the dormitories.

Such is the general relation of the teachers to the pupils and to the household needs. For purpose of oversight and in order to give the necessary relief to individual teachers, the staff is divided into three sections which take supervision duty in daily turns. Each third day the same section is on duty. In this way, all the teachers become familiar with the general needs of the place as the centre of common life, and with the individual dispositions of the pupils. I lay particular emphasis on these things in order to show how we try to give the institution the characteristic features of home, both for teachers and pupils. It is a home education we are aiming at, such as ensures the really warm sympathy of everybody for everybody, and thus develops in each individual genuine interest in the whole organisation.

The pupils are further divided for more particular supervision. Each of the older teachers takes charge of twelve to fifteen boys who are handed over to him as his special care. He is their particular tutor and they address themselves to him in all their difficulties and in all their wants. The teacher is expected to use this position in such a way as to make himself intimately acquainted with all that is necessary to the happiness of the child as a child and as a human being.

Once a week, after supper, a masters' meeting is held; these meetings often last several hours. One week we discuss the curriculum and the methods of teaching; another time we are concerned with the progress and position of individual pupils, and so on, alternately. At one meeting reports on particular branches of instruction are read and discussed, at the next reports on the children are similarly dealt with.

Masters' Meetings.

Discussion between me and my staff on these occasions is absolutely free and unreserved. Each teacher is glad to lay his experience, his observations, his particular opinions and wishes before his colleagues, with whom he may then talk them over in complete confidence. Observations and decisions arrived at are entered into books kept for that purpose, and the reports to parents on individual pupils are based on these discussions. The free interchange of views is particularly helpful in the further development of the teachers themselves. Such perfect community of sentiment and action results from them, that to the pupils the staff appears as one person.

In this way, too, it is possible for the best amongst the teachers to understand the individuality of the children in the same direct way as an intelligent mother understands her child. Similarly our procedure prevents the partial treatment of and hasty judgment about the solitary expressions and actions of individual children. The teacher is not dazzled by a child who appears on occasion in a particularly favourable light. Nor is he misled into wrongful severity through occasional lapses. He learns to distinguish apparent from real strength, a transient inclination from a definite disposition. He can be fair, and he is so, because he has grasped the child's nature and estimates the significance of any particular action or attitude in the light of the boy's character and capacity as a whole. He never loses sight of this.

The general interchange of impressions concerning the boys ensures not only a sound and trustworthy view of present character and outlook, but, through bringing physical and mental condition into relation, we find out the times and circumstances in which the child made no progress or seemed indeed to be going backwards, and we observe the noteworthy influence of age and health upon the mind and vice versa, as well as the mistakes that arise through the false conclusions of one or other teacher.

Generally speaking, the benefit that comes to the teacher from these meetings in all matters which concern his judgment of the children is infinitely important.

Besides these two weekly meetings of the teachers, they foregather every Saturday after supper in order to bring together the observations they have made in the course of the week on the children, the instruction, and the necessities that have arisen in this connection. At this meeting the more external sides of the common life of the boys are considered and the way in which they take their part therein—we discuss everything which should properly be brought to public notice.

The records of our meetings furnish subject-matter for my addresses to the whole school. These are School Assemblies. designed to bring before the school the general regulations in force, to warn against mistakes and to call for improvements in special directions. This assembly takes place on Sunday evenings. I generally take advantage of the occasion to dwell upon the progress that is being made, but, whilst emphasising the good, I also call attention to dangers which it is necessary to avoid; should a child need personal exhortation, it is given as judiciously and gently as possible, so as to arouse better ideas without causing him unnecessary pain. But I use this means of correction very rarely, and always avoid particularisation. On this account it has been extraordinarily successful.

In addition to all this I myself live in intimate and unbroken personal intercourse with all the teachers; with each one of them I talk confidentially about his work, about himself, and the duties of his post. I do the same thing with the children. Once a week each tutor brings his particular group of boys to me, having previously given me a private report upon them. At these times I am careful to speak to them simply and as a father might do, drawing their attention to points in which they are not progressing, leading them in all earnestness and love to a sense of these things, teaching them to be conscientiously critical of themselves, to be sincerely sorry for their past mistakes, and to make good resolutions for the future. Usually they promise solemnly, often with tears in their eyes, to continue to be diligent, attentive, and, on necessary occasions, to improve. I meet two small groups every day in this way.

Further, I take prayers with all the children morning and evening. This service usually begins with a hymn of praise. In my address I try to put before them, in ways that they will remember, those ideas which are best calculated to arouse and to encourage earnestness, piety, and wisdom.

On Sundays the children attend the German or French service in the city church. Besides this, the **Religious Instruction and Exercises.** older children have two lessons a week for religious instruction. We follow the line laid down in the Bible, namely, that of the religious development of the human race, from the Mosaic beginnings to the teachings of Jesus Christ as given in the Gospels. We make the Sermon on the Mount the basis of the doctrine of duty, and the Gospel of St. John the basis of our teaching of faith. These are read in connection with each other, and explained by means of the text itself, and from Christ's own words about God and about Himself as God's representative on earth, and as representing in His person the relationship of Man to God and of God to Man. Through Christ and His example, through the way in which He regarded and dealt with things and with men, we try to awaken in the children a lofty sense of the eternal realities of religion, in the hope that God may reveal Himself in them as He revealed Himself in Christ. We do not controvert religious heresies ; we only try to implant the spirit of true religion. We seek the foundation of dogma and of all religious opinion in the essential character of religion in human nature, its impulses, its relationships, its capacities and its necessities, in order that the children may recognise the truth in any disguise, and grasp the essentials in any form.

Our methods in the preparatory stage of religious instruction are based on the answers to the following questions :—

(1) What elements of true religion are native in men— what germs of true religion has God implanted in him ?

These elements are man's intuitive feelings.

(2) How are these feelings awakened to life and revealed to consciousness ?

The specific agencies in this matter are the child's intercourse with his parents, with Nature, and with society.

(3) In what way do these feelings find expression once they are awakened ? And in what directions do they tend ?

Religious feelings are expressed in our demeanour, religious ideas are expressed in words, religious experience is expressed in symbols. The first appears as, or is developed into, ceremonious institutions, the second becomes the subject of instruction, the third develops into image worship. In the course of these changes the development of all that is eternally true in religion is intimately bound up with that which leads to sensuous degeneracy, painful error, gross superstition and unbelief, to godlessness and contempt for all that is holy. The immature child finds the key to clear insight in regard to these things in his intuitive knowledge of his own feelings, in his attitude towards things, and in the religious institutions and sentiments in the midst of which he lives. The whole truth is to be found from the outset in the history of religion. The method of presenting it to the children is ready to hand in the language of the people. With this means at our disposal, we must make up our minds on this point: the child must obtain a grasp of the eternal truth in its very foundations; he must learn to regard himself and men generally as essentially religious, and to picture man as an organic whole, self-developing in accordance with divine law. Knowing of man's fall from God in the beginning and in his later developments, he must devote himself the more to the cause of return to God and to life in Him in order that the true meaning of the Gospel may be revealed in him, and that his inner life may be holy, as his outer life is intelligent.

The more sacred this matter is to us, the more devotedly we busy ourselves in regard to it, and the higher our aim is, the more do we owe it to the parents of our children and to the general public to explain that we are still far from its attainment, and that in these indications we think we have only pointed to a method of religious instruction which is capable of further development, and is in accordance with the unchangeable laws that underlie education. In some such way as this, we are in confident hope that we shall be able shortly to bring our practice into line with our ideals and with the general progress of instruction in the Institution. Nor shall we neglect to made known what we have done, and our judgment thereon, so soon as it has reached sufficiently ripe a stage.

The older pupils may also be prepared in the Institute for Holy Communion; to that end they receive special religious instruction for six months. This is, at the moment, going on with a group of fourteen boys.

In general, I may say that we try to wake and to foster the spirit of peace, of love, and of brotherly helpfulness. Things are going well with the house as a whole. Everywhere there breathes a spirit of peace and of effort. Much in our midst is really excellent. Some of our boys have angel hearts full of love and the promise of a higher life. Evil does not accord with what we do and what we stand for: on the other hand, every trace of good which is present even in ill-doing finds such encouragement and nurture as is its due. We do not harden the disposition of our children by punishments, nor do we make them superficial and vain by rewards. The gentleness of the tenderest home life pervades the whole school. The children are not lightly injured. The weaker ones are not encouraged to compare themselves with the stronger. We never ask a child " Can you do what so and so can do ? " We only ask him " Can you do this ? " And then " Can you finish this ? " Quarrels are as rare between our children as between brothers and sisters who are fortunate enough to have an affectionate mother. The range of views, of feelings, and of talents which comes to light amongst the many members of the house is very wide ; it all contributes to the general spirit of harmony and freedom.

It cannot be otherwise. The size of the establishment, the absolute necessity of strong effort, the variety of characters all working, in the light of their special capacities and interests, in a spirit of unity towards a common end, make an environment far richer than the home, in the stimulus and material it offers for individual development. There is, of course, a wide difference between the most senior and the most junior members of the school community, both in respect of age and of training. But, in spite of that, there is no obvious gap, for the intervening stages

The Training of Character.

are all filled up. Each individual finds the particular
environment he needs for the satisfaction of his own
powers. The boy who needs young and cheerful com-
panionship finds it in children of his own age and in the
younger teachers, full as they are of good spirits, adaptable, kindly, and encouraging. In a like way, the older
teachers provide the atmosphere of quiet strength which
is best for the boys who take a serious view of life and of
their own future. This is a point of vital import in an
educational organisation which aims at being at once
human and complete. Our experience in this regard must
influence other residential schools very considerably.

The womenfolk of the establishment work in unison with
our general pleasure. My wife takes charge of the younger
children, and takes especial pleasure in gathering them round
her to comfort and encourage them. My daughter-in-law,
Frau Custer, herself the mother of several children, devotes
herself to the physical care of all the others with as much
devotion as if they were her own children; in which work
she is assisted by a first-rate practical person, who has
been in the service of my household for thirty years. I
have noticed with pleasure that the maid-servants themselves improve, their ideals of work and of conduct are
affected by the spirit which pervades the establishment.

In quite a special way also we endeavour to watch over
and make use of the social relationships of the boys in
order to humanise them in the best and widest sense of
the word. All important events, all festivals, all changes
afford opportunities for bringing to their notice in a concrete and impressive way the sacredness of the bonds
which unite men. These extraordinary occasions only
emphasise the things that belong to their daily experiences,
but this connection of the ordinary with the rare gives

them a truer view of actual life ; by bringing their customary intercourse into connection with things outstanding and noble, it raises their whole conception of what life
can offer for them to think about. To this sort of thing
we ascribe the kindly warmth of feeling which prevails,
and which, in happy moments, as we often find, rises in
many to the point of an enthusiasm which bears fruit in
producing victories over self, and in detailed and patient
effort in the common cause.

We make absolutely no difference in the treatment of
our children owing to external and fortuitous difference
between them. We recognise, in this regard, no advantage of one child above another, except such as is based
on purity of will and effort to self-realisation. We honour
the humanity in each child in an equal degree. We are
far from wishing to put limits on outstanding ability.
But we desire as little to favour such ability at the
expense of any other boy, and we think we owe it to the
parents, to the children and to ourselves to watch over
the dull child and the clever child in such a way that
each may become all that is possible for him, and that all
the capacity with which Nature has endowed him may
be unfolded. The same principle applies in the relationships of teachers and pupils. Each stands for what he
is. Each is just what he makes of himself. Each takes
the position among his fellows which Nature decides for
him. He takes no other rank than that which he wins
through his insight, activity, and love. To that extent he
is certainly recognised, and we have many striking
examples of the regard and influence which distinguished
pupils possess, and of the respect and honour in which
they are held. Such distinction is accidental. It is not
a favour. It is not the gift of fortune or of disposition,
nor is it the result of anything external. It is, on the

other hand, the free natural result of virtue which is
unselfconscious, and, for that reason, also unpresuming.

This account of the present arrangements for the care
of the children, for their proper treatment, for the recognition of their individual characteristics and needs, for
the preservation of their innocence and for the elevation
of their feelings, and the statement of certain fundamental
principles on which these arrangements are based, will
give to our friends a concrete picture of our efforts to turn
out good, manly, and religious men.

But, whilst I regard these endeavours as fundamental
and as the ultimate measure of the value of
our Institution, it should be understood that
the physical welfare of our boys is in no way
allowed to suffer. Our arrangements for preserving the
Institution from danger in this respect are not less carefully thought out. As to food, it is simple, sufficient,
and nourishing. For breakfast the boys have soup, a
different kind each day. For the midday meal we provide a very good soup made from meat, joint, and vegetables, and bread in unlimited quantities, and a glass of
wine. At four o'clock seasonable fruit and bread is served.
For supper at eight o'clock we give them soup, vegetables,
or milk puddings, and, twice a week, meat, with as much
bread as they wish, but no wine.

The general health and appearance of our boys strikes
everybody as extraordinarily good. It is sufficient to say
that not one boy has died here since we settled in Yverdun,
although our numbers have risen from sixty to close on
one hundred and fifty. Illness is very rare, and many
delicate boys have improved in health in quite an astonishing way. We are, moreover, fortunate in having an excellent doctor at hand, as well as a famous spa in our near
neighbourhood where the children can take baths occa-

Care of
Health.

sionally, even in winter. Whenever a child complains of feeling ill the doctor's advice is sought, and the boy is nursed in a special room by my daughter-in-law and her assistant, who has had much experience in these matters. Further, the children are kept clean and well kempt by daily washing and combing, and by frequent changes of linen.

We ascribe the good health of the boys not only to care in matters of food and cleanliness, but also and especially to the free active life which they lead the day through, even in their lessons, but more particularly in recreation times. Though much depends on the organisation of the Institution and on the activities of the teachers, it is natural that the children's own doings make the most difference in achieving the physical and intellectual results at which education aims. Free activity, order and regularity, well regulated effort, the proper alternation of work and play and of subjects of instruction, the proper regulation of the hours of sleep and so on, must necessarily be provided for them. I think I can give a short and clear picture of these things as they affect my boys from day to day. It is as follows :—

The first lesson begins at six in the morning. At seven o'clock prayers are held. Afterwards the children wash and make themselves tidy in preparation for the personal inspection which follows. This is done in small groups, each in charge of an older boy of recognised carefulness. Afterwards comes breakfast. At eight o'clock classes begin again, and go on until twelve. For a quarter of an hour the children are now free, after which follows dinner. When the meal is over, the boys are free until half-past one, when lessons begin again and continue until half-past three. From half-past three to five they are free once more, during which time they have their third meal.

After this, and until eight o'clock, they are in class; supper is at eight; prayers and bed follow immediately.

Of course, the healthy situation of Yverdun and of the castle in particular contributes a great deal to the health of the school. The town lies on Lake Neuchatel, in a pleasant valley swept constantly by health-bringing winds from the north and east. Yverdun has the reputation of being unhealthy, but this is a complete mistake. All sorts of arrangements have been made to drain the swamps left by the diminishing lake, and it is a fact that, during the last twelve years, infectious diseases and recurrent fevers have been less frequent here than in neighbouring towns, and the death rate is lower than it is elsewhere. Nor are the children's ailments more frequent than in other places, the best proof of which is the good health of the school.

Our method of teaching, and the freedom we give in the lessons themselves, account largely for the cheerful vivacity of the boys. If you recognise the absolute necessity of movement and speech to children, and you know, at the same time, how these native impulses are repressed in the ordinary schools where silence and order reign, then you will understand how we avoid this evil by our procedure. We make the first advances in education and in instruction, and escape the pitfalls commonly attendant on both.

In recreation times we devote ourselves to the physical life of the boys. During the summer's heat we give the evenings from six to eight to this side of our work. The teachers on duty for the day take the boys for a walk, or, in summer, for a bathe; in winter they go sliding and skating on the snow and ice. The lake is perfectly safe, as the water is not more than three or four feet deep for more than a hundred

Physical Training.

yards from the side—and the water does not freeze beyond the shallow margin. When none of these things are possible, the boys go to the public square, which is admirably suited for physical exercises. There they divide up into groups and enter vigorously into self-chosen games or exercises. The teachers are with them, and add to the boys' enjoyment by playing amongst them on the common footing. In bad weather physical exercises are taken in the castle itself on the plan which is detailed in the *Wochenschrift*.[1] The school is, for this purpose, divided into five groups with a teacher in charge of each. Attention, adroitness and endurance are the chief points kept in mind in these exercises. The after-noons of Wednesday and Sunday are given up to long walks, which harden the boys' muscles and introduce them to the joys of wild nature. The keenness and fulness of each day's doings makes bedtime welcome. The boys are tired without being exhausted or over-heated; they quickly fall asleep. It is this which is, in our view, the most important factor in preserving the purity of their minds and the soundness of their health.

When parents desire it, special instruction is given in deportment, in dancing, in fencing, and especially in military drill. Already there are eighty boys in the cadet corps in charge of a teacher who has been satisfactorily through the military school of Lausanne. He is keen about the work, and the boys are extremely fond of their captain.

I take this opportunity of informing parents that I am in a position to provide muskets and cartridge pouches at an exceedingly low price. The fees for the military train-ing are so low as to be not worth considering in comparison

---

[1] *Vide* p. 106.

with the advantage to be derived from it—at any rate, as
it is carried on here.   Three months ago I introduced a
uniform for the school as a whole, and I should be grateful
if parents would help me in the matter,—trousers and
coat of grey cloth, without facings ; overcoat in another
colour and of different material ; black stockings.   The
uniform will help in the cultivation of *esprit de corps*, and
simplify the work of supervision.   Whilst I should be glad
if parents would approve of this new regulation, I wish it
to be understood that they are quite free to do as they
like in the matter.   Boys who do not wear the prescribed
uniform will suffer in no way.   On the other hand, I may
say that we can provide the uniforms here at a low rate to
those children whose parents desire it.   Our orders are
given for large quantities, and each suit is provided with
an extra piece of cloth for mending.   In this way considerable economy is effected.   Uniforms will only be
provided on the receipt of a definite order from the
parents.

What I have now said will, I hope, suffice to assure
everybody that the organisation and equipment
of the school is such as to merit to the full the
rank of an " Educational Establishment."
But on the side of instruction opinion is not
so united.   On the contrary, we are always meeting objections—old ones over again at times, despite what we have
written and proved ; at other times new ones which it is
urged are of great importance.   In order to clear away
misconception, I will endeavour to give a short account of

**General
Features of
Curriculum.**

        1. What we teach,
and
        2. The principles which govern our procedure.

    1. First, on some general points respecting the curri-
culum I have to say the following :—

The child learns first of all to know himself, to realise and put to use his capacities and powers in all their variety—physical, intellectual, aesthetic, moral and religious. These things are taught "concretely," and step by step with instruction of like kind in external Nature. From his knowledge of himself, his lessons carry him to the observation of others, and thus he learns something of the more superficial characteristics of Human Nature in general. Similarly, his external experiences are gradually extended from his immediate environment outwards over the whole range of physical nature. He is led, on the one hand, to a knowledge of men, the various features of their character and their relationships one to another; on the other hand, he arrives at a knowledge of the interaction between man and his environment. Man and Nature, their relations one to the other, and whatever from the observation and knowledge of these things is likely in any way to advance the training and improvement of the children, constitutes the ground-work of the curriculum, and, from this ground-work, individual subjects are developed.

It is, however, necessary to emphasise the fact that this early work is not merely external and sensory. It is not, that is to say, a logical course that is offered, in which a carefully arranged series of isolated facts is taught. On the contrary, I have in mind the direct acquaintance with things as they actually occur in nature and in life, such as will enable their harmonious and intimate interdependence to be realised. I have in mind a process in which the complexity of a great and apparently simple whole is gradually revealed, leading finally to a clear conception of the principle of cause and effect in the universe. Not formal abstraction, but direct concrete experience is the basis of this process; abstractions merely express the results of experience; they should therefore follow it.

I must, however, postpone the further explanation of this principle. It makes too many assumptions to be clear to most of the parents of my boys, and, moreover, would take more space than is here at my disposal. I proceed, therefore, to the individual subjects in which the children are instructed, and I will enumerate these less in accordance with their inner connection than in accordance with customary divisions, in order to make it easier to understand the range of that which parents may expect their children to know.

Language is a most important part of the curriculum.

Language Teaching. Instruction in this subject is divided into (i) Knowledge of and skill in the production of the elements (sounds and words); (ii) Linguistic relationships, *i.e.* grammar and the philosophy of speech; (iii) Language as significant or as the universal means of expression of those mutual relationships between man and Nature, and of all that man necessarily sees and names in himself, and in the external world. In this third branch of the work the two first branches are united, and they both develop out of it. I have already set out the elements of it in *The Mother's Book*.[1] This way of looking at it gives that book a meaning different from that which is commonly given to it, namely, that it is merely a means of teaching the parts of the human body, and an example of how the parts of other objects must be brought to notice and learned by name. We are busy now in trying to bring all our language work to a complete and ordered whole. I shall, however, omit the details of this work, partly because they would take too long to

[1] *Vide* p. 177.

describe clearly, partly because it would presume a knowledge of the nature of mental life as a whole. I will only
say that the organisation of our elementary language work,
when it is once completed, as a means of introducing men
to a knowledge of themselves and of Nature, will be far-
reaching in its results, both on the nature of knowledge
itself, and still more on the general preparation for studies
of a more general kind.

As our children, for the most part, speak either German
or French, these two languages are kept chiefly in view, and
instruction is given in both equally during several lessons.
Further, special lessons in each language are also separately given. Thus the children learn to speak, read, and
write in both languages, and to express themselves about
their doings and about what goes on around them orally
and in writing. Moreover, these lessons are not treated as
mere lessons in speech and writing, but also as a means of
stimulating their general intelligence and emotional life.
The procedure has certain unavoidable drawbacks. The
wider view of the purpose of such lessons prevents our
pupils making as rapid progress in particular parts of the
language in question as is made when the language itself
only and its particular divisions are taught and practised.
In these cases more time is given to the subject than we
can spare.

Of the classical languages, Latin is taught to those
children whose parents desire it when they are sufficiently
advanced in the knowledge of their native tongue. Very
young children and those who have received no language
lessons do not take the subject. A few boys who are to
proceed to the University have made a beginning in Greek.
Our procedure in these cases is based on our general organisation of language teaching, and cannot be published
until we have succeeded in working it out.

We also teach descriptive geography. This begins in directing the attention of the boys to the things they can see, and to their geographical relations. It advances to (i) elementary geography, which is treated from the physical, mathematical, climatological, and political point of view, and (ii) the topographical section, in which the geographical features of the environment are treated more systematically, their mutual relations being developed. In this way the boys are prepared for wide generalisations concerning the history of the world and of men, the interconnections of States and of peoples, the history of human culture, and finally for natural science in its wider outlines. Statistical geography—that is to say, that which concerns productions, modes of government and population—is learned by the children from general tables. All the boys learn geography (either in German or in French), if they have sufficient previous knowledge and are intelligent enough. In natural history the course follows the three natural kingdoms—animals, plants, and minerals. The chief point aimed at is to connect the course with the things the boys can see about them in the behaviour of the animals and plants, their peculiarities of form and structure.

Geography and Natural Science.

We are also trying, at the same time, to organise the teaching of experimental science. So far we have demonstrated to the boys the principal facts concerning Electricity and Magnetism, and the behaviour of certain gases. We are, in this connection, trying to establish a satisfactory course of instruction in the language of physical science.[1] A local doctor gives weekly lessons in this direction to the older children with the aid of excellent apparatus in his possession.

[1] Cp. *The Learning of Words*, p. 189.

We teach the main outline of universal and national history, together with the biographies of the most famous men, to those of our pupils who complete their education in our school and are not therefore condemned to move from one institution to another; further, when pupils are sufficiently advanced in Latin and Greek, we teach them the history of classical times and of classical literature.

History.

Special attention is given to knowledge of and practical skill in Mental Arithmetic, and our pupils reach a high degree of attainment. Practice in the observation of number (quantitative) relations is the basis of the work. Similarly, practical acquaintance with the square and its properties leads to the calculation of square roots. Written exercises develop out of this work, the same principles being followed; bookkeeping and the elements of general commercial arithmetic are treated in connection with these exercises. The more scientific treatment of the subject leads to the study of Algebra, progress in which is made both sure and easy by the preparatory course. This progress is also due to the fact that the boys do not merely play with formulae, as so often happens, using them as they are given, without being able to develop anything further out of them. On the contrary, the rigour of their procedure gives them a keen feeling for the subject. They do not merely know the foundation and origins of the subject, they are keen enough to discover for themselves new relationships, and, from them, to develop new principles.

Arithmetic.

This is true also of the practical work in geometry and surveying. Thanks to the outstanding talent and rare devotion of the teacher, who is entirely a product of the school and of the method, the teaching in this subject has been thoroughly systematised. It opens

Geometry.

up a very important scheme of practical teaching, whether at home or in school, which promises to be of the greatest service not only in general mental development, but also in the practical and vocational training of the people. We have, moreover, great hopes of its usefulness as a source of ideas of the greatest importance for the teaching of science. The subject called the A B C of Spatial Experience (*Anschauung*) is taught under the following heads: the Apprehension of Form, the Apprehension of Size, the Apprehension of Quantitative Relations, and, to some extent also, the Geometry of Solid Bodies. The course is more educative, more carefully graduated, and more complete than has ever been offered before. The foundations, on the one hand, of the higher scientific study of geometry, and, on the other hand, of wide applications to mechanical and vocational needs, are carefully laid.

The pupils practise linear drawing in the lessons on Form, and make great progress. When the aesthetic of form is separated from the mathematics of form, and the pupils are clearly conscious of the difference, they are trained in the manifold ways of artistic expression. Now they learn perspective. The purely artistic side of the work is taken by a specialist teacher with the older boys. Since the " forms " for the elementary drawing will be published shortly, I will say nothing further on the subject except that competent artists tell us that we are so far successful in this work that any of our boys who takes up Art as a career is in a position to enter an artist's studio when he leaves us—further than this a general school training could hardly be expected to go.

Drawing.

The A B C of Observation (*Anschauung*) proves to be an excellent foundation for training in penmanship—an important subject in these days. What is still more important, it promises to make drawing

Writing.

and the elementary mathematical way of looking at things which affect the mind and life of the citizen so profoundly as common as reading and writing now are.

The boys have also special opportunities for studying the mechanical arts. Skilled mechanicians in **Workshop Training.** the town have opened their workshops to them and given them lessons. Already ten boys receive instruction of this kind.

All the boys learn Singing, except those who are naturally tuneless. At present, instruction in the **Singing.** subject is divided into exercises in time and tune, lessons in harmony, in musical notation, and in composition. Spontaneous musical activity is encouraged. A society for vocal music meets every Sunday morning. Visiting teachers give lessons in instrumental music—violin, flute, clarionet, and piano.

This concludes the list of subjects actually taught in the school. I might have extended it considerably by the addition of such ambitious names as stagger one when reading the prospectuses of many trumpery establishments. In such cases the name of the subject is the only reality. Even of names there are too many; their multiplication is only a proof of the melancholy subdivisions of knowledge and of the weakness of the human mind; apparent opulence is indeed only the greatest proof of poverty.

The school time-table is so arranged that whenever possible the same subject is taken throughout the **Time-table.** school at the same time. This makes it possible and easy to classify the boys differently for each subject. The number of classes varies from subject to subject—sometimes it is only six, sometimes there are as many as ten. Each division has its own teacher. This plan enables a visitor to understand the organisation of the teaching in each subject—the arrangement of the syllabus, and how the work of each class leads up to that of the next.

2. So far I have said little or nothing of the relation of the individual pupil to the scheme as a whole; still less have I said anything of our specific aims in regard to the individual boy. I shall try now to say something on this last point.

The Consideration of Individual Capacity.

In general, we try to avoid such over-pressure as might come from a boy working at too many things at the same time. We take pains to make everything they learn appeal to the boys in as many ways as possible, so that their whole nature is stimulated and given practical direction, in harmony with the stage of development it may have reached.

What I have said about equality of treatment in other matters applies especially to the question of instruction. We recognise only one principle of procedure—that which, whilst it is in complete harmony with the development of the mind, is based upon the nature of the subject-matter. This is of course constant for all children who study the subject; the only difference is that a clever child gets through the course much more quickly than a dull one. The dull boys may only complete a few stages, whilst the clever ones obtain a complete and commanding view of the whole subject. The genius works as it were creatively ; he makes discoveries on his own account, whilst the ordinary boy has to work hard in order to gain an insight into the self-same things, arriving nevertheless at the same point in the end. We try on the one hand to put the genius on the right way and to give him freedom, and, on the other hand, to make sure that the less gifted boy should master the elements perfectly in the hope of making his future progress sound. We desire above all things to avoid superficiality and the mere appearance of progress. Rapid advance in such cases means superficiality and uncertainty in the end, both in actual knowledge and in capacity for putting it to practical use.

For this reason we emphasise the importance of finding out what each boy is really capable of. We make his particular capacity the centre so to speak of his intellectual activity and use it as the means of introducing him to the intellectual life, of stimulating within him an effort to widen his general outlook. On this point we have collected observations of the utmost importance, if only we could persuade parents to adopt our point of view and to give us their confidence. No boy can master everything, nor is there any boy who does not show power in some direction, and who, if he were given the opportunity, would not excel in it. One lad lives as it were for Number and Form (Mathematics), and regards everything else with indifference. Another throws all his energy into his language lessons. A third enjoys nothing so much as Art : he draws beautifully, though he is behind in everything else. Others seem to be equally capable in every direction ; they need an alternation of subjects ; change stimulates them to enjoyable effort. Boys differ too in their "times and seasons." A pupil will suddenly develop a taste for a subject which previously made no appeal to him. Are these things not Nature's finger-posts? Would it not be a great advantage if, instead of making every boy work in several directions at the same time, we let boys do the things towards which they showed definite leanings as long as the impulse lasted or until the feeling that other things were necessary awakened in them.

It is of course essential that every boy should master all the subjects of an elementary course up to a certain point. But questions arise as to the order in which and the time at which this should be done, and as to whom the decision is to be left to. Obviously, the nature of the child himself should be decisive, and a school should be so organised that the native impulses and needs of each boy are properly catered for. Courses should be adapted to the boys, and not the boys to the courses. But if this claim be admitted, and if then the welfare and progress of the boys and the reputation of a school are estimated by whether or not the usual subjects are taught in the usual order without reference to the boys' desires, without asking whether or not they would, in the future, learn in a month what they now labour in vain over for years, without troubling whether pupils are allowed to do the things that are right for them without the teacher's will being continually forced upon them, then it will be understood why Nature and the fortuitous demands of men are at variance, why teachers and pupils are in like despair, and why education puts fetters upon the progress of boys rather than brings them the joys of satisfaction. To put this on right lines would take much time and give much trouble. The whole organisation of schools would have to be changed and set upon new foundations. Current views concerning the aim of instruction and what ought to be done at school would have to be radically altered. I have only just touched on a point which has received much attention here and has given occasion for many misconceptions concerning the school, because I hope to make myself clearer about it on some other occasion. I must now go back to the real subject of this paper.

The unfolding of capacity is in everything our first object. We regard the various subjects of the curriculum rather as different means of intellectual training than as means for increasing knowledge. If increase of knowledge in any direction is to be of use, the intellectual powers of the child must first of all be equal to the task of grasping its true significance. It is a principle of ours that the teacher should aim rather at increasing the powers of his pupils than at increasing their knowledge. Unless we stand by this principle absolutely, there is an end to the idea of effecting the harmonious development of the child. Instead of producing men of solid worth, their education will only make them at once pitiably weak and excessively presumptuous. Even to know what is right and what is best, unless it is combined with the will and the capacity to act accordingly, can only be a source of weakness; it is in fact rather a hindrance than a help. Learning in youth should always be a spontaneous process, a result of free activity, a living and original product.

All this is true of our school in a very rare degree. The boys give themselves wholly to their work; they feel no ill results from their strenuous efforts, just because there is no compulsion. On the contrary, they are extraordinarily well, and they enjoy their work keenly. Learning is a pleasure, not because it is disguised as a game which makes no serious demands upon them, but because nothing is asked of them that is not in due relation to their capacity. Difficulties increase as their powers of attention and thought grow. What we teach is determined by the demands of the developing powers of the child. It is intimately connected with the things he can already do. Learning is for him an affair of life. He is filled with the spirit of it, hence the joy it gives him. Instead of dissipating his activities, we concentrate them; instead of amusing the boys, we fill them with enthusiasm; instead of stifling their powers, we breathe into them the breath of life.

Only those persons who have experienced nothing of this kind in their own education, or who have no idea how

such results are brought about, could ascribe these mani-
festations amongst the boys to mechanical process. If
you prefer to call it by such a name, well and good; that
at any rate is the course which Nature herself lays down
for the teacher. The teacher cannot of course become a
mere mechanical tool, applying inanimate force to an
inanimate object. He must enter wholly into the child's
point of view, identifying himself completely with the
purpose in hand, and march in company with the child
from truth to truth, from discovery to discovery. This is
admittedly much harder than to stand at a desk with a
text-book in your hand, dictating or demonstrating its
contents to the boys.

But whilst we make the unfolding of capacity our prime
purpose, instruction in particular subjects is not excluded,
as indeed the account of our curriculum has already shown.
On the contrary, we believe that the soundest way of
training capacity is provided by the absolute fundamentals
of knowledge. It could not be otherwise. As the child's
power grows, so does his knowledge increase—the latter
always proportioned to the former. As far as it goes, his
knowledge is always thoroughly reliable, harmonising with
the full range of his developed capacities and powers of
judgment. The child of my method is not wise beyond
his years. He knows his limitations. His judgments in
matters with which he is acquainted are sound; of other
things he does not speak. He is put in the path of the
discoverer, and follows the course the discoverer followed.
We put into his hands the threads of its extension; we
lead him through the course of its development as it has
been followed by the race, that he may, by intelligently
and independently employing the means at hand, himself
continue the historic course as far as his powers will allow.

In most schools where science is taught the course is

very definitely prescribed. The pupil never sees beyond
the narrow limits within which he is set to work. Such a
procedure puts a stop to spontaneity of thought. It is
deadening in the extreme to all boys of ordinary capacity—
exceptional boys may be strong enough to burst the bonds.
We pursue the opposite plan. From the very beginning
the boy is free. He is put, so to speak, at the heart of
things, and he follows his own course, ever widening his
field of knowledge, knowing no limits except those which
Nature herself has fixed to his own powers. The very
feeling of freedom exalts his ideas and stimulates his zeal
for genuine knowledge. He is conscious of power, and
eager to put it to use to a degree which would in no other
way be realised.

The principles and methods which we follow in teaching
the various branches of knowledge apply also
Training in Art. to the training we give in art. The boys are
introduced to practical exercises before rules
and principles are learned ; they acquire in this way a
varied knowledge of the peculiar characteristics of the
world of art and a mass of practical experience which,
together, put them in a position to appreciate fully the
meaning of principles, and, when there is talent, to discover
them for themselves on occasion. Just as a youth brought
up in our way can never gossip on subjects of which he
knows nothing, so can he never talk volubly about art
without being in some degree an artist himself. Harmony
and completeness, the basis of all artistic education, spring
from these fundamental principles. Experience confirms
what psychology teaches in advance. The boy who has a
genius for art rapidly develops under our hands. The
boy who has no capacity in that direction, and in whom
higher artistic impulses are unthinkable, nevertheless
reaches by these means a high degree of practical skill,

limited perhaps in scope, and mainly mechanical and imitative in character.

I should not forget to mention the influence of my methods on vocational training. I know that many parents are by no means indifferent on this subject; that, on the contrary, they are greatly troubled about the relations of our work to the future life of their children. I am happy to be able to speak with definiteness on this point. Our boys develop such a degree of physical, intellectual and practical power that they enter upon any work which may fall to their lot with confidence and self-reliance. Although it is impossible for the school to give itself up to special industrial pursuits, nevertheless, as must happen when human power is being developed, the spirit of industry, which is fundamental to every branch of work, is awakened all round. The more active minds accumulate a large number of ideas and opinions, the application of which to the vocational life of the citizen at once strikes the intelligent observer. What I say is supported by our experience in the case of several older pupils, and it is impossible not to see how decisively helpful the ideas developed in the school are in relation to the betterment of the conditions of life of the industrial classes.

The very essence of the problem of the right way of educating is how to convert the various activities of industry into educational instruments. This can, however, only be done when the development of mind and heart precedes any particular branch of industry; that is to say, we need first of all a general education of head, heart, and hand. Industry which is mere routine, mere mechanical skill in a particular direction, which has its origin in external conditions and is based upon primitive impulses, exalts and ennobles neither individual men nor the people as a whole.

But the spirit of industry which is produced by a comprehensive "Elementary" Training brought into harmony with the higher capacities of man's essentially spiritual nature is ennobling; for it brings contentment to man through reality. It beautifies activity through the purity of the soul and consecrates life through love. The closer application of these principles still awaits the time when I shall be in a position to carry out my pet scheme; that of a school for poor boys. Then I shall hope to produce results for the lower classes which will appeal to the hearts of high-minded folk as surely and as powerfully as the methods we employ in the "Elementary Training" of the mind have appealed to them.

Generally speaking, I can say with certainty that our idea of what "Elementary Training" should be **Relation of Elementary to Higher Courses.** needs testimony from no man. As sure as that there is light wherever the sun is, as certain as is the beneficial influence of light upon plant and animal life, so sure are the benefits which sound "Elementary Training" brings to mental life. For this reason, it is important in the preparation for the study of special subjects and of art, as well as for the needs of home and community life. The principles of "Elementary" instruction have, however, taken so strong a hold on the methods of technical and scientific instruction that it is no longer possible to speak of "Elementary" education ending at a point at which scientific education begins. We have now reached the point in which men must either be unfaithful half-way and leave our principles altogether, or they must conduct higher instruction absolutely on the same principles as govern the lower. In the latter case the method of teaching each subject needs to be specially worked out.

That is at present far from being accomplished, and

nobody is more conscious than we ourselves of how much remains to be done. The task is not, however, a matter of a few years or of a few men. It is enough for the present to say that we are in a position to give instruction in all the subjects essential for any rank of life, or for the university. We may also say that the higher instruction will be in complete harmony with the general principles which govern our procedure in the elementary work; that the higher work is based upon that Elementary training of head, heart, and mind which is our pride; that this later work is the necessary outcome and continuance of that training. We would venture to say further that this instruction is free from the superficiality which results from the isolated treatment of particular subjects. We keep in mind the essential unity of aim in education which underlies our Elementary methods, and endeavour to keep up the solid human effectiveness of our early work. We are, however, not in a position to speak of these things as accomplished facts—nor, for that matter, is any other person in such a position.

It is nevertheless certain that the principles of the "Elementary Method" point the way, and that we have already got some distance in the desired direction. In many respects we are in a position to achieve much more than those who do not recognise our first principles.

It would be of enormous assistance if parents, when they are satisfied with the school and its **Co-operation of Parents.** methods, would say definitely how long they propose to keep their boys at school and for what profession they would especially like them to receive preparatory training. If we knew this, we could tell parents how much we thought their boys could accomplish in the time. We should of course have to give closer attention to the particular measures taken and to assume responsibility for them. I should like very much to have a clear understanding with parents on this matter.

Taking all in all, the school has accomplished a good deal. It could not be otherwise. During the last eight years a considerable number of young men have gathered around me to devote themselves to the study of education, prepared to abandon the confusion of contradictory experiences in favour of a science based on incontrovertible first principles. We might without boasting say that we devote ourselves to the work in absolute wholeness of heart, and, what is certainly not unimportant, we are all perfectly fresh-minded.

We have no faiths, no attachments to antiquated ideas as such; we have no economic, no civic, no moral axe to grind which might obscure the simplicity of the issue in which we are interested. There are no complications of any sort arising from our views about our position, our knowledge or our skill. No pride of rank or of knowledge divides us from those for whom we are working. As brothers we live in complete unity, happy in each other's society, devoted heart and mind to the one thing we think essential. We may well be so. Our pupils feel that we treat them as parents would treat them. They recognise that we not only give them lessons, but that we are interested in them as human beings and in anything that is likely to be useful in their education. They also are keen to enter into everything we do. They never forget their own capacity for doing. They are manifestly happy and unrepressed in their intercourse with us. All of us, young and old, take much pleasure in this. I rejoice to be able to say again here how much I owe to the confidence of the parents. Without this, it would have been impossible to carry on, and I should have been the most miserable of men.

The means at my disposal are limited; I am not rich; I shall indeed never be rich, nor do I deserve to be so. I have been too neglectful of the things that might have helped me in that direction. Indeed I have no wish to reap where I have not sown. Nor does the empty honour which is paid now to my work constitute my happiness. I know well enough that the world praises the appearance of things and leaves their substance unnoticed. I do, however, rejoice in the success of my efforts to attract attention to the problem of education and to have warmed the hearts of thousands of parents in this matter. It is my greatest joy, even in the midst of pressing cares, to live amongst my boys, to encourage them in all good, to pray with them, to touch their hearts and to make them love me. My only desire is that these dear boys would use the means which have been so successful with them in an endeavour to found the welfare of their fellow men.

Boys Must Remain Full Time at School.

If that is to be so, I must speak again of the necessity of keeping the boys at school the full time. My methods do not lend themselves to rapid results, nor can I promise anything of the kind. Man is the one creature whom Nature takes time to educate and we must not hurry. Nature will have nothing to do with appearances; unripe results are nothing to her; she insists on time and on reliance upon preparatory work amongst realities. It is the soundness of the early results that makes later success so marked. To withdraw children before the foundations have been laid is to run the risk of losing all the advantages of our work. In the hands of men who do not know our ideas, who do not use them, or who perhaps work in the opposite direction, what we have done must of necessity tumble to pieces. Children who leave the school early are as little use for demonstrating the advantages of our principles and the soundness of our results as are the mistakes of those who unintelligently imitate our methods without having any idea of the principles on which they are founded.

Finally I should like to appeal for close and continuous attention to the work of the school. In the very beginning I invited parents and friends to watch us as closely as possible. The school is and always has been perfectly open. Access is possible from the moment of rising to the moment of going to bed. We do nothing of which we are ashamed. We have no desire even to cloak our mistakes. We regard criticism as the first proof of friendship when it is given in the right spirit. We do not wish for confidence and approval which we do not deserve. I wish to move on as far as it is possible to go. In spite of my sufferings and my anxieties, I have confidence in the cause and in God. All my activities are consecrated to parents and friends of children; my whole life is devoted to my object. I beg you, my friends, to give me your confidence in return. Watch the school and put it to the test. Parents, I beseech all of you to come and see us. Your coming is in our interest, and in that of the boys; we would have you enter into the closest relations with us. Do not hide any truth from us, do not conceal your slightest wish; demand of us the closest care, the utmost performance of duty. Look on the school as yours; indeed it is more yours than mine. Live with your children; share the life of the school as I and my colleagues share it; then I shall look to the future with confidence; whether I live or die my work would then continue.

CHAPTER XX.

A book on Pestalozzi's Life and Work would hardly be complete without some further attempts to picture the man and his doings. There are many contemporary documents written for the most part by men who worked with him as students or assistants.

The most objective and perhaps the most instructive account of Pestalozzi at Burgdorf is that given by Soyaux, who spent several days at the Institute in August 1802.[1] It is obviously the record of an impartial observer and clear thinker.

He writes : "I admit that at first everything seemed to me so new, and had so little connection with Burgdorf: my few pedagogical ideas, that I could not Pestalozzi's make up my mind about it. Pestalozzi's un-Personality. ceasing experiments give evidence of the extraordinary boldness of his intellect. It was not, however, the elastic, cheerful, easy flight of genius, but rather the straining of undisciplined power. It is a hard and foolish judgment which pronounces him a visionary or praise-seeking reformer. Because Pestalozzi feels more deeply, thinks more boldly, and desires more courageously than the majority of us, he is to belong to the fanatics ! Because

[1] Morf, vol. i., p. 302 ff.

the old school reforms appear rotten to him, and because, with all the force of his noble dissatisfaction, he breaks through the barriers of custom in order to fight and obtain for the babes and sucklings a place of exercise where the mind may move with pleasure and freedom, for this reason the ambition of the reformer is said to sway him. Perchance his method deserves little approval; but the *spirit* of his principles, the *tendency* of his method, will certainly have a beneficial effect.

" The machinery of his thoughts is always in constant and strong motion—he lives more within himself than outside—more in his world of ideas than in the world of reality—a spirit of restlessness, an inner impulse drives him sometimes from one room to another, from one companion to another. It seems then as though he desired to chase a flying thought, or to make clear by main force a perplexing doubt. Often the countless visits of strangers make him restless. At other times he passes days together in his room, thinking and writing in total oblivion of himself and his affairs. It is easy to commence a conversation with him; but a stranger is seldom successful in maintaining it and in bringing it to a satisfactory result. Only momentarily does he break the thread of his meditations, pronounce a friendly word; then he retires within himself once more.

" Meanwhile, if one is successful in drawing his attention to real complaints or doubts, he grows lively and communicative—he speaks quickly, decidedly, keenly, with emphasis and confidence—contradiction does not irritate him, but usually only establishes him still more firmly in his own opinion—love and friendship fill his whole heart. It often seems as if he preferred to speak to his friends and pupils through their feelings, rather than in thoughts and words ; a hearty slap, a hearty handshake, an affectionate glance, a sympathetic or grateful seizing of the hand, are more natural to him than wordy remarks and superficial communications. Strangers are treated just in the same way as his colleagues, he rejoices in his visitors in proportion as he sees them display an interest in the doings of the school.

"No sacrifice seems to him too great for good and noble aims; altogether forgetful of himself and of his family, he takes many children without fees. He considers it his first duty to be grateful to benefactors, helpers, and friends.

"The decided, independent character of his mind is also visible in the external man. He can lay but little claim to social culture. What he thinks and believes, what he feels and wishes, he gives out unreservedly and in his own fashion. Unacquainted with the forms of European politeness, he depends upon the natural impulses of his mind and heart. He is silent, true, serious, open-hearted, modestly firm, lively without sensory distraction, attentive when sympathetic, unrefined, making no demands on outside help in word or deed. Since he has lived very little amongst people, he does not know how to work directly upon them. He lacks the quiet thoughtfulness, the never-failing sympathy in regard to the small things of life, the certain touch in action, and the social skill of the teacher who knows his way about in the world of children; he knows better how to think than to educate.

"The whole house is in activity by six o'clock in the morning, and in the evening, at the stroke of ten, the young people assemble in a large room —Pestalozzi enters their midst, and holds a fatherly enquiry into their behaviour. Since he likes to be alone at this moment, I did not venture to satisfy my own desire at his expense.

"The little river Emme, near at hand, makes a famous

place for bathing, and is diligently made use of by the whole school. In the evenings, in the hours of recreation, the merry throng assembles in the school-yard. The teachers start the singing of a patriotic song, and all who can use their legs march up and down in rank and file to the tune.

"The children enjoy perfect health. Everywhere they breathe pure mountain air, and rejoice in beautiful nature. Nothing pampers their palate, debilitates their body, intoxicates their senses, narrows their heart, or spoils their morals. The daily occupations have so taken possession of their minds that they think of nothing else but drawing and arithmetic. Even on Sunday they assembled voluntarily in the class-rooms and undertook singly and in groups arithmetical exercises. I often overheard boys repeating energetically to themselves the 'tables of observation.'

"In discipline, the rule is to allow the young people as much freedom as possible, and only to guard against the misuse of it. The compulsion and limitation of *rules* is nowhere felt. Teachers and pupils are as simple and natural in their manner as isolated mountain dwellers. Nothing is known of studied politeness, of fine gestures, of fine-sounding formulae, of conventional custom. The children follow the pure promptings of nature. They do not think about what they are to do. In the full enjoyment of their freedom, they spontaneously recognise certain bounds; obstinacy, ill-natured teasing, quarrelling, etc., are seldom seen. Since the Institute was founded no punishment has been necessary. There is no trace of 'piousness' or of the repulsive pedantic school-tone. Pestalozzi's principles in regard to moral education are excellent. The germs of good are not unfolded by means of moralising. 'Act before the child and towards him according to the views which you desire him to adopt; put yourself in such a relation to him that he will love you and trust completely in you.'

"Teachers and pupils thus live in pleasure-giving harmony. The former do not dream of expressing their authority by commands, by scoldings, or by encouraging the children to be perpetually dependent on them. They forbid little acts of naughtiness in a gently warning tone; their praise is a glance of approval or a pressure of the hand. The children look up to them with confidence, and never forget the respect which is due from them to a sensible, even-tempered, well-meaning teacher. It is, however, always difficult to steer a middle course. Here, too, this is true. The boys are a little too free. There are scarcely any rules. During instruction they may sit or stand in any order they please; no one pays any attention to that. Naturally youthful spirits have their free play, and the company resembles a crowd that has collected together and struggles for the first place, rather than a body of learners amongst whom lawful order must reign if the aim of the instruction is to be reached.

"On the other hand, the character of the method puts certain bounds to high spirits; it concentrates the liveliness and claims all the activities of the pupils. Here there is no answering in turn, nor consideration of capacity. It may have its good points that all the boys should speak with one voice and in one tone, but the piercing yells in which they thoroughly rejoiced should not be permitted. At times I did not know how to find refuge from the deafening noise, when it echoed penetratingly from several rooms at once. The ear becomes accustomed to noise, and at last the boys cannot speak at all without shouting.

"The whole household amounts to 102 persons, among whom are 72 pupils, who for the most part come from Switzerland. There are eight Roman Catholics from

Appenzell among them. About ten teachers give instruction. To mention several by name : *Krusi* from Appenzell, *Buss* from Swabia, *Weiss* from Switzerland, *Neef* from France, *Blendermann* from Bremen, and *Reinhardt*. In addition, there are several strangers here learning the method.

"The institution is young. Pestalozzi's principles are in germ and outline, rather than matured and complete. Therefore one must not yet expect perfect organisation.

"Director and teachers are working with concentrated power at the building up of the whole. One is correcting the 'tables,' the other is following up the tracks of nature in the reading and arithmetic lessons.

"Would that all schools were animated by this beautiful spirit of unity and the ceaseless striving after improvement!

"The Institute aims in the first place at elementary instruction, but the period immediately following is not excluded. The steps in the education are connected as *cause* and *effect*, consequently the teaching, the subject-matter, and the method must be thought out in this relation. The pupils are from five to thirteen years of age, usually of the middle classes. The majority are from seven to nine years.

Instruction in the Institute.

"There is as yet no thought of definite division into classes. There are five or six groups of children, who separate after each lesson, and form again differently, according to their various intellectual needs.

"School books presuppose a certain amount of knowledge and skill, without which they rather confuse than explain; therefore they are banished from the first stages of instruction. Only those who can spell have an A B C book given to them. In every room hang tables (of words, etc.).

"The smallest children learn to count with pebbles, leaves, etc., and to draw lines on a slate. Others add and subtract the strokes on the first table.[1] In their first lessons, the teacher, pointing to the table, repeats the process to them until they have understood it. One after the other now comes forward and teaches the rest, just like the teacher; thus the boys learn and teach at the same time. Since the counting proceeds according to definite and necessary rules, the teacher has only to take care that no leaps are made, and that no confusion arises. The more experienced boys are busy with the three other tables[2] at the same time.

" Here are some problems solved instantly by eight and nine year old scholars; they were set not only by the teacher, but also by strangers.

" Take $\frac{2}{9}$ from $\frac{3}{8}$, how many quarters remain ? $\frac{11\frac{11}{18}}{4}$.

" How many thirds are $\frac{2}{11}$? $\frac{6\frac{6}{11}}{3}$.

" How many eighths in $\frac{5}{6}$? $\frac{6\frac{2}{3}}{8}$.

" How many fifths are $\cdot 7$ times the eleventh part of $\frac{11}{15}$? $\frac{2\frac{1}{3}}{5}$.

" How many times does $\frac{\frac{3}{4}}{9} = 11$ times the twelfth part of $\frac{1}{3}$? $3\frac{2}{3}$ times.

" Of what sum is nine 7 times the eighth part ? Of $10\frac{2}{7}$.

" Thirteen times the nineteenth part of 19 times the twenty-fourth part of 24 times the twenty-ninth part of $\frac{3}{4}$? $\frac{13}{36}$.

" Seven bottles of wine cost 15 fl.: if I break 3 bottles, for how much must I sell each of the others in order to lose nothing ? $3\frac{3}{4}$ fl.

---

[1] The Table of Unity, etc. ; *vide* p. 195.   [2] *Ibid.*

"If I spend $\frac{1}{3}$ and $\frac{1}{4}$ of my money and have 3 fl. left, how much had I at first? $7\frac{1}{5}$ fl.

"Younger and older boys alike reckon with figures, and I noticed that the more practised only wrote down the final results of their mental calculation.

"In another lesson the A B C of observation is given; several boys draw lines, others quadrants, others again divide these into new figures; the most expert draw hands, eyes, heads, etc., on paper. The method of the A B C is as follows. When the teacher says the words, 'I draw from left to right a horizontal line,' the pupils repeat it as they make the stroke. The teacher continues: 'I divide this horizontal line by a dot, into two equal parts,' and so on, until the intended figure is completed. *Then the teacher measures each drawing with a compass.* The boy whose drawing proves most accurate is very proud. Some of them are wonderfully skilful. They draw quadrants in the most exact proportions, as though they had used a compass. One of them copied in freehand a map on a smaller scale, as exactly correct as if he had traced the outline with an instrument. They can describe circles which satisfy every test."

One of the most interesting accounts of the work at
Yverdun is that given by Vulliemin in his
Yverdun: *Souvenirs racontés à ses petits enfants.*[1] He
Father entered the school as a pupil at eight years
Pestalozzi. old. "Imagine, children, a very ugly man whose hair stood on end, whose face was deeply pitted with small-pox and covered with red blotches, with a ragged, untrimmed beard, without a necktie, with trousers half unbuttoned and hanging in folds over stockings that were

[1] *Vide* Morf, vol. iv., pp. 21-3. Cp. also the various pictures of Pestalozzi at work in De Guimp's *Biography of Pestalozzi*, translated by Russell (Sonnenschein).

down over his clumsy shoes. Add to this an unsteady, jerky walk, eyes which sometimes opened wide and blazed with fire, and sometimes were half closed as if given up to inner observation. Think, too, of features which now expressed deep sadness and now the most benign happiness, and of a voice whose utterance was sometimes slow and sometimes quick, sometimes soft and melodious, and sometimes thunderously loud. This is a picture of him whom we called *Father Pestalozzi*.

" Him we loved; we all loved him, for he loved us all. Occasionally we did not see him for a time, and we were quite sad, so heartily did we love him ; when he appeared again we could not take our eyes away from him.

" There were from 150 to 200 of us young people of all nations united in the castle. In turn we received instruction and gave ourselves up to happy games. In winter we used the snow to build fortresses, which were attacked by one party and defended by another. There were never any sick ones among us. We all went bareheaded. Once on a winter's day, when the stormwind which blows so icily over Yverdun caused everyone to flee before it, my father, who pitied me, put a hat on my head. Unhappy headgear ! My comrades had scarcely spied it when they cried ' A hat ! a hat.' One hand drove it far away from my head ; a hundred others threw it in the air, in the yard, in the corridors, in the barn, where finally, sent by a last kick, it fell through a hole into the brook which flows by the walls of the castle. I never saw it again ; it swam away to tell the sea of my woe.

" Our teachers were for the most part still young men. They had grown up under Pestalozzi, and he was like a father to them. Then, too, there were some learned men among them, who had come to help Pestalozzi in his work. The teaching was

Lessons : How Geography was learned.

more for the intellect than the memory ; it had as its aim the harmonious development of the capacities which God had given us. 'See that you educate the children,' Pestalozzi would repeat continually to them, 'not train them as one would train a dog, and as children are often trained in our schools.' Our lessons were specially concerned with Number, Form, and Language.

"Speaking was taught by means of observation; we were taught to see things rightly, and in this way we obtained a correct idea of the relations of objects to each other. What we had grasped well we could express clearly without difficulty.

"For the first elements of geography we were taken into the open air. They began by turning our steps to an out-of-the-way valley near Yverdun, through which the Bûron flows. This valley we had to look at as a whole and in its different parts, until we had a correct and complete impression of it. Then we were told, each one, to dig out a certain quantity of the clay, which was embedded in layers on one side of the valley, and with this we filled large sheets of paper, brought with us for the purpose.

"When we got back to school, we were placed at large tables which were divided up, and each child had to build with the clay, on the spot assigned to him, a model of the valley where we had just made our observations. Then came fresh excursions with more explorations. Thus we continued, until we had worked through the basin of Yverdun, and had observed it as a whole from the heights of Montela which command it entirely, and had made of it a model in relief. Then, and then only, did we turn to the map, which we had only now gained the power of correctly interpreting.

"Our teachers let us discover our geometry, contenting

themselves with merely giving us the goal to be reached, and putting us on the way to it. They proceeded in the same way with arithmetic. We did our calculations mentally, without the aid of paper. There were some among us who gained a surprising facility in these exercises, and, since charlatanism creeps in everywhere, we were the only ones who had to appear before the numerous strangers who daily appeared in Yverdun, attracted by the name of Pestalozzi.

" I have said that we saw visitors nearly every day, sometimes famous visitors, who came to pay to Pestalozzi the tribute of their admiration.

" One day he received the visit of a man who gained later a great reputation as a man of science—Karl Ritter —the moderniser of geography. Ritter was even then no ordinary traveller; he was honoured with a great reception. He stayed a week,—a real pedagogic feast—in converse with Pestalozzi and his chief helpers, Niederer, Tobler, Muralt, Nieg, Schmid, and Krusi. Each day they met and discussed education from every point of view. But it was in the confidential conversations with Pestalozzi alone that Ritter felt himself imbued with sympathy and honour for him. He saw that he was in the presence of a nature which soared far above the ordinary—of a great soul of powerful originality, absolutely given up to one idea. In the presence of Pestalozzi's remarkable simplicity, combined with his unbounded confidence in the greatness of the task he had set himself, Ritter felt personally elevated and honoured."

CHAPTER XXI.

Two Lessons by Pestalozzians in England.[1]

1. From Biber: *Henry Pestalozzi and his Plan of Education* (pp. 375-7).

The Feelers of Insects.

Having a number of specimens, among which care should be taken not to omit any of the characters to be compared, we should direct the attention first to the part of the head from which the feelers spring, and the pupils having found that they are always near the eyes, we should then ask for the different positions which they can hold towards the eyes.

This would give the following result.

The feelers spring either from within the eyes, or from some place near the eyes.

In the latter case they are either before or behind, above or below the eyes; or half before and half above, half before and half below, half behind and half above, half behind and half below the eyes.

To impress this clearly upon the mind, we should set it out as follows :—

---

[1] Cp. Chapter XV., p. 284 f.

Considering their *position to the eyes,*

Feelers are
- in the eyes,
- near the eyes,
  - above, — half above and half before,
  - before, — half below and half before,
  - below, — half below and half behind,
  - behind, — half above and half behind.

After this the pupils should be asked again with reference to all the different specimens, under which of the above nine characters each comes, until they can determine them with facility.

In the same manner we should proceed with the other characters.

Considering their *mutual position,*

Feelers are
- connected,
- unconnected,
  - near,
  - distant,

Considering their *length,*

Feelers are
- longer than the body,
- equal to the body,
- shorter than the body,
  - longer than the head,
  - equal to the head,
  - shorter than the head.

Considering their *shape,*

Feelers are
- round,
- flat,
  - with two sides,
  - more than two sides.

Considering their *structure,*

Feelers are
- jointed, consisting of several pieces ;
- not jointed, consisting of one piece.

Considering their *thickness,*

Feelers are
- the same thickness throughout, threadlike,
- the thickness increasing
  - towards the top, clublike,
  - towards the root, tapering.

In *clublike feelers,*

The club is $\begin{cases} \text{solid,} \\ \text{divided} \end{cases}$ $\begin{cases} \text{into flat leaves} \begin{cases} \text{connected at the end,} \\ \text{connected in the middle.} \end{cases} \\ \text{into tile-shaped leaves.} \end{cases}$

Considering their *appendages,*

Feelers are $\begin{cases} \text{simple, without appendages ;} \\ \text{garnished, with appendages.} \end{cases}$

In *garnished feelers,*

The appen-
dages are $\begin{cases} \text{irregular, like thorns,} \\ \text{uniform} \begin{cases} \text{single,} \begin{cases} \text{like the teeth of a saw,} \\ \text{like the teeth of a comb.} \end{cases} \\ \text{double,} \begin{cases} \text{spread out like a double comb,} \\ \text{clasped together, like a pair of} \\ \quad \text{eyelashes.} \end{cases} \end{cases} \end{cases}$

Concerning their *carriage,*

Feelers are $\begin{cases} \text{straight,} \\ \text{bent,} \\ \text{rolled.} \end{cases}$

In a similar manner the distinctions between the different orders, families, genera, etc., should be illustrated in diagrams.

2. From Mayo: *Lessons on Objects* (p. 5).

GLASS.

Glass has been selected as the first substance to be presented to the children, because the qualities which characterise it are quite obvious to the senses. The pupils should be arranged before a blackboard or slate, upon which the result of their observations should be written. The utility of having the lesson presented to the eyes of each child, with the power of thus recalling attention to what has occurred, will very soon be appreciated by the instructor.

The glass should be passed round the party, to be examined by each individual.[1]

Teacher.—What is this which I hold in my hand?

Children.—A piece of glass.

Tr.—Can you spell the word *glass*?

(The teacher then writes the word "glass" upon the slate, which is thus presented to the whole class as the subject of the lesson.)

Tr.—You have all examined the glass; what do you observe? What can you say that it is?[2]

Ch.—It is bright.

(The teacher having written the word "qualities," writes under it—"It is bright.")

Tr.—Take it in your hand and *feel* it.[3]

Ch.—It is cold. (Written on the board under the former quality.)

Tr.—Feel it again, and compare it with the piece of sponge that is tied to your slate, and then tell me what you perceive in the glass.[4]

Ch.—It is smooth—it is hard.

[1] By this means, each individual in the class is called upon to exercise his own powers on the object presented; the subsequent questions of the teacher tend only to draw out the ideas of the children, which he corrects if wrong.

[2] This question is put instead of asking "What are its qualities?" because the children would not, at first, in all probability, understand the meaning of the term; its frequent application, however, to the answer to this question, will shortly familiarise them to it, and teach them its meaning.

[3] The art of the teacher is to put such questions as may lead successively to the exercise of the different senses.

[4] The object of the teacher here is to lead the pupil to the observation of the quality *smooth*, and he does so by making him contrast it with the opposite quality in another substance; a mode of suggestion of which frequent use may be made.

Tr.—What other glass is there in the room?

Ch.—The windows.

Tr.—Look out at the windows and tell me what you see.

Ch.—We see the garden.

Tr.—(Closes the shutter.) Look out again, and tell what you observe.

Ch.—We cannot see anything.

Tr.—Why cannot you see anything?

Ch.—We cannot see through the shutters.

Tr.—What difference do you observe between the shutters and the glass?

Ch.—We cannot see through the shutters, but we can see through the glass.

Tr.—Can you tell me any word that will express this quality which you observe in the glass?

Ch.—No.

Tr.—I will tell you, then; pay attention, that you may recollect it. It is transparent.[1] What shall you now understand when I tell you that a substance is transparent?

Ch.—That you can see through it.

Tr.—You are right.[2] Try and recollect something that is transparent.

Ch.—Water.

---

[1] The fact of the glass being transparent is so familiar to the children that they will probably not observe it till its great use in consequence of that quality brings it forcibly to their minds. They then feel the want of a term to express the idea thus formed, and the teacher gives them the name, as a sign for it, and in order to impress it upon their minds. To ascertain whether they have rightly comprehended the meaning of the word, they are called upon to give examples of its application.

[2] It is but too common a practice to call a child *good* because he gives a right answer; thus confounding intellectual truth and moral virtue.

Tr.—If I were to let this glass fall, or you were to throw a ball at the window, what would be the consequence?

Ch.—The glass would be broken.   It is brittle.

Tr.—If I used the shutter in the same way, what would be the consequence ?

Ch.—It would not break.

Tr.—If I gave it a very heavy blow, with a very hard substance, what would then happen?

Ch.—It would then break.

Tr.—Would you, therefore, call the wood brittle ?

Ch.—No.

Tr.—What substances, then, do you call brittle ?

Ch.—Those which are *easily* broken.

These are as many qualities as would occur to the children at their first attempt : they should be arranged on the slate, and thus form an exercise in spelling.   They should then be effaced, and if the pupils are able to write, they may endeavour to remember the lesson, and to put it down on their slates.

CHAPTER XXII.

PESTALOZZI'S CHIEF EDUCATIONAL WRITINGS.

The most satisfactory edition of Pestalozzi's collected works is that which appeared in 1899 under the editorship of Seyffarth (12 vols.). The writings distinguished by * are included in Mann's edition of Pestalozzi's selected works (Pestalozzi's *Ausgewählte Werke*, 4 vols.).

1. **Aspirations.** (*Wünsche.*) Published in the *Erinnerer*, the weekly newspaper in which for eighteen months (1765-1767) the young men of Bodmer's circle expressed their political and social aspirations. (*Vide* pp. 25-6.)

2. **How Father Pestalozzi Educated and Observed his Three-and-a-half year old Son.** (*Wie Vater Pestalozzi anno 1774 sein drey und einhalbjähriges Söhnlein Jacobli unterrichtet.*) Published by Niederer in 1828. Extracts from Pestalozzi's diary to which reference has already been made. (*Vide* text of the diary, p. 28 f.)

3. **Essays on the Education of the Children of the Poor.** (*Aufsätze über Armenerziehung.*) 1775-78.

(i) "An appeal to philanthropists for the support of the Institute at Neuhof." Dated 1775. Appeared in the *Ephemerides*, Vol. I., 1777. (*Vide* De Guimp, Chap. V.)

(ii) "Three letters to N. E. T. concerning the education of poor country children."

Seventeen letters by Tscharner had appeared in the *Ephemerides*. They are summarised in Seyffarth's edition of Pestalozzi's works, Vol. III., pp. 237-241. Tscharner is generally supposed to have been the person whom Pestalozzi portrayed as Arner, the good squire of Bonnal in *Leonard and Gertrude.*

Pestalozzi's letters were written directly to Tscharner, who handed them over to Iselin for publication in the *Ephemerides.* (*Vide* pp. 48 f. and 286.)

(iii) **Report upon the work of the Neuhof Institute.** Dated 1778, written for the Society of Economics in Berne, and published in extracts in the *Ephemerides.*

It contains a complete list of the thirty-seven children then in the Institute, with a statement of their origin, age, health, character, and previous life. (De Guimp, Ch. V.)

4. **Evening Hours of a Hermit.*** (*Abendstunde eines Einsiedlers.*) *Ephemerides,* 1780. (*Vide* pp. 27-29.) The full text in translation is given in G., p. 15 f.

5. **Leonard and Gertrude.*** A book for the people. (*Lienhard und Gertrud. Ein Buch für das Volk.*) Part I., 1781, Part II., 1783, Part III., 1785, Part IV., 1787. (*Vide* p. 54 f.). This book went through three revisions at the hands of its author. The first was published in 1790-2, and the second revision appeared in 1819-20. These revisions, especially the third, were drastic in their nature. For an account of the changes introduced *vide* W. Roste, *Pestalozzi's Lienhard und Gertrud: Vergleichende Darstellung der drei Ausgaben* (1909).

6. **Christopher and Elizabeth. My second book for the people.** (*Christoph und Else. Mein zweytes Volks Buch.*) 1782. (*Vide* p. 60.)

7. *Ein Schweizer-Blatt.*** A weekly paper appearing every Thursday during the year 1782. It was almost entirely written by Pestalozzi; its contents deal solely with social questions. (*Vide* p. 60.)

8. **Researches relating to the Course of Nature in the**

Development of the Human Race. (*Nachforschungen über den Gang der Natur in der Entwickelung des Menschengeschlechts.*) 1797.

Most of Pestalozzi's biographers find little that is good to say of this book. Herder reviewed it enthusiastically in the *Erfurter Gelehrte Nachrichten*, 1797, and expressed the hope that it might be reprinted in a more attractive style. The wish remained unfulfilled until Hunziker's edition appeared. (Zürich, 1886.) (*Vide* pp. 131-134.) A translation of the most important parts of the book is given in G., p. 53 f.

9. **Pestalozzi and his Institute in Stanz.*** (*Pestalozzi und seine Anstalt in Stanz.*) Written in 1799 at Gurnigel. (*Vide* p. 69 f.)

10. At Burgdorf Pestalozzi wrote a number of short accounts of his methods as reports to ministers, societies, and friends. In addition to these he published

Instructions for the Teaching of Spelling and Reading. (*Anweisung zum Buchstabieren und Lesenlehren*). 1801.

This is the book he intended to publish when his work in Stanz was finished. (*Vide* p. 83.)

11. **The Method. A Monograph.** (*Die Methode. Eine Deukschrift Pestalozzi's.*) Written in 1800. The text of this important document is given in Chapter XVII.

12. **How Gertrude Teaches her Children.*** (*Wie Gertrud ihre Kinder lehrt.*) An attempt to give guidance to mothers in the instruction of their own children. 1801. (*Vide* p. 95.) A translation of the most important parts is given in G., p. 85 f.

13. **The Essential Character and Aim of the Method. A Monograph written for Friends in Paris.** (*Wesen und Zweck der Methode. Eine Denkschrift Pestalozzi's an seine Pariser Freunde.*) 1802.

The text is printed in Vol. 8 of Seyffarth's collected

edition. It is largely occupied with the problem of the avoidance of all one-sidedness in education.

14. Pestalozzi's Elementary Books. (*Elementar Bücher.*)

(i) **The Mother's Book,** or "A Guide for Mothers in Teaching their Children to observe and to talk." (*Buch der Mütter, oder Anleitung für Mütter ihre Kinder bemerken und reden zu lehren.*) 1803. (*Vide* p. 177 f.)

(ii) **The A B C of Observation, or Lessons in the Observatio of Form**. (*A B C der Anschauung oder Anschauungslehre der Massverhältnisse.*) The book is really the work of Buss. "The child is taught to notice and to name the differences in form and relation between several objects."

Pointing to the horizontal lines the child is told, "These are horizontal lines," and, pointing to the top line, "That is the first top horizontal line." The child repeats this, and learns also to reply in answer to questions, "That is the second, fifth, seventh line," etc. The same occurs with the perpendicular lines. Next they are compared according to their length or shortness and divided into equal parts, to the measure of the first line. For example, the child repeats "The first line is as long as the half of the second line." For correcting the drawings transparent sheets of horn were used, upon which the figures were scratched. After the straight line comes the square, and then the circle. The instruction progresses until the pupil can draw correctly both these figures, without ruler or compass, in the most varied combinations, and until finally he frees himself from the leading-strings of the method by feeling "the necessity for independent progress," and becoming conscious of having in himself the independent power for such progress. See also Dean Ith's Report (p. 97).

(iii) **Lessons in the Apprehension of Number Relations**. (*Anschauungslehre der Zahlverhältnisse.*) (*Vide* p. 193 f.)

15. **Educational Journal** or **Pestalozzi's Views, Experiences, and Means in respect of the promotion of a method of education based upon human nature.*** 1807. Printed in Mann's edition as *Ansichten und Erfahrungen die Idee der Elementarbildung betreffend*. The only number of a second journal projected by the Institute. Written in the interval between Münchenbuchsee and Yverdun. Like *How Gertrude Teaches her Children*, it takes the form of a series of letters (eight). Six of these —Nos. 3 to 8—are part of a larger plan to publish a revised edition of the Gessner letters, which should take account of the advances he had made since that book appeared. The MS. of the whole, if it ever existed, is now lost. It contains an interesting review of his life-work up to the time of writing, and a forecast of what he hopes may come in the future. Many of his principles are set forth with greater clearness than in any other of his writings; *e.g.* his views on moral education and on the need for experimental schools (*vide* p. 257). The text in translation is given in G., p. 155 f.

16. *Wochenschrift für Menschenbildung,** 1806-1810 (*vide* p. 106).

The Stanz Letter, the *Report to Parents*, and the Lenzburg Address are the most important writings that appeared in the *Wochenschrift*. The **Lenzburg Address*** was written as a reply to many criticisms which had been directed against the Institute at Yverdun. It opens with an appeal to the critics to come and see. He calls his method "the organic-genetic elementary method which aims at seeking out and establishing the unchangeable starting-points and the unchangeable lines of progress in all instruction and education." It is an unconditional principle of the method that it cannot put into the child what is not already there in germ. The child is made in God's image. He is not a *tabula rasa* on which one may write from without, nor is he an empty barrel which has to be filled with strange matter, but a real, living, self-active power which from the first moment of its existence is busied with its own development, using the materials presented to it by circumstance to that end.

In this regard, this method is *positive*. It is not occupied in preventing the development of the bad, but in actively stimulating the good, thereby indirectly keeping down weakness and error. The teacher inspired by the method is too conscious of his own weaknesses to wish to interfere forcefully in the boy's development. His particular part is to bring to birth the child's human and intellectual independence, in other words his individuality. The individuality of the child must always be the starting-point of his procedure.

The method is *positive* also in respect of instruction. It presupposes that all branches of human knowledge have starting-points, and it endeavours to seek them out. From this point of view the method is *general*, not however in the sense that it treats all men alike, irrespective of powers, character, and position.

The mother is the natural type of an educator who follows this method, and the Elementary Method in education consists in an uninterrupted continuation of the mother's methods in all the directions education takes.

As Christianity belongs to us all, rich or poor, so is the Elementary Method in intellectual education applicable to all men. Even the poorest of men may by its means be raised to the highest development of the powers which God has given him.

The method declines to use such feelings as love of honour and emulation. The child brought up on its principles compares himself with nobody but himself. Those who have seen his boys in the moment when they have finished a particular task will quite realise that no such stimulus to effort is necessary. The same spirit rules in play-ground and school alike.

The method rests absolutely upon love. It recognises no forms of intellectual, physical, or moral education which do not find in love and faith a common point of agreement.

After pointing out the difficulties to be overcome in practice, Pestalozzi once again outlines the development of the child as Nature and a good mother would determine it, though he admits finally that such mothers are rare.

17. **Report to the Parents and the Public concerning the present condition and arrangements of the Pestalozzian Institute at Yverdun.** (*Bericht an die Eltern und das Publikum über des gegenwärtigen Zustand . . . der Anstalt.*) 1808, in the *Wochenschrift*. The full text is given in Chapter XIX.

18. **Pestalozzi's Addresses.** * It was Pestalozzi's custom to address the whole school in a more formal way on special occasions. Some of these addresses have been lost, but we have still over twenty. The chief are the New Year and birthday addresses of 1808, 1809, 1810, 1811, 1812, and 1818.

It is impossible to summarise these eloquent addresses, which mirror so faithfully Pestalozzi's moods at the time they were uttered, and show clearly his humble trust in God and his unconquerable belief in his ideals. The address of 1818 is specially interesting, as it contains Pestalozzi's appeal for funds to establish a great educational institute. (*Vide* p. 112.) A not dissimilar appeal was printed in English as "The Address of Pestalozzi to the British public soliciting them to aid by subscriptions his plan of preparing schoolmasters and mistresses for the people, that mankind may in time receive the first principles of intellectual instruction from their Mothers" (Sept. 1818).   (Text of 1818 Address in G., p. 187 f.)

19. **Swansong**. (*Schwanengesang*.) This work, which was not published until 1826, was written in the period 1811-13. It is divided into two parts—the first part is a re-statement of Pestalozzi's doctrines intended originally for separate publication under the title "Education according to Nature" (*Uber die Naturgemässheit der Erziehung*). It occupies about two-thirds of the *Swansong*. The second part he intended to publish as a message from "The sick Pestalozzi to the healthy public." It is in the nature of an apology for the failure of his efforts to realise his own ideals.

The work opens with a discussion of the meaning of elementary education. He defines it as the result of the efforts of humanity to offer such guidance to the course of nature in the unfolding of the capacities and powers as would confer upon the individual the enlightened love, the cultivated intelligence, and the practical good sense of the race.

He then asks and discusses the answers to the three questions :—

(1) How do the bases of our moral life—Faith and Love—actually and naturally reveal themselves in humanity ?

(2) How do the bases of our intellectual life, of our thought powers, naturally unfold ?

(3) How do the bases of our practical capacity reveal themselves in nature—the power, that is to say, by means of which we give expression to the results of our intellectual activity and successful effect to the impulses of our hearts, and upon the

cultivation of which our domestic and civic efficiency depends.

A perfect scheme of elementary education exists nowhere, and he sums up the results of his own researches into the practical means which bear upon it in the principle "Life Educates." He examines this principle and sets forth its truth in respect of intellectual, moral, and practical education.

The educational value of subjects of instruction—history and geography being taken as types, the meaning of human nature, which is not a mere conglomeration of powers, the education suited to particular social rank, and the necessity of organising education on a religious basis are then each in turn discussed.

In the last part of the *Swansong* he endeavours to sum up the results of his work. He recognises its incompleteness, but he feels still that some good has come from his efforts at Burgdorf and Yverdun. He closes his review with the words "Examine everything, hold to that which is good, and if you conceive anything better, add it to that which I, in truth and love, have endeavoured to give you in these pages, and, at any rate, do not cast aside the whole of my life's effort as a thing of the past, deserving no further attention." The chief parts of the text are given in G., p. 267 f.

20. **A Word concerning the present Condition of my Pedagogical Efforts and the new Organisation of my Institute.** (*Ein Wort über den gegenwärtigen Zustand meiner pädagogischer Bestrebungen. . . .*) It is in part an explanation of the changes brought about by the re-union of the Institute at Clendy with that of Yverdun. (*Vide* also p. 113.)

21. **Life's Destiny.** (*Lebensschicksal.*) 1826. Written and published after Yverdun was closed. Pestalozzi's last

work, in which he enters into the painful details of the
quarrel between Schmid and himself on the one side, and
Niederer and Krusi on the other.   An unhappy publication
which all Pestalozzi's friends regretted.

22. **Letters on Early Education.** Addressed to J. P.
Greaves, Esq., in 1818, and published in translation in
1827.   Thirty-four letters referring chiefly to mothers'
education of their children.   (See also p. 245 f.)   The
chief of these letters are reprinted in G., p. 211 f.

Of other writings less directly concerned with education
the chief were :—

1. **Yes or No ?** (*Ja oder Nein ?*)   An enquiry into the
true sources of popular discontent, a sort of concrete
application of the doctrines of the *Enquiries* to the general
circumstances of his time, with particular reference to the
French Revolution.   It was probably written before the
Enquiries, but, on Fichte's advice, its publication was de-
ferred.   It did not see the light until Seyffarth's collected
edition of Pestalozzi's writings was published.

2. **Views of Subjects which demand the Special Attention
of our Legislators.** (*Ansichten über die Gegenstände, auf
welche die Gesetzgebung Helvetiens ihr Augenmerk vorzüglich
zu richten hat.*)   (*Vide* p. 100.)

GENERAL INDEX.

INDEX OF NAMES.

PRINTED AT THE BURLINGTON PRESS, CAMBRIDGE.

SELECTED TEXTBOOKS

IN

PHILOSOPHY, AND THEORY AND PRACTICE OF EDUCATION

PUBLISHED BY

University Tutorial Press Ld.,

HIGH ST., NEW OXFORD ST., W.C.

Philosophy.

Ethics, A Manual of. By J. S. MACKENZIE, LL.D., Litt.D., M.A., sometime Professor of Logic and Philosophy in the University College of South Wales and Monmouthshire, formerly Fellow of Trinity College, Cambridge. *Sixth Edition.* **9s. 6d.**

An outline of the most important principles of ethical doctrine, so far as these can be understood without a knowledge of Metaphysics.

Ethics, Groundwork of. By JAMES WELTON, D.Lit., M.A., sometime Professor of Education in the University of Leeds. **3s. 6d.**

Logic, A Manual of. By Dr. JAMES WELTON. Vol I. *Second Edition.* **10s. 6d.**

Contains a treatment of the whole of Deductive Logic, except Fallacies.

Logic, Intermediate. By JAMES WELTON, D.Lit., M.A., and A. J. MONAHAN, M.A. *Third Edition, Revised* by E. M. WHETNALL, Ph.D., B.A. **10s. 6d.**

A textbook of University Intermediate standard.

Logic, Groundwork of. By Dr. JAMES WELTON. **5s.**

An elementary textbook of Logic, suitable for London Matriculation and similar examinations.

University Tutorial Press Ld., London, W.C.

Philosophy—*continued.*

Logic, Exercises in. By F. C. BARTLETT, M.A., Fellow of St. John's College, Cambridge, and Director of the Cambridge Psychological Laboratory. **4s.** KEY, **3s.**

Logic, Questions on, with Illustrative Examples. By HENRY HOLMAN, M.A., late H.M.I., and M. C. W. IRVINE, M.A. *Second Edition.* **2s. 6d.**

Psychology, A Manual of. By G. F. STOUT, LL.D., M.A., Fellow of the British Academy, Professor of Logic and Metaphysics in the University of St. Andrews. *Fourth Edition, Revised,* in collaboration with the Author, by C. A. MACE, M.A., Lecturer in Logic and Psychology in the University of St. Andrews. **12s. 6d.**

Psychology, The Groundwork of. By Professor G. F. STOUT. *Second Edition, Revised* by R. H. THOULESS, Ph.D., M.A., Lecturer in Psychology in the University of Glasgow, late Fellow of Corpus Christi College, Cambridge. **5s. 6d.**

Social Psychology: A Textbook for Students of Economics and of Social Sciences. By Dr. R. H. THOULESS. **5s. 6d.**

Education.

Teaching, Principles and Methods of. By JAMES WELTON, D.Lit., M.A., sometime Professor of Education in the University of Leeds. *Third Edition.* **8s. 6d.**

CONTENTS: General Function of Teaching—Material of Instruction—Form of Instruction—The Teaching of English—Reading, Grammar, Composition, Literature—The Teaching of Music—The Teaching of History—The Teaching of Geography—Nature Study—The Teaching of Mathematics—The Teaching of Form—The Teaching of Needlework—The Teaching of Modern Languages.

Teaching: Its Nature and Varieties. By BENJAMIN DUMVILLE, M.A., F.C.P., late Master of Method and Lecturer in Education in the Islington Day Training College. *Second Edition.* **6s. 6d.**

Principles and Methods of Moral Training, with Special Reference to School Discipline. By JAMES WELTON, D.Lit., M.A., and F. G. BLANDFORD, M.A., late Lecturer in Education in the Cambridge University Training College. **3s. 6d.**

Education—*continued.*

Principles and Methods of Physical Education.
By W. P. WELPTON, B.Sc., Master of Method in the University of Leeds. With a Sketch of the History of Physical Education by JAMES WELTON, D.Lit., M.A. **5s. 6d.**

Also issued at 4s. 6d., without the chapters on Hygiene.

Experimental Psychology, An Introduction to.
By C. W. VALENTINE, D.Phil., M.A., Professor of Education in the University of Birmingham. *Second Edition.* **4s.**

Psychology, Fundamentals of. A brief account of the Nature and Development of Mental Processes for Teachers. By BENJAMIN DUMVILLE, M.A., F.C.P. *Second Edition.* **6s. 6d.**

Child Mind. An Introduction to Psychology for Teachers. By BENJAMIN DUMVILLE, M.A., F.C.P. *Second Edition.* **4s.**

The Hygiene of the School. By R. A. LYSTER, M.D., Ch.B., B.Sc., D.P.H., late County Medical Officer for Hampshire, and Chief School Medical Officer and Chief Tuberculosis Officer, Hampshire County Council. [*In preparation.*]

An up-to-date work based on the author's *School Hygiene.*

School Organisation. By S. E. BRAY, M.A., late Inspector of Schools to the London County Council. *Fourth Edition.* **4s. 6d.**

School Training. By R. E. HUGHES, M.A., B.Sc. **3s.**

The Life and Work of Pestalozzi. By J. A. GREEN, M.A., late Professor of Education in the University of Sheffield. **6s. 6d.**

Synthesis of Froebel and Herbart. By R. D. CHALKE, LL.D., M.A. **5s.**

The book traces the relation of Pestalozzi, Froebel, and Herbart to each other and to the progress of modern education.

History of Elementary Education in England and Wales, from 1800. By CHARLES BIRCHENOUGH, M.A., late Lecturer in Education in the University of Sheffield. *Second Edition, Revised and Enlarged.* **6s. 6d.**

Educational Handwork, or Manual Training. By A. H. JENKINS, Inspector of Schools under the Manchester Education Committee. *Second Edition.* **4s.**

Gives for the first time in a single volume an account of all the different branches of Handwork commonly practised in schools.

Education—*continued.*

Nature Study, The Aims and Methods of. *A Guide for Teachers.* By JOHN RENNIE, D.Sc., F.R.S.E., late Lecturer in Agricultural Zoology and Parasitology in the University of Aberdeen. With an Introduction by Professor J. Arthur Thomson. **5s.**

The greater part of the book is devoted to model courses and model lessons dealing with typical studies and designed for all grades in the school. All branches of nature study are included.

Nature Study, The Aims and Methods of (South African Edition). By JOHN RENNIE, D.Sc., F.R.S.E., and GEORGE RATTRAY, D.Sc., M.A., Principal of Selborne College, East London, S.A. **5s.**

School Lessons in Plant and Animal Life. By Dr. JOHN RENNIE. **6s. 6d.**

A course of eighty lessons in Nature Study.

School Gardening, A Teachers' Handbook of. By ALBERT HOSKING, Garden Superintendent, the John Innes Horticultural Institution, Merton, Surrey. With numerous illustrations and plans. **4s.**

The Teaching of Geography. By W. P. WELPTON, B.Sc., Lecturer in Education and Master of Method in the University of Leeds. **3s. 6d.**

The Teaching of Drawing: Its Aims and Methods. By SOLOMON POLAK and H. C. QUILTER. **3s. 6d.**

The Teaching of Needlework: Its Aims and Methods. By Miss H. M. BRADLEY, B.A. **2s. 3d.**

Voice Training in Speech and Song. By H. H. HULBERT, M.A., M.R.C.S., L.R.C.P. *Second Edition.* **2s. 3d.**

The Science of Speech: an Elementary Manual of English Phonetics for Teachers. By BENJAMIN DUMVILLE, M.A., F.C.P. *Second Edition.* **4s.**

First Studies in Dramatic Art. By ENID ROSE, Royal Academy of Dramatic Art. **5s. 6d.**

1000 Questions in Music for Teachers. By J. H. WHITELEY, Mus. Bac., L.Mus.T.C.L. **2s. 3d.**